LANGUAGE ARTS
IN THE
ELEMENTARY SCHOOL

• A MODERN LINGUISTIC APPROACH

GERTRUDE B. CORCORAN

SAN JOSE STATE COLLEGE

THE RONALD PRESS COMPANY • NEW YORK

Library of Congress Catalog Card Number: 77–110546

Preface

This text for courses in the teaching of language arts is designed to provide teachers and future teachers with a balanced view of the kinds of experience children will need both for *learning* a language and for *learning about* a language. It is also intended to provide a foundation for the newer linguistic emphasis on language learning.

A body of verifiable knowledge from linguists has made it possible for the schools to approach instruction in grammar in new and exciting ways. The new emphasis on grammar is creating grave concern on the part of many teachers who recognize distressing similarities between old teaching methods and new linguistic concepts. Without an understanding of the importance of the linguistic concepts or the purpose of instruction in grammar for elementary school children, teachers are backing away from the threshold of the promising possibilities which understanding one's language holds for each human being.

The major concern results from the fact that teachers have not before made explicit the difference between *learning* a language and *learning about* a language. The child spends the first two or three years of school learning to read and write, becoming literate. He continues to expand his language ability as he participates in oral communication activities such as listening, speaking, and dramatic interpretation to further develop skills in each of these areas. Teachers provide classroom opportunities to develop skill in the social aspects of language, to develop and extend vocabulary, to promote ability and enjoyment in reading through the use of literature, and to increase facility in written expression. In all of these experiences the child continues to *learn* his language.

Teachers are now being urged to provide the child an opportunity to *learn about* his language as well. Previously, a kind of haphazard inclusion of certain bits of knowledge and terminology in language arts texts have given lip-service to the idea that children should know something about their language, but now linguists have made available a body of knowledge which will make it possible for the child to discover the system of his language. Linguists have joined together with psychologists, anthropologists, and other behaviorial scientists in an effort to further understand man. Each of these groups recognizes the awesome mystery of language, and each seeks to use its knowledge of language to unlock the complexities of man's deepest nature.

Learning about one's language will undoubtedly help one to learn important things about himself, but this must not become the entire language arts curriculum. Elementary school children have need of extending their ability to use language effectively as well as to know something about it. This text is concerned with both of these aspects of language.

The Questions for Study at the end of each chapter are intended as guides for further study. The Suggestions for Further Reading provide important background for answering the questions, and the Teacher's Aid sections at the end of each chapter include teaching ideas, activities, and suggestions for specific techniques to be used in the classroom.

The writer wishes to express her deep appreciation to Professors Donald H. Alden, Edith Trager Johnson, and Philip H. Cook of the Department of English and Linguistics, San Jose State College, for their help and advice in preparing portions of the manuscript. The author is also indebted to Professor J. N. Hook, Professor of English, University of Illinois, for his careful reading of the manuscript and extensive suggestions for its improvement.

GERTRUDE B. CORCORAN

San Jose, California
January, 1970

Contents

LANGUAGE ARTS
IN THE
ELEMENTARY SCHOOL

1

Linguistic Concepts
for Language Learning

In the beginning was the word . . . and since the beginning language has been examined and discussed in a variety of ways. In John Carroll's book *The Study of Language* [1] one is confronted by a host of subdivisions of language study including descriptive linguistics, psycholinguistics, historical linguistics, comparative linguistics, and structural linguistics. All of these disciplines have made interesting and valuable contributions to the understanding of language and its use. In addition, the social sciences have investigated language. Psychology, sociology, and anthropology have found it necessary to study language as a type of human activity and as a system interacting with personality, society, and culture. Technological problems in modern society have driven engineers to basic research on human speech. As all of these and many other disciplines have concentrated on language investigation, certain basic attitudes toward language have emerged, giving direction to the elementary school teacher, who has two main areas of concern (1) how to help the child use his language with ever-increasing facility and (2) how and what to teach the child about his language.

Language as Speech

Perhaps the most fundamental statement derived from linguistics is that language is speech. The spoken form of language is the basic form. The written form is simply an effort to symbolize what has

[1] John B. Carroll, *The Study of Language* (Cambridge, Mass.: Harvard University Press, 1959).

3

been said. Such symbolizing is almost never able to depict exactly what has been said. The stress, pitch, juncture, intonation patterns, facial expressions, and gestures of the speaker that frequently give meaning to speech cannot be captured in writing. Because of a recognition of the primacy of speech, linguists now attempt to describe language by carefully analyzing speech, and they recommend that teachers help children discover the system of language rather than teach language prescriptively by rules.

The Systematic Nature of Language

The second tenet agreed upon as a result of linguistic study is that language is systematic. Specific principles, intertwined and interrelated, govern the operation of language. The former belief that children learned their language chiefly through imitation has been challenged. It is now recognized that no individual memorizes the almost infinite number of combinations that are possible in language. Even small children use structures that they have never heard before, and such usage both amuses and charms adults. The grammar of a three year old is different from that of an adult, but it too will be systematic. For example, the child who has discovered that the *ed* suffix is usually added to form the past tense form of an English verb will normally apply it to irregular verbs as well as regular, and his vocabulary will include words like runned, flied, and singed. When the system has been completely mastered the child will be aware of the fifty-two possible modifications of the inflectional system for the past tense in English.[2] Most of the distinctions will be learned through usage, but a few verb forms such as those of *sit–set* and *lie–lay* will probably take direct teaching and be used fluently and accurately only in the later years of school, although home environment may affect the choice of these verb forms.

The Symbolic Nature of Language

A third premise for understanding the nature of language is that language is symbolic. Many English words refer to objects. *Chair,* for example, is a word that blends with the object almost instantly

---

[2] George H. Owen, "Linguistics: An Overview," *Elementary English,* vol. 49, no. 5 (May, 1962), pp. 421–425.

in one's mind. When one looks at a chair and uses its word referent, the word and the object seem to unite in the mind in such an unconscious stimulus-response pattern that one tends to forget that the word is not the object but only a symbol for the object.

The first symbol for the object is the sound symbol, the second symbol is the written symbol. This symboling creates many problems in communication. There is less chance of misunderstanding when the first or sound symbol is used because the sound symbol is usually used in a meaningful context. If someone says, "Look at the chair," "Please have a chair," or "That chair is an antique," the person listening is obviously in a position to see what chair is being talked about. There is less chance of misunderstanding, although still some chance if more than one chair is in sight, than if one simply sees the symbol *chair* written as a word without specific context, i.e., "John sat on a chair near the door." When one sees the written symbol *chair*, he might refer back to any one of a great variety of chairs with which he has had contact in his lifetime. Of course, this is possible also if one hears the sound symbol for *chair* out of context with any other sound symbols and in a situation in which no chairs are present. The probability of hearing the sound symbol for *chair* completely out of context is much more remote than the probability of seeing the word written in a less than specific context. In summary, a particular sound symbol or written symbol can elicit a variety of responses depending on (1) the situation in which the symbol is used and (2) the individual receiving the symbol. The possibility of semantic misunderstanding increases with the degree of symboling (i.e., primary or secondary symbols), as well as with the degree of abstraction of the symbol (i.e., *love, good citizenship*).

A careful scrutiny of symbols such as the *ed* morpheme for the past tense of the regular English verb shows that the symbols are clearly arbitrary. Nothing about the sound of *ed* or its appearance in writing relates it in any way to the past. A person learning this ending must learn it from some other person, either directly, from tapes or books, or from some human-oriented device. It cannot be learned by observing nature or listening to its sounds. There seems to be no relationship between the words of a language and the objects they symbolize.

Language in Time

Language, then, is an organized system of sound used by people to communicate ideas. It is used by people at a specific time and in a specific location. The language of 1970 is not the language of Shakespeare. "Stand not upon the order of your going" is not a grammatical expression for contemporary usage. Could the language of Shakespeare be called ungrammatical? Yes, if grammar is a description of the way in which language operates. Lady Macbeth's exhortation to speed the parting guests tells them to hurry on out, to ignore protocol, to stop worrying about who should go first. Today's hostess, if she wished to hurry guests on their way, would probably say, "Don't stand on ceremony," or "Don't insist on being polite and waiting your turn; feel free to go right on out."

Does this make Shakespeare bad and the modern utterance good? Not at all. One must be careful not to equate ungrammatical with bad and grammatical with good. This kind of verbal relationship leads to false assumptions. Shakespeare's English, far from being an inferior language, is a different sort of language from today's with different grammatical rules. It is English of another time.

Language and Dialect

Children learn the language of their parents and their peers. If the language or dialect they speak when they come to school is not the language or dialect used by educated members of the community, they may have to learn a second language or dialect. Dialects of language are part of social behavior. The child speaks the way he does because he has to learn his language in order to become an integral part of his group. When the teacher invites the child to learn a second language or dialect, the child is in fact being invited to join another group. This is real motivation if the person inviting the child to join his group is sincere, and if the child wants to join the group. If either of these factors is not the case, the child will probably have little success in mastering the new language or dialect.

Teachers who ask children to learn their dialects are actually asking children to join their social group. Do they mean it? Do they have any intention of encouraging these students to become an integral part of their lives? If not, why should the child learn the teacher's dialect? It is frequently not necessary nor even applicable to membership in his peer group or family group.

Perhaps it would be helpful to clarify the difference between a language and a dialect. Descriptive linguists have attempted to describe individual languages or dialects in terms of their own characteristic structure. The use of phonemic analysis based on a single dialect of English and overall patterns based on a wide range of dialects have produced a definition of language that results from delimiting the language and defining the system. Any statement of overall pattern will be a less adequate treatment of any given dialect than a statement based exclusively on the dialect with equal care and methodological accuracy. Phonemic analysis will be discussed at length in Chapter 8, but for the present, language may be termed any form of speech of which a workable description can be made. Language is usually considered to be an orderly sequence of sound resulting in a complex set of patterns that form its structure. Dialect is a variety of language, also describable in an overall pattern. Grammar is the system of the language, and dialect is a system of grammar used within a particular social group. Grammar, an important part of social behavior, and dialect, the system of language used by a particular social group, both refer to systems of language.

The metaphor frequently used to define levels of language, pointing up the overlapping of the levels, is in fact very confusing because the different levels are not the same in different social groups.

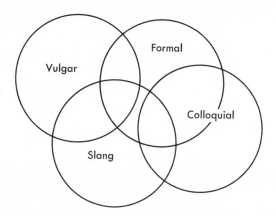

Actually, the common elements within the levels exceed 80 percent, and the word *level* tends to be misleading. *Level* is not a qualitative word in this context; in certain circumstances colloquial language may be preferred to formal language. There are indeed degrees of formality and informality in language, but these are not the same in different social groups. Social psychology demonstrates different language patterns for different social groups, and the sanctions placed upon language forms within the groups are heavy and severe. No sentimental liberalism can overcome these actualities; group membership requires conformity. The teacher in today's school must be prepared to teach second dialects in many instances. This is a new field, and although much is being done in this area at the University of California in Los Angeles, the best single source for teachers is probably English Language Services.[3]

Language Habits

Linguists share with other intellectual disciplines the concept that language use is habitual rather than logical. When one is fluent in language, he can manipulate it without conscious effort. Yet English teachers constantly ask students to think about rules and apply them as though the use of language were logical. In spite of generations of English teachers, when people speak they concentrate on what is being said, not on the way it is being said. Because writing provides greater opportunity for misunderstanding, a great deal more care is given to how something is said, and form and structure are more closely adhered to when one writes. Yet even in writing, *what* is being said gets the emphasis.

If language use is habitual, and one is attempting to teach a new language or dialect, it must be done by providing enough practice so that the new patterns of usage become a habit. No longer are old language habits broken down before new ones are achieved, but children are taught to use both, each habit as appropriate. Contrasting analyses of the various aspects of the phonological and syntactical components of both languages, or the forms within the language, greatly aid the child's grasp of the new language or dialect.

The Grammar of the Language

Finally, linguists have made teachers aware of the necessity of a scientific study of the way in which a language operates, which is the grammar of the language. Linguists are using a variety of tech-

---

[3] English Language Services: A division of Washington Educational Research Associates, Inc., Rockville, Md.

niques in their pursuit of knowledge. Machines are making it possible to observe, collect, and analyze language in a manner heretofore undreamed of. As patterns begin to emerge, equipment is available that makes possible the testing of hypotheses concerning these patterns against new data. Ever-widening possibilities for hypothesizing and testing bring to light new patterns and new categories and subcategories of words. Man has long recognized the changing nature of language, but the rapidly changing descriptions of language are finding most teachers and laymen quite unprepared for the onslaught of new information. Although most people are truly thrilled to be living in an age of exploding knowledge, the task of understanding, organizing, and teaching is so overwhelming that one can hardly be surprised if this onrush of new data is viewed with at least apprehension and at most, resistance.

The next chapters of this text will attempt to analyze rather specifically what linguistic knowledge to date has contributed to language learning in the elementary school. The distinct difference between learning a language and learning about a language will be made increasingly explicit as the book progresses.

QUESTIONS FOR STUDY

1. What is linguistics? How does it contribute to the understanding of English?
2. What does linguistics contribute to the teaching of language?
3. How have linguists used scientific procedures to inquire into the role of language in human affairs?
4. What are some contradictory views regarding the nature and use of the English language today?
5. How are the two facets of language study, learning a language and learning about a language, organized in the elementary school language arts program?

SUGGESTIONS FOR FURTHER READING

Board of Public Instruction, *Miami Linguistic Readers,* Dade County Materials, Miami, Fla. (Boston: D. C. Heath and Co., 1965).

Bloomfield, Leonard, *Language* (New York: Holt, Rinehart & Winston, Inc., 1933).

Carlsen, G. Robert, "How Do We Teach?", *English Journal,* vol. 54, no. 5 (1965), pp. 364–369.

Fries, Charles Carpenter, *Linguistics and Reading* (New York: Holt, Rinehart & Winston, Inc., 1963).

Gleason, H. A., *Linguistics and English Grammar* (New York: Holt, Rinehart & Winston, Inc., 1965).

LaFevre, Carl, *Linguistics and the Teaching of Reading* (New York: McGraw-Hill Book Co., 1964).

Marckwardt, Albert H., "Linguistics Issue: An Introduction," *College English*, vol. 26, no. 4 (January, 1965), pp. 249–254.

McDonald, James B., ed., *Language and Meaning* (Washington: Association for Supervision and Curriculum Development, N.E.A., 1966).

Wilson, Graham, *A Linguistic Reader* (New York: Harper & Row, Publishers, 1967).

TEACHER'S AID

1. Do-it-yourself grammar. Write each of the following words on a separate piece of paper: he, the, washed, never, Donna, car, Peter, a, ball, boat, desk, his, toy, my, she, Jane, seldom, saw, moved, pushed, sometimes, rarely, painted, frequently, her.

    Put the slips of paper into a box and draw five words out at random to make a sequence. Record your results. Your chances, mathematically, of getting a grammatical sentence are few. For example:

X	X	X	X	X
his	Peter	seldom	played	frequently

   Now arrange the slips into piles of words that will substitute grammatically for each other. For example:

he	frequently	washed	his	desk
she	sometimes	pushed	her	car
Donna	rarely	painted	my	boat
Peter	never	moved	a	toy
Jane	seldom	saw	the	ball

   Draw one word from each pile and arrange the words in a five-word sequence. Every sentence drawn this way should be grammatical.

2. Take the following set of words:

father	his	your	somewhat
very	a	short	this
ladder	seemed	strange	pretty
looked	rather	appeared	building
the	old	ugly	quite
became	grew	umbrella	stride

   There is a common five-word sentence pattern which can be composed from these words. Determine what the pattern is. List the words in each of the five-word classes involved. Make ten sentences by choosing at random from each word class in order. Your sentences must be grammatical, they need not be sensible.

Answers to Exercise 2

1st Class	2nd Class	3rd Class	4th Class	5th Class
a	father	looked	very	old
the	ladder	became	rather	short
his	umbrella	seemed	quite	strange
your	building	grew	somewhat	ugly
this	stride	appeared	pretty	pretty

For additional ideas for developing an understanding of grammar, see Paul Roberts, *English Sentences* (New York: Harcourt, Brace & World, Inc., 1962).

2

How Children
Learn Their Language

The problem of how children learn their language is an intriguing one for both psychologists and teachers. The most recent and exhaustive theory of language learning has been found highly questionable. In Noam Chomsky's review [1] of B. F. Skinner's *Verbal Behavior*, the concept of learning language through imitation and practice is challenged. Very young children produce hundreds of sentences daily. Many of these are entirely original; the child has never heard the sentences before. There seems to be some kind of sentence-producing mechanism in each human being.

Although how children learn their language is still a mystery, certain generalizations can be made regarding the present knowledge available on this topic. Nelson Brooks makes the following points about language learning: [2]

1. Language is universal and universally adequate to the conduct of human life.
2. No language has been discovered that is less systematic or less fluent than any other.
3. The infant learns the knack of language through reinforcement rather than by imitation.
4. The child of five throughout the world is thoroughly familiar with the structure of his mother tongue.

[1] Noam Chomsky, "Review of B. F. Skinner's Verbal Behavior," *Language*, vol. 35, no. 1 (January–March, 1959), pp. 26–58.
[2] Nelson Brooks, *Language and Language Learning: Theory and Practice*, 2d ed. (New York: Harcourt, Brace & World, Inc., 1964), pp. x, xi.

5. The usual response to words is to the conception of the things they stand for, not to words themselves.

6. When language is in action, grammar performs at an unconscious level; grammar is difficult to learn consciously, and if it is thus learned, it is equally difficult to forget when language is put to actual use.

7. Language is a phenomenon of sound, despite auxiliary help from gestures, pictures, and writing.

8. Language cannot be equated with communication. Communication takes place without language, and language, in both origin and function, goes far beyond the limits of communication.

9. The use of verbal symbols is exclusively human. Man and language are inseparable, and life without language is nonhuman.

In the process of language three levels of analysis are possible. The interaction of phenomena upon the senses is the first level. The second level involves recognizing concepts within the phenomena as common to certain groups or classes, and categorizing these. The third level is the formal, logical, or mathematical system with which the concepts seem to agree. Although some aspects of the system of language are beginning to emerge clearly, its vast complexities have not yet been unified. Physics, psychology, and descriptive linguistics become involved in any attempt to analyze even a simple specimen of language.

Language learning involves the establishment of a set of habits, neural and muscular, that can function automatically. In addition to the physiological and psychological nature of language, the social or cultural aspect is equally evident. Within a few months after a baby is born, he breaks the code of the language being used around him, and within a few years he masters its spoken form. Through the magic of language a human being gains knowledge about the environment in which he lives and gains insight into himself and his own nature. Without language this universal event would be incomprehensible.

Language is dual in nature. The *intake* or receptive aspect of language involves direct experience and observation, viewing pictorial representations, listening, and reading. The *outgo* or expressive nature of language demands a precise and fluent expression of ideas in oral communication or writing. An adequate experience in either speaking or writing requires (1) something to express and (2) someone to receive the ideas expressed.

The Child and Language Development

During the first school years (grades K–3), the child demonstrates steady progression in the nature of his interests, the mastery of his environment, and his ability to express ideas. His first period involves dynamic learning, and he moves from this stage to one of more channeled and more assimilative behavior. As the child progresses, he becomes increasingly aware of others. He begins to assimilate and organize learning experiences. In grades one and two the child is almost completely engrossed with learning to read and write his language. By grade three, a child learning his native tongue is ready to begin to learn something *about* his language.

Language development in the middle grades (grades 4–6) includes reaching out toward adulthood and increasingly independent control of personal and social behavior. The middle grade child is ready to polish and perfect skills, and his language contributes to and is developed through group process. This child is ready and eager to unlock the mystery of the system of his language, and through his study of the language he becomes increasingly aware of the great number and variety of resources possessed by every speaker of every language.

In a stage of rapid and uncoordinated growth the self-conscious upper grade child (grades 7 and 8) may seem listless, bored, and uncooperative. His interests fluctuate and his moods and taste are unpredictable. As he strives to change from childish ways to adult behavior, the upper grade child forms close friendships and joins clubs, groups, and gangs. Although he is interested in social conventions, he frequently feels insecure about the proper thing to do and needs frequent opportunities to practice social responses. His increasing knowledge about his language can help him realize his own amazing potential and help him appreciate those around him as he considers the fantastic ability of every speaker of every language.

Any learning situation involving the use of language needs a social situation with people, context, purposes, and communication needs. Children need to learn the community's approved social form for conversation, notes, letters, and telephone calls. The related skills, mechanics, usage agreements, and conventions needed in these experiences can best be taught in actual social situations requiring them. Elementary school children need to converse with each other. Many genuine opportunities arise which require the children to write invitations, and notes of appreciation or sympathy. Children should plan, organize, and direct their own school parties with much supportive guidance from the teacher. Telephone courtesy can be well taught using the fine equipment, and frequently personnel, made available to the schools by the local telephone companies.

Learning situations involving learning about the language include a recognition of the major strands of language and their relationship to each other. Spoken language, literature, and composition are the three main areas in which an analysis of phonology, morphology, and syntax are possible. Discovering the writing system through the use of literature, and the speaking system through the vehicle of dialogue can greatly enhance the learning experience.

The Teacher's Role

Because the teacher must organize and develop all aspects of language—listening, speaking, reading, and writing—in relationship to each other, these should be consciously planned for in each language experience. It is much more difficult to move the child from an isolated skill to its use in a meaningful situation than to move from a social situation to a meaningful skill. The problem, of course, is to learn how to pay the attention necessary to all aspects of language at a time and under the conditions which will make the learning situation efficient and meaningful.

One solution to this problem might begin with an effort to identify both things and activities which children usually enjoy, and to use these interests as the bases for language experiences. Various developmental materials available to the teacher in the form of reading texts, language texts, programmed learning materials, films, film strips, and records may be effectively used through this procedure.

Second, teachers must develop some judgment concerning the range of maturity found in groups of children, to provide experiences and materials which will meet their needs.

A third possible step involved in organizing all aspects of language into an efficient and meaningful learning experience, and related to the second stage, requires the teacher to obtain evidence of how rapidly each child can move within the language program.

Remembering that language develops in direct proportion to the child's opportunity to practice words and sentences, and that the children in any given classroom come from a range of environments, some of high linguistic level, some bilingual, and some in which little opportunity is present for saying words or being heard, the teacher will be conscious that fixed patterns of language development exist only in the minds of the writers of instructional materials, not in the language patterns of children.

The fourth step in organizing an effective language experience includes identifying and relating the important forces acting upon the development of language. Language patterns and interrelationships operate differently over periods of time. The forces and tensions which result from a maturing physical organism may make a child seem bored, uncooperative, or listless. Demands being made upon the child by a dynamic social environment may motivate and encourage language growth at one time and discourage it at another stage of development. Also, the experiences which encourage one child may discourage or even defeat another. The purposes and goals which evolve from a maturing concept of self are perhaps the most powerful forces influencing language development. The teacher must work closely with the child to help him discover, articulate, and extend his goals. This simultaneously keeps the teacher aware that all learning experiences must be organized and developed for the purpose of helping the child to achieve *his* goals, rather than to promote some artificial, imposed standard or requirement.

Last, the teacher must determine the adequacy of the child's language development. Evaluation is an integral part of every learning experience, not an arbitrary anticlimax to it. To evaluate language development, the teacher must follow each child over a period of time. Is growth in language facility obvious? Are there spurts of growth and then plateaus? Is the child aware of and encouraged by his progress? In addition, the teacher must compare the progress a child is making in the classroom development of specific language skills with his ability to use these skills to achieve his purposes in listening, speaking, reading, and writing. Progress in one aspect of the child's language development should be compared with progress in the other areas for each child, and all present achievement examined in the light of what can be done to improve future language development.

In summary, the amount and quality of language experiences are significant to children at all levels. Language development is (1) dependent upon opportunities for language uses and (2) positively related to cultural development. Because language power and thought power go hand in hand, language is the most important means of dealing with emergent concepts of self and the rapidly expanding environment.

Factors Influencing Language Growth

Psychological Factors in the Environment. An influential factor in the school's language program is the classroom climate. The classroom in which the child feels respected and accepted, and which provides adequate opportunity for him to acquire a rapidly growing and functional store of language meanings, certainly contributes to the development of communication skills. The psychological factors involved in language development, often difficult to cope with, are even more significant than the physical factors. Attitudes within the learner such as egocentricity, preoccupation with personal problems, prejudice, disinterest, and boredom may adversely affect language development.

When a teacher is sincerely interested in the potential growth of each child in the classroom, his understanding is immediately felt by the pupils. Teachers' attitudes are revealed not only by what they say and do, but also by the tone of voice used and facial expressions. The successful language teacher is poised, gracious, and friendly. Pupils are treated with respect, their mistakes are met with understanding rather than with derision. They are accepted "in spite of" rather than "because of" what they can do at any given time during their development. The teacher's competence in stimulating and guiding pupils in their activities gives them a feeling of confidence and belongingness as they work toward the realization of their goals. In such a climate the *self* begins to emerge. Children begin to think, to express, to create, and to evaluate. Growth in language results!

Physical Arrangement of the Classroom. The physical arrangement of the classroom probably affects in some manner the extent to which the child is able to relate to his peers and to establish within himself a concept of his acceptance and self-worth. It also affects his op-

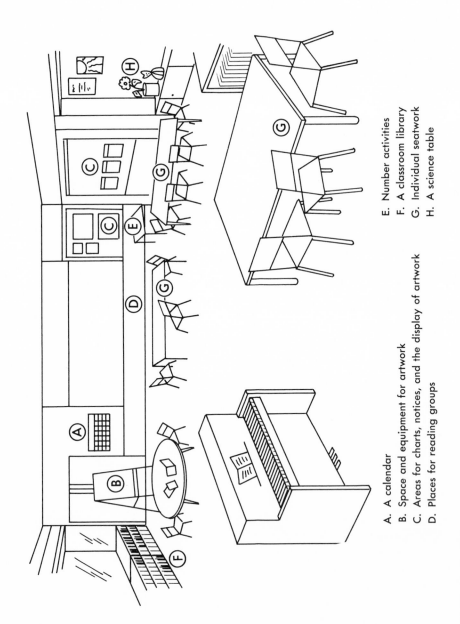

A. A calendar
B. Space and equipment for artwork
C. Areas for charts, notices, and the display of artwork
D. Places for reading groups

E. Number activities
F. A classroom library
G. Individual seatwork
H. A science table

portunity for language growth and use. The elementary school classroom needs to provide children with a wide variety of materials to explore, manipulate, and utilize if interests are to be tapped, information gained, and the child provided with "something" to say.

Colorful bulletin boards, whether developed by children or the teacher or both, should be attractively arranged to create interest and extend learning experience. Questions are excellent captions because they at once interest and involve the student. Realia tables may include questions on cards—"What is it?" "How is it used?" "By whom is it used?" "For what purpose is it used?"—placed beside the realia. Pictures, maps, globes, and charts should be displayed in a fashion to arouse curiosity and evoke response, and the teacher should provide experiences which require their use. Arithmetic materials and games such as quizmo, flash cards, pegboards with colored pegs, counting frames, number charts, a variety of abacuses, number lines, integers, common fractions, decimal fractions, bases (other than ten), relationship rods, and slide rules encourage children to develop new terminology and extend number concepts. A science corner including materials and directions for exploring and experimenting, as well as a variety of specimens to observe, can provide excellent background for language experiences. Books can be attractively displayed to encourage children to browse. Books should be many, easily available, and selected with the needs, interests, and abilities of the children in mind.

The seating arrangement of the classroom is extremely important. Today's tables and desks are movable and should be moved according to function and purpose. Children should not sit in five rows of eight desks or six rows of six for every learning experience. For adequate communication, children should be able to see and hear each other.

The example of classroom arrangement illustrated on page 18 provides for adequate language development. In this example the child is not too far away from the speaker to hear or to see visual aids. The speaker can move quickly and easily around the group to show pictures or realia. At tables children can face each other directly, an arrangement of utmost importance for the early years during which listening and speaking are the primary language vehicles for learning. If the classroom is too warm, too chilly, or too noisy, children may be distracted. Conversely, if outside noises are minimized, if desks and tables are free of attention-distracting materials, if the teacher's voice is pleasant and he is poised, gracious, and friendly, the classroom environment will be conducive to developing adequate foundational language skills.

Physical Factors Within the Child. The teacher must also remember that physical conditions within the child, such as hearing loss, speech impediments, and eye problems, may deter language growth. In addition, malnutrition, fatigue, or any bodily ailments which interfere with the general output of energy can create problems for the child as he attempts to listen, speak, read, or write.

Language and Human Relationships

Have you ever heard an argument that didn't get anywhere or a conversation which was based on a complete misunderstanding of a point of view? In all probability the block in communication was caused by:

1. The way in which ideas were expressed.
2. Particular words which aroused hostility or caused confusion.
3. Strong feelings which blocked thought.

Language creates problems which extend far beyond the problem of acceptable usage into the intricate problems of structural meaning and semantic meaning.

The Function of Language

The dual function of language makes it possible to refer simultaneously to a fact or situation and to the expresser's feelings about the fact or situation. Both functions are legitimate, but they frequently become confused in the mind of the expresser as well as in the mind of the receiver. In separating these language functions, the first use is called *referential* because it refers to a fact or situation. The second function, which is *emotive* or *affective*, both expresses and affects feelings. This dual function of language operates within a dual world, the world of words and the world of fact. Confusion concerning the relation between the two language functions creates overwhelming misunderstanding.[3]

---

[3] S. I. Hayakawa, *Language in Thought and Action,* 2d ed. (New York: Harcourt, Brace & World, Inc., 1964).

Language reflects life. Sometimes the reflection is clear and precise, sometimes confused and confusing. Originally language attempted to state what the senses perceived. Nouns and verbs stated verifiable facts. The complexity of today's world, and its reflection, makes verification so difficult that it seems at times impossible.

Meaning in Language

Words, lexical units, have meaning only as they are used in patterns. The context of the patterns may be physical, social, or verbal. No word has precisely the same meaning twice. It depends entirely on the context in which it is used. People frequently disregard context and misinterpret meaning, and this creates great confusion and misunderstanding in human relationships.

Words both name, or identify, and suggest. Thus meaning is both denotative and connotative. **Denotative language,** which names, identifies, and describes, is the language of science, the language of accurate reporting. **Connotative language** extends the actual experience and affects the emotions of the receiver. This is the language of literature. Dallas Lore Sharp believed that only a combination of the denotative and connotative aspects of meaning could complete an utterance.

> Experience and expression are the same thing or the complete thing—clay and form and molded jar; one does not have all the experience, not until one has given form to it, meaning, and so invested it with the image of oneself that writing thus becomes a second life, a way of living twice, now in the spirit with the word—revisiting the scene, recalling the incident and, free from accident and extraneous detail, recalling what was at first hazy and half a dream.[4]

Words may be true in two basically different ways, they may be literally true or scientifically accurate; or they may express a true feeling or a sincerely held idea. When these two types of meaning conflict, confusion and resulting tensions create problems in human relationships.

Language seeks to state what the senses observe. Thus the basic form of language expression reports what has been seen, heard, tasted, smelled, or felt. An accurate report includes the three criteria listed at the top of the next page.

[4] Dallas Lore Sharp, "Five Days and an Education," *Harper's Magazine,* vol. 151, no. 1,101 (August, 1925), pp. 273–280.

1. The facts may be verified and there are words which fit the facts.

2. The reporter excludes judgments concerning the facts because the report should not include what the reporter thinks or how he feels, as these judgments stop thought on the part of the receiver.

3. The report avoids "loaded" words, words that arouse feelings, slant ideas, or direct judgment.

The good report lets the facts speak for themselves. Because people tend to disregard these rules, good reporting is rare and confusion common.

Words also legitimately communicate feeling. The tone of voice with its dramatic variations of rhythm, rhyme, and repetition; the context and resulting atmosphere of association in which words accrue; devices such as metaphor, simile, personification, irony, and humor—all are employed in the communication of feeling. These devices are part of the affective use of words. They affect people by encouraging pleasant or hostile feelings.

In summary, the basic language problem involves recognizing the difference between facts and inferences about them, between scientific and poetic truth, and between denotative and connotative language. Misjudging the intended meaning, or confusing the two types of meaning, interferes seriously with communication.

Generalizing and Abstracting

Two language processes essential to thinking, generalizing and abstracting, often lead to empty talk. Generalizations drawn from too few facts are not only meaningless but can also be misleading. For example, "The students rose up in protest," is said, when in reality four students spoke out in protest. High-order abstractions like democracy, faith, and love can be meaningless words. When these words are used, specific questions involving who, when, where, what, and how need to be asked. For example, a group of teachers have little conflict in accepting good citizenship as a goal of elementary education. However, when they are asked to describe the specific behavior which makes a good citizen, they are in an area of immediate disagreement. Is a good citizen a quiet child who does not interrupt, or one who is actively and sometimes noisily engaged in solving problems?

The Minneapolis Public Schools Communication Guide suggests that language may be viewed from the following four angles:

1. Sense (literal meaning), the principal factor in referential language.
2. Feeling, the attitude of the speaker or writer toward what he is saying.
3. Tone, the attitude of the speaker toward his audience as revealed through language, e.g., sarcastic tone, casual tone, belligerent tone.
4. Intention, the purpose that lies behind an utterance.[5]

The Guide points out that almost every utterance can be viewed from each of these four angles. Feeling and tone are especially important in poetry. Intention is the dominating motive in politics and advertising. Sense is the principal factor in referential language, the language of work, business, science, and education.

Only as man understands language and its function can he hope to look beyond the utterance and comprehend its meaning and intent and thus really communicate. Only as he is able to communicate can he have satisfying human relationships. Man needs to understand and appreciate value systems, basic ideas, and concepts which are different from his own. Different words are not simply different labels for the same ideas. If satisfactory human relationships are to be achieved, man must seek to know his neighbor's heart as well as his neighbor's mind. Both the denotative and connotative aspects of language must be developed, together with an awareness of the difference between the two, and a sophistication concerning when, where, how, and with whom to use each.

In summary, it is obvious that the elementary school teacher has a tremendous responsibility in helping pupils gain increasing facility in the use of language as well as teaching the system of language. To accomplish this goal the teacher must be able to speak fluently

[5] Minneapolis Public Schools, "Communication: A Guide to the Teaching of Speaking and Writing," reprinted in Anderson, et al., Readings in the Language Arts (New York: The Macmillan Co., 1964), pp. 40, 41.

[6] The "accepted dialect of the community" is a term used in this book as a synonym for standard English. Man lives in a series of expanding communities within the world community. Each of these communities influences and is influenced by the other communities. For example, the neighborhood both affects and is affected by the town or city, which in turn relates in a similar manner to the county, state, region, nation, international, and world communities. Community, for purposes of this text, however, refers to the language area of a group of people. Linguists discuss language boundaries in terms of isoglosses. These are statistical abstractions representing lines which indicate the limit of some stated degree of linguistic change. For purposes of this text, the much less precise concept of language community may suffice. Accepted dialect or standard English as used throughout the text stands for the language used by educated people. Hence, the "accepted dialect of the community" means the language used by the educated people of a given group of people who speak one dialect of one language.

and effectively the "accepted dialect of the community." [6] He must have a thorough knowledge about the system of the language and be consciously aware of the difference between knowing a language and knowing about a language. In addition, the teacher should know each individual child, his abilities, interests, attitudes, and needs. Finally, he should be a competent artist in guiding children through the learning process.

QUESTIONS FOR STUDY

1. What cultural influences are reflected in language learning?
2. What are the various ideas expressed in the literature regarding how children learn their language?
3. How do schools attempt to meet the language needs of very young children, children in the middle grades, and upper-grade children?
4. How do schools provide for individual differences?

SUGGESTIONS FOR FURTHER READING

Cronbach, Lee J., *Educational Psychology* (New York: Harcourt, Brace & World, Inc., 1963).

Gagne, Robert M., ed., *Learning and Individual Differences* (Columbus, Ohio: Charles E. Merrill Publishing Co., 1967).

Havighurst, Robert J., and Neugarten, Bernice L., *Society and Education*, 2d ed. (Boston: Allyn and Bacon, Inc., 1962).

Jespersen, Otto, *Language: Its Nature, Development and Origin* (New York: Henry Holt and Company, Inc., 1922).

Jones, J. Charles, *Learning* (New York: Harcourt, Brace & World, Inc., 1967).

Piaget, Jean, *The Language and Thought of the Child* (New York: Harcourt, Brace, and Co., 1932).

TEACHER'S AID

1. Miss Jones has a neat, cheerful fifth grade classroom. There are plants at the windows. Pictures from an art lesson are displayed above the chalkboard. There are several colored photographs of wheat harvesting and a sheaf of wheat displayed on the bulletin board. Also on the bulletin board under the label *Our Best Writing* are eight writing papers. At desks which are arranged in orderly rows, each student is working quietly in his fifth grade workbook.

   Do you think that the climate of this classroom provides for language learning? Why or why not?

2. Select a child to observe in language situations during the next two weeks. Select one who is somewhat average for the group in mental age but who is having some problems related to school progress. You will be tempted to select an aggressive child because he will be demanding much of your time and taxing patience. Please do not overlook the quiet child who makes no effort to get help when he needs it.

Use the following outline form to describe the child's behavior and the reaction of the child's classmates and teacher to his behavior.

Psychologists tell us that the self can be understood only from the study of both internal and external data, thus the outline offers you an opportunity to describe not only the child's behavior but the reaction of the teacher and pupils to his behavior.

Be sure to keep your descriptions objective. Make no attempt to analyze or interpret the behavior. Simply record the specific behavior. For example: Notice the difference in the following reports of the same observation:

Record A. Jimmy arrived at nine-fifteen this morning. He walked around the inside of the planning circle, tripping over several pairs of feet. He made considerable noise as he sat in his chair. He is chairman of the street scene committee. Today he shouted answers to each question his committee members raised. When the class started work the teacher asked Jimmy not to join his committee today until she was sure that he could move and speak more quietly. She suggested several things with which he might occupy himself: number cards, a library book, a crayon picture.

Record B. Jimmy arrived at nine-fifteen this morning. He deliberately tried to upset the planning circle by disturbing others. To add to the confusion, he was clumsy and noncooperative. To show off further, he shouted answers to all the questions his committee asked about the work on the street scene. The teacher told him the group could do better work without such a noisy chairman and had him take out his number cards for study.

What the observer reported in B may have seemed true from the observer's point of view, but remember to record only factual happenings on the outline.

Description of Classroom Activity in Progress & Specific Time	Description of Child's Behavior	Description of Classroom Reaction to Behavior	
		Children	Teacher

3

Curriculum Organization
and Language Learning

The citizenry of today's world needs more than the two-way process of communication in which men talk, write letters, and direct personal ideas to specific individuals or small groups. Although this two-way process, speaker-receiver, is still basic to communication, additional competencies in communication are necessary today.

The average man of the last century could read a little, write his name, phrase a simple note or letter, and add a column of figures. Today's citizen must at least be aware of the historical background of present-day life, know about the mechanical processes and tools which he uses constantly, understand human relationships, and know some scientific facts if he is to function adequately. This knowledge provides a basis for understanding the information presented in current publications and news broadcasts, and it gives man sufficient background to understand the conversations of his neighbors. Modern man is also faced with the problems of distinguishing among a variety of values. In order to evaluate a constant avalanche of propaganda, he must be able to grasp the total idea involved in an argument and recognize the specific contributions of subordinating points.

Today's child, then, must be equipped with adequate knowledge and skill, positive attitudes, and the power to think as well as to speak, listen, read, and write. He needs these abilities, if he is to help solve socioeconomic and scientific problems for himself and other individuals, communities, states, and nations in a world that will be so radically different from today's world that leaders and teachers find it nearly impossible to visualize or predict it.

Education for today's child involves learning to solve problems of significance at his own maturational level, not only because psychologists have pointed up the positive relationship between learning and meaningful goals,[1] but also because it is pointless to train children to meet the adult needs of today's world when their own adult world will be so different.

Today's child must learn:

1. The verbal skills of oral and written communication.
2. The problem-solving skills of analyzing problems; gathering, verifying, and evaluating data; formulating and applying conclusions.
3. Reading skills involved in all kinds of experiences, including pictures, cartoons, and illustrated charts and maps.
4. Discrimination skills for use in listening to radio and television.
5. The interpersonal skills of insight and understanding needed for meeting and getting along with people of varying backgrounds.

These are the "arts of communication," and teachers must constantly modify the curriculum to teach these language arts.

Providing for Individual Differences

Perhaps the most difficult problem teachers face in the classroom is that of providing for individual differences. Because children have a wide range of needs and abilities, teachers must motivate different pupils, find materials suited to the children's various levels of ability, differentiate assignments, diagnose and correct difficulties, test and evaluate achievement, and make success possible for every pupil.

As early as 1927, Hull's study of the variability in amount of different traits possessed by the individual provided insight into the impossibility of designing a curriculum for uniform mass-instruction procedures.[2] *Individual differences* include dissimilarity among various children in any characteristics such as subject matter (i.e., reading ability, spelling ability), interests, cultural background, physical characteristics. *Trait differences* refer to the variability

[1] Ernest R. Hilgard, *Theories of Learning*, 3d ed. (New York: Appleton-Century-Crofts, 1966), pp. 469–472.

[2] Clark L. Hull, "Variability in Amount of Different Traits Possessed by the Individual," *Journal of Educational Psychology*, vol. 18, no. 2 (1927), pp. 97–104.

within the individual concerning his own relative standing in reading, spelling, arithmetic, music, and art. For example, a child might be reading above grade level but functioning below grade level in arithmetic. Today's schools are obligated to furnish instruction and materials of difficulty commensurate with the range of ability in a given class. The great emphasis on individualizing instruction is simply an attempt to make education more than the low-order, rote-memory mental process required to name, describe, or define. This type of learning substitutes information for education and cannot possibly equip man to live in the space age.

Retention of Learning. Tyler and Wert investigated the relative permanency of different types of learning, and their experiments indicated that, in general, learning that involves problem-solving relationships and the operation of the higher mental processes is relatively permanent, whereas learning unrelated facts and unorganized information is relatively temporary.[3]

Learning must involve differentiation and integration of old and new behavioral responses into a meaningful, purposeful problem-solving type of mental process, or into an organized behavior pattern, if it is to have permanence or value for the individual. For example, if a student is taught to develop a usable vocabulary it will remain with him. If the student develops the ability to read literature and social science materials at a given level of difficulty and with a given degree of comprehension, he will retain this ability. If a student has developed the ability to write effective business letters or interesting personal letters, to think on his feet and speak effectively to a group, to use the library and basic reference materials, to organize ideas for effective presentation, to conduct a meeting, to get along with people, and to maintain harmony in social groups, these abilities will be maintained.[4] These same abilities, essential to man's effective existence in the space age, must be provided for in school curriculums.

Grouping to Individualize Instruction. The practice of grouping pupils according to some measure of general ability (intelligence, general

[3] Ralph W. Tyler, "Permanency of Learning," *Journal of Higher Education*, vol. 4, (1933), pp. 203–204.
[4] Robert H. Beck, Walter W. Cook, and Nolan C. Kearney, *Curriculum in the Modern Elementary School*, 2d ed. (Englewood Cliffs, N.J.: Prentice-Hall, Inc., 1960), pp. 48–49.

achievement, teacher opinion, or a combination of these) in order to minimize individual differences was extensively adopted throughout the United States following the rapid development of group intelligence and achievement tests in the early 1920's. Such grouping ignored trait differences. Research carried out during the following ten-year period provides substantial evidence that general-ability grouping, if perfectly done, still reduced the variability of classes only 20 percent. In other words, instructional groups formed by general ability groupings are not sufficiently homogeneous to warrant designing a curriculum for instructing an entire group.[5]

Effective educational experiences encourage rather than eliminate individual differences. The typical range of ability in relevant educational traits is four years for first graders. In the sixth grade it approaches eight years. Schools have tried to find some procedure that might make instructional groups homogeneous so that mass instruction of large classes and the use of uniform texts, instructional procedures, and standards of achievement could be possible. This, of course, would educate great numbers of children with minimum expenditure of money. Because no way has been found to achieve true homogeneity in grouping, if the most effective teaching is to take place schools must accept the wide range of ability found in all classes as inevitable, accept it as something good, highly desirable, and necessary in the scheme of things, and determine procedures for meeting individual needs of children in classroom groups.

Adjusting the Pace of Instruction

The position that certain common learnings should be attained and that everyone should stay in school until he masters them, requires teaching for specific educational outcomes. Such a policy, followed in the days when a child stayed in the first grade until he could read his primer, is evident to some extent in the nongraded primary unit that some children complete in two years, some in three years, and some in four years. It appears in linear programmed instruction which brings all learners to fixed content, each at his own rate. The nongraded primary organization, programmed instruction, and homogeneous grouping are all based on adjusting the pace of instruction.

[5] *Ibid.*, for a complete discussion of individual and trait differences.

These programs invoke a concept of "rate of learning," which is highly debatable. Woodrow [6] spent twenty years compiling evidence that rate of learning is inconsistent from one task to another and that there is no justification for identifying mental test scores with ability to learn. Humphrey's [7] findings are in harmony with this position.

Cronbach [8] hypothesizes that when several intellectual tasks are to be learned under the same instructional conditions, there will be some individual consistency in time needed to reach the criterion. This hypothesis implies that the person's learning rate will vary, depending on the nature of the instruction. Therefore, adapting instructional technique would be expected to be more important than altering the duration of exposure.

Changing Programs to Meet Individual Needs. Schools have sought to provide for individual differences by altering programs. Certain high school students are counseled into general mathematics rather than algebra on the assumption that algebra will be too difficult. Yet many primary grade curriculums include algebra. Unquestionably, the variety of techniques as well as the organization of content make it possible for even young children to grasp basic algebraic concepts.

Frequently, schools add onto existing programs instead of redesigning them to teach new concepts and extend new skills. Supplementary instruction is often provided as remedial treatment to fill in gaps in skill, and to put the student back into the regular pace. Such treatment seems intent on erasing individual differences. Branched programmed instruction, with its continuous diagnosis of misconceptions or gaps in recall, and the assignment of a short linear program covering a single topic or subskill for independent study in an area of weakness, are kinds of remedial instruction that attempt to remove individual differences. The compensatory education programs now in progress are remedial in nature. The goal of these programs is to develop skills and attitudes that will constitute normal readiness for primary school.

[6] H. A. Woodrow, "The Ability to Learn," *Psychological Review*, vol. 53, no. 3 (May, 1946), 147–158.

[7] L. G. Humphreys, "Some Investigations of the Simplex," *Psychometrika*, vol. 25, no. 4 (1960), pp. 313–323.

[8] Lee J. Cronbach, "How Can Instruction Be Adapted to Individual Differences?" *Learning and Individual Differences*, ed., Robert M. Gagne (Columbus, Ohio: Charles E. Merrill Publishing Co., 1967).

Adapting Teacher Response to Individuals. The teacher is constantly faced with adapting classroom experiences to the needs of the individual. One child will be told where to get information when he asks for help; another will be helped directly because the teacher has decided to encourage the first child to develop increasing independence and to minimize the frustration of the second child. The teacher may barely acknowledge one comment, and then praise a lesser contribution. He allows options for term papers and projects, and plans individual projects for people of special ability or limitations. These adaptations are informal, based on a variety of cues from test records, daily work, and observations of work habits and social interactions. Do teachers overdifferentiate? Can differentiation based on impressions from cues be inefficient or even harmful to pupils? Can adaptation be systemized and error reduced?

Studies [9] show that students who are high on achievement motivation and low on anxiety need simple instructions in dealing with problems where there is moderate risk. Their work improves when they are told that they have done poorly, and they seem to operate effectively in homogeneous grouping situations. However, adding pressure through competition lowers their scores. On the other hand, students who are low on achievement motivation and high on anxiety are most persistent when they think the chance of success is very low. Pressure such as a cash prize, pacing, and stern supervision improves the work of these students, as does favorable comment on their progress.

Perhaps one day pupils can be diagnosed with the aid of computers. Then the computer might suggest activities appropriate to the student's interests and abilities based on empirically validated rules. Both differential and experimental approaches to learning will need to be used to build the adaptations. In the meantime teachers must accept individual differences and deal with them honestly and effectively, realizing all of the problems involved.

The Concept of Individual Worth

The 1965 Annual Conference of the Association for Supervision and Curriculum Development presented several topics which crystallized the concept of the preciousness of people. Harold Hand [10]

[9] *Ibid.*

[10] Harold Hand, University of South Florida, addressing the Fourth General Session of the ASCD 20th Annual Conference (Chicago, February, 1965).

presented two beliefs basic to the "righteousness" of democracy. First, all human beings are supremely precious simply because they are human beings, and second, all human beings are of equal as well as of supreme moral worth.

Ernest D. Melby [11] told the second general session of the Conference that for a third of the children in our schools, the available offering is so ill-adapted to the maturation and previous life and experience of the children that they not only fail—they develop dark self-images, and often become so alienated that they are unemployable or delinquent.

Melby believes that teachers are still more interested in what children study than in what the study does to children. He stated that a true educational system would honor and respect every child, rich or poor, black or white. It would educate the parents so that they could give the child a good home life. It would work to make the community a better place in which to live. School would begin for large numbers of children when they are three years of age, and our best teachers would go to the children in greatest need of their help.

Such education would be more concerned with the child's liking for what he studies than either the facts he remembers or the skills he acquires. The child who likes school, his teacher, and the subject he studies will always learn. He is learning that he *can* learn, and this is about the most important thing he can learn.

Arthur Combs [12] extended the concept of the preciousness of individuals, and the resulting challenge to teachers, by pointing out that literally bushels of evidence are available to demonstrate that intelligence can be changed. Creating intelligence has been accomplished and teachers need to do much more of it. Experts are reasonably certain that man is not the victim of heredity. Rather, he is the victim of his own limited experience. Whatever restricts experience and free exploration limits an individual's intelligence. Whatever reduces a person's self-image, or feelings about himself, also reduces his intelligence.

[11] Ernest D. Melby, Michigan State University, addressing the Second General Session of the ASCD 20th Annual Conference (Chicago, February, 1965).

[12] Arthur W. Combs, University of Florida, addressing the Second General Session of the ASCD 20th Annual Conference (Chicago, February, 1965), based on evidence presented by J. McV. Hunt, *Intelligence and Experience* (New York: The Ronald Press Co., 1961).

Professor Combs further stated that intelligence is made up of one hundred twenty qualities of which present tests measure no more than eight. Whether a person can behave effectively and efficiently depends on the extent and availability of experience which in turn are determined by:

1. The individual's health.
2. The individual's opportunity for experience.
3. The individual's need for fulfillment.
4. The question of values.
5. The degree of threat and challenge.
6. The self-concept.

Attitudes of teachers can limit or strengthen the self-concepts of children. Language teachers then will accept both the child and his language. There will be no attempt to eradicate the language which the child brings to school, his first dialect. Instead, the school will teach a second dialect as though it were a foreign tongue. The advantages of learning and using standard English should be pointed out early in the child's school career.

Teachers need to remove any element which limits an individual's growth and reduces his self-image, substituting in its place whatever enhances and strengthens the self, whatever opens up a person's experience, whatever encourages the individual to try, and whatever interests and excites.

In addition to individual and trait differences found in children, cultural differences also create problems for education. The present emphasis on the culturally disadvantaged child indicates at least an awareness of such problems.

A number of levels of culture prevail in the Western world. These include the Judeo-Christian culture, Western European culture, North American culture, South American culture, Midwestern or Southern culture, and even cultures of academic or occupational groups.[13] Although nearly every individual has had some experience with each of these levels of culture, the precise nature of the experience differs for each individual and is largely determined by who he is, where he lives, and what he does—his position in society.

[13] William O. Stanley, B. Othanel Smith, Kenneth D. Benne, and Archibald W. Anderson, *Social Foundations of Education* (New York: Dryden Press, Inc., 1956), p. 21.

An unmistakable characteristic of the current social scene is the increasing insistence of minority groups for social, political, and economic equality. As the nation works toward increasing measures of equality to all its citizens in the areas of job opportunities, housing, voting rights, and utilizing public and private services, the schools must be ready to extend some promises to children in line with an open and flexible social system.

The Disadvantaged

At this point it is probably advisable to discuss that group of children, newly discovered in a sense, and known by various labels such as the culturally different, educationally deprived, underprivileged, and disadvantaged. For a long time these children have been lumped into a slow-learner category, and teachers have failed to distinguish the divisions among pupils in the lower academic levels of the class or school. Disadvantaged children often are *not* slow learners.

The disadvantaged children are those children who come from America's slums, both rural and urban, and they include blacks, Puerto Ricans, migrant whites, Mexicans, and American Indians.

Most of the disadvantaged children come from families that have no job security, little or no schooling, and annual incomes which fall below the established minimum subsistence level of the nation. More than half of these children have only one parent, and many have never known either parent. The families of these children live on the rim of society, and make up one-quarter of the population.

Among the disadvantaged is a group of children from foreign-speaking or otherwise different cultures. These children are slow, average, superior, and gifted, just like the rest of the school population. Many of these children could succeed in college and most could at least be contributing members of society. However, conventional intelligence tests fail to measure their ability, and the curriculum of the average school frequently hastens the decay of their self-concepts and reduces their ability to deal successfully with ideas, language, and books. The measured intelligence of these children usually declines as they progress through school, and few of them ever attend college.

The disadvantaged child is multiplying at a disproportionate rate, as science and automation increase minimal education requirements for labor. Increasing numbers of unskilled and semiskilled fall below the subsistence level. This threatening and nationally reprehensible condition has resulted in the present national war on poverty.

Somewhat over half of the disadvantaged children share two special characteristics: they are Black, and they live in urban slums. Although there is wide acceptance of the belief that well-prepared, interested teachers are essential to an effective program of education under normal conditions, good teachers can rarely be attracted to the schools of disadvantaged children, where they are most sorely needed. The teacher in the school of the disadvantaged must not only understand and believe in the culture of the community and be sensitive to the methods most practicable for transmitting its values, but he must also be a working sociologist, psychologist, and anthropologist. He must learn to understand the structure of the culture of his students, he must be able to look with compassion and understanding on a way of life that is the only life they know, not one which they have chosen.

The Task Force of the National Council of Teachers of English has studied nationwide projects and programs for the disadvantaged and offers the following ten guidelines for adapting educational experiences to the special needs of the disadvantaged:

1. Every reasonable measure should be taken to establish, especially at the local level, lines of communication and bonds of cooperation among persons, organizations, and institutions working with the disadvantaged.

2. Children should be permitted to operate in the dialect of their community at the lower levels of elementary school education, and direct instruction in the use of standard informal English should be begun no earlier than the intermediate elementary grades.

3. Oral language should receive greater stress in language instruction for the disadvantaged at all levels of education, from preschool through adult.

4. All levels of instruction in the English curriculum for disadvantaged students should include appropriate imaginative literature chosen and presented with these students in mind.

5. Policies of teacher placement should be revised where necessary to enable school principals and project directors to play a direct role in recruiting teachers for positions in schools for the disvantaged.

6. Greater financial support should be given to school programs for the provision of ample materials and personnel.

7. Administrators and project directors should develop deliberate programs to make available to teachers reports on new research and experimentation.

8. Both pre-service and in-service teacher education programs should develop courses dealing with the application of current educational theory to classroom teaching, especially in the study of language.

9. The problem of developing adequate structure and continuity throughout all levels of school, from preschool through twelfth grade, should be the responsibility of the school district.

10. Teachers of the disadvantaged should possess at least a working knowledge of developments in structural and transformational grammar, in social dialectology, in psycholinguistics, and in language and cognitive development.[14]

Gifted and Fast-Learning Children

Gifted children, who are capable of a consistently high level of performance in one or more areas of human behavior, and fast-learning children present a special challenge to education. It is still extremely difficult to identify gifted children. Psychologists draw attention to the "late bloomers" and "early faders" and have difficulty in spotting consistently superior performers. In addition, as early studies regarding intelligence indicated and as later studies verified, giftedness seems not to be a general thing, but quite specific with the individual. If the development of all of the child's potential calls for an educational setting from the beginning, then indeed the school is faced with a continuous challenge. Because the idea of equality of educational opportunity is seen as something different from identical educational experience, schools are also faced with finding a workable program which provides for the special needs of fast-learning children, who have a wide variety of educational experiences outside school, whose skills in reading are highly developed, and who are eager to learn. (See the suggested enrichment practices at the end of this chapter.)

[14] Richard Corbin and Muriel Crosby, cochairmen, *Language Programs for the Disadvantaged.* The Report of the National Council of Teachers of English Task Force on Teaching English to the Disadvantaged (Champaign, Ill.: NCTE, 1965), pp. 271–281.

Foreign Languages

Modern elementary education, burdened with the load of mushrooming knowledge, population increase and mobility, and the need for meeting varied individual needs of children in this highly dynamic society, faces concurrent pressures when disciplines such as geometry and foreign language seek admittance to the present overcrowded curriculum. Is a foreign language essential for children growing up in today's world?

The Modern Language Association of America claims that:

1. The learning of a foreign language contributes to the general learning process of the child.
2. Because language is a vehicle of culture, the child who commits to memory jingles, songs, and verse in a foreign language is cultivating a taste for and a love for literature.
3. The learning of a foreign language can be an element of enrichment and support for many parts of the curriculum.
4. Foreign language serves to cultivate the child not only as an individual, but also as a member of his own society,[15] particularly in the United States, since numerous words are borrowed or derived from other languages.

In addition, the Modern Language Association cites numerous experimental programs as evidence that the five-year-old child is ideally equipped to begin to learn the skills of a foreign language.[16]

It is interesting to note that research is also available to "prove" the following:

1. Bilingualism in young children tends to retard their learning of the mother tongue.
2. Some children with language disabilities are further hampered academically and emotionally by instruction in a second language.
3. Older pupils learn a foreign language more rapidly than do younger children.

The childhood years have advantages in linguistic flexibility, but the late high school and college years are the period of greatest learning ability in general and are closer to the time of possible use. Prob-

[15] Reports of Work Conferences (December 11–13, 1953 and June 11–12, 1954) as reprinted by permission of the Foreign Language Program Research Center, Modern Language Association of America in Anderson et. al., *Readings in the Language Arts* (New York: The Macmillan Co., 1964), pp. 431–432.

[16] *Ibid.*, p. 432.

ably the truth is that dependable research is insufficient to indicate conclusively the best age to introduce a second language.[17]

An examination of the literature shows many writers in agreement concerning the desirability of a bilingual American society in order to enhance international understanding. Opponents of this point of view present the antagonism existing between certain European nations whose citizens are bilingual and multilingual as evidence that friendship, cooperation, and mutual respect are related to attitudes rather than a person's ability to speak another language.[18] Educators also disagree on the reasons for teaching foreign language at the elementary school level. Should the purposes of this language teaching include (1) the ability to communicate in a foreign language, (2) the development of a foundation for high school or college language experiences, (3) the ability to communicate with minority groups in the area, or (4) to learn about a foreign tongue and culture rather than to speak and understand the language?

If and when goals can be agreed upon, some questions of organization still remain:

1. Does it seem possible to make the second language functional? Will children be able to use the language, and if it is started at the elementary level, will there be consistent follow-through in the progression of the language experience? Repetition eventually results in boredom, while lengthy gaps create loss of facility in using the language.[19]

2. What is the probable long-range cost of the program? One suburban district, providing a modest estimate based on minimum salary figures, calculated that it would cost $42,000 to provide instruction from grades one through six and at least two hours per week.[20] Do the children need twenty-five minutes per day of French or Spanish more than they need other experiences which equivalent time and money could buy?

3. What language will be offered? At what level? To whom? How will the experience be evaluated? Of course the answers to these questions will be determined largely by the goals of the programs

---

17 *Enclyclopedia of Educational Research.*

18 Harold G. Shane and June Grant Mulry, *Improving Language Arts Instruction Through Research* (Washington: Association for Supervision and Curriculum Development, N.E.A., 1963), p. 112.

19 Edward Diller, "Sequences of Growth and Instruction in Foreign Language in the Elementary Schools," *California Journal of Elementary Education,* vol. 30, no. 2 (November, 1961), pp. 115–120.

20 Anne S. Hoppock, "Foreign Language in the Elementary School," *Education Digest,* vol. 22, no. 2 (February, 1957), pp. 9–12.

which presently vary from community to community. Sufficient evidence for absolute answers is certainly not available, but research in the field does provide some direction.[21]

There seems to be general agreement that elementary school children could profit from many vital experiences with several cultures, including their languages. These experiences are intended to provide interest and readiness for future intensive foreign language training. If, as the Modern Language Association suggests, a study of language is introduced at the earliest possible time, a program based on the oral–aural approach should probably be designed in such a manner that children can learn to communicate rather than simply to learn a smattering of phrases. Such a program seems of little value unless children have an opportunity to use the language and develop continuing facility and skill in its use.

Probably any child who is interested should be allowed to learn language. There seems to be no reasons for limiting foreign language experiences to the academically gifted.

In some districts a foreign language may be educationally unsound. No program may be a better policy than a program which lacks continuity, adequately trained teachers, or sufficient time for development. Foreign language programs for elementary schools hold much promise, but their adoption should be preceded by carefully planned and objectively evaluated studies to determine specific needs and establish clearly defined goals.

In summary, the actual planning of the language arts curriculum calls for general decisions in selecting content and determining methodology as well as specific planning concerning the kinds of learning experiences to be provided, the amount of time to be spent on teaching, practicing, and using the new knowledge and skills, and the possible ways of providing for individual differences. The teacher needs to be aware of the choices available, and then to make decisions based on his ability and experience as well as on the particular needs and abilities of the pupils, the physical environment of the classroom, and the instructional materials available to him.

QUESTIONS FOR STUDY

1. How are the various areas of language arts organized for instruction in today's elementary schools?

[21] Shane and Mulry, *op. cit.,* pp. 111–125.

2. Some suburban neighborhoods tend to group people of similar socio-economic backgrounds, interests, and abilities. How does this influence the language program?
3. How should the use of slang in the classroom be handled? How should the teacher deal with (1) children who swear and (2) children who use English considered to be substandard by the educated community?

SUGGESTIONS FOR FURTHER READING

Anderson, Paul S., *Language Skills in Elementary Education* (New York: The Macmillan Co., 1964).

Brooks, Nelson, *Language and Language Learning,* 2d ed. (New York: Harcourt, Brace & World, Inc., 1964).

Lado, Robert, *Language Teaching* (New York: McGraw-Hill Book Co., 1964).

Tiedt, Iris M., and Tiedt, Sidney W., *Contemporary English in the Elementary School* (Englewood Cliffs, N.J.: Prentice-Hall, Inc., 1967).

TEACHER'S AID

Read the following case study and consider the aspects of lesson preparation, arranged environment, curriculum organization, and teacher-pupil interaction which affect learning.

Case Study

The teacher, Mrs. Combs, was busy making last-minute preparations before the children came into the classroom at the conclusion of the first morning recess. She had planned to show a filmstrip on the Indians of South America, but the third grade teacher was still using the projector. Mrs. Combs decided to present an extended introduction to the strip, as it would be at least fifteen minutes after the next period began before the projector would be available.

The children were lining up outside of the room at the sound of the first bell when Mrs. Combs, who had opened the door to admit them, noticed Mr. Packard, the principal, coming toward her. As he approached, Irene Combs nodded and said, "Good morning, Bill."

"Good morning, Irene, I hope you won't mind if I sit in on your social studies lesson during this next period," responded Bill Packard.

"Of course not, Bill," she replied. "That is, if you don't mind putting up with a few inconveniences, such as the setting up of the film strip projector in the middle of the lesson. You know our standard complaint about not having enough A-V equipment."

"Yes, I know," said Bill. "It will be a relief when the P.T.A. finishes their fund drive to finance the new projector."

By this time the children had assembled in two lines, boys on one side and girls on the other. When they were reasonably quiet and orderly, Irene Combs asked them to move into the room and take their seats.

Mr. Packard followed the last child into the classroom, and sat down in the back of the room. Mrs. Combs walked to the front of the room to begin her hastily constructed but lengthy introduction to the filmstrip. Mr. Packard, understanding the situation, began to take visual inventory of the classroom environment.

As his eyes roamed about the room, his attention fixed on a bulletin board in front of the room. It was entitled "Citizenship" and was artistically produced. A large apple tree displayed beautiful apples, each with the name of a child printed across it. Some of the apples (names) appeared near the top of the tree, others were scattered throughout the many branches. Some apples were on the ground under the tree. Several of the apples contained yellow worms. Bill Packard wondered about the utilization of the bulletin board, and he jotted a note to himself to ask Irene at the first opportunity.

His eyes moved on around the room. He noticed a display of six arithmetic papers with perfect scores neatly arranged under the title "Our Best Work."

There was a daily schedule on the chalkboard for Mrs. Combs's sixth grade. Bill noticed that no time had been allotted for art, and that only fifteen minutes had been reserved for Phys. Ed. Bill jotted down additional notations to help him remember questions that he wanted to ask in his follow-up conference with Irene.

A portable easel held a tag board chart which listed eight positively worded class standards.

The social studies bulletin board displayed a large colored construction-paper map of South America. Bill knew that this was a newly erected project, because Irene had asked for his help to carry the opaque projector to her room two days before. Two students had stayed to help her project the map on the paper, and outline it so that it would be accurate.

Irene had a reputation for keeping the cleanest classroom in the school. She was the custodian's best friend. In addition to keeping the room picked up, Irene's desks were in neat rows making it possible for the custodian to sweep without moving too many desks.

Although Mr. Packard had come to observe the social studies lesson, he had unconsciously missed the introduction to the filmstrip. His survey of the room stopped abruptly when some third grade children wheeled in the projector. Mrs. Combs hurriedly inserted the filmstrip, had the room darkened, and began showing the filmstrip.

Several children volunteered, at the teacher's request, to read the captions. Bill noticed that the volunteers were sitting in the two rows on the left side of the room. Mrs. Combs selected Jim to do the reading. As Jim read the third frame, three children stood up and said, "I challenge." Jim had made a mistake in pronouncing a word. The children who were standing corrected Jim's mistake. This happened four more times during the filmstrip viewing.

After the lights were turned on and the shades were opened, Irene continued her lesson. Her first question called for a comparison between the Indians of North and South America.

Dale, sitting in the middle row, volunteered to answer and was called on by Mrs. Combs.

"There is little likeness because most of the Indians in South America live in big stone houses, and the North American Indians live in teepees," he responded.

Before Dale had finished his sentence five children on the left side of the room leaped to their feet and shouted, "I challenge! All the Indians in North America do not live in teepees!" A protesting Dale attempted to correct himself, but the teacher interrupted with, "Yes, only certain tribes—the nomadic ones. Now can anyone think of any other contrasting characteristics of the Indians?"

At this point Dale resorted to muttering to himself and poked the unsuspecting boy in front of him. This resulted in a slight commotion and Irene said, "Dale, settle down. I don't want any more disturbance from you." Her meaningful stare accented the words.

Dale slid down into his seat, mumbling. As the boy in front turned around to snicker, Dale struck him again.

"Dale, that's just about enough from you! You come with me!" shouted Irene as she grabbed Dale by the arm and marched him outside.

The class became quite noisy until they remembered that the principal was sitting in back of the room, then they quickly settled down.

In a few minutes Irene and Dale reentered the room. Dale sheepishly settled down in his seat, and Irene marched to the front of the room. Before she could resume her discussion a child handed her a piece of paper which she read carefully. Her voice was firm as she remonstrated, "I find that I cannot trust certain children while I am out of the room, therefore, I'll have some company with me after school. We have wasted enough of our time and we should now return to our lesson, rather than wasting any more of our valuable time on issues that should not be included in our social studies period."

Obviously Irene was frustrated. She sighed a breath of relief when the second recess bell rang. As the children left the room Bill said, "Let's go to my office and have a cup of coffee. We can talk about ten minutes concerning your lesson. I have several questions I'd like to ask you."

As Irene followed the principal to his office, she apologized for the lesson. "Things seemed to come apart at the seams today. I can't quite understand what went wrong! I've had some exasperating times in my past two years of teaching, but this past hour has completely exhausted me."

"Some days are like that," responded Bill, "but try to compose yourself. You still have about four hours to teach, so try not to worry about it!"

The coffee was ready when Bill entered his office and as he poured two cups he said, "I'm sorry to rush you, but I do have several questions and only ten minutes! Let's see—oh, yes, I made a note about your citizenship board. How does it work?"

"Each week we hold an election via secret ballot to find out who the good citizens are. The names of children receiving the most votes are placed near the top of the tree, while those receiving negative votes are placed on the ground. When a child, whose name is on the ground, redeems himself, a worm is put in his apple and he is allowed to progress back up the tree," answered Irene.

"I see," said Bill. "How about the process of children challenging children? Also, I noticed that most of the challengers seemed to be sitting in a group, the two rows on the left side of the room."

Irene responded, "As you know my major goals in teaching are to emphasize accuracy and individuality. To achieve these goals I encourage the children to challenge and correct anything said in the classroom with which they disagree. Even I have been challenged by several of the children. Also, I find it convenient to seat children according to reading achievement. In addition to having the highest reading achievement, the children on the left side of the room have the highest I.Q.'s."

"That certainly explains the activity from that side of the room," replied Bill. "One other question—why only fifteen minutes for P.E., and no time for art on your daily schedule?"

"The art supervisor comes to the classroom once a week," answered Irene, "and because I'm not too confident with the subject, I decided to eliminate it from my schedule. The Phys. Ed. period is shortened five minutes a day because I need the extra time for arithmetic, and I feel that the children get enough physical exercise and not enough mental activity. Sometimes I use the extra time for language arts."

Even as Irene spoke the bell rang. Bill said, "Ten minutes can surely go by in a hurry, but I feel that I now have a good overview of your class, your organization, and some idea of your teaching methods. I now think that I can be of real help to you with your program. May I see you after school to continue the conference?"

"Of course," answered Irene, "I will appreciate anything you can offer."

"Fine," Bill replied. "I'll see you in your room at 4:00 P.M."

What suggestions can you make for Mrs. Combs's classroom in the following areas?

(a) Physical environment
(b) Class organization
(c) Handling of Dale
(d) Curriculum
(e) Attitude toward art and physical education

Enrichment Practices for Able Children

1. Utilize gifted students to plan a hobby show; a book fair.
2. With your help, have gifted students organize and edit creative writing of students, reproducing it as a magazine for the school.
3. Utilize gifted students in the staging, lighting, production, and costuming of plays.
4. Cut out six cartoons from a magazine. Cut off the captions. Paste the cartoons on a large sheet of paper and have children write new captions.
5. Establish one reading group basing reading and research on individual interests. (Suggested activities: pupils organizing their own projects, writing their own reading books, making their own vocabulary lists, illustrating their own books.)
6. *Give these activity suggestions to the children:*

   Catalog the books in the classroom. Make book cards and file them alphabetically.

   Read many books and share with the class.

   Read books on mythology to obtain background for classical literature and share with class.

   Prepare favorite poems or short stories for oral reading in class.

   Write an original poem about (1) a holiday soon to come, (2) the social studies unit, (3) the science unit, etc.

   Prepare a calendar showing birth dates of American poets or writers; choose selections to read each month on their birthdays.

   Prepare descriptions of characters in stories that the class has read; have the other pupils guess the identity of the characters ("What's My Line?").

Use the thesaurus to obtain as many synonyms as possible for words in a given sentence.

Write original poems about stories you have read.

Write a talk, imagining you are a guide, taking visitors around the school, the community, or the world. Present this to the class, together with pictures.

Write dramatic plays, a radio script, or a TV broadcast of countries or industries being studied.

Do advanced dictionary work—find the etymology of words.

Express in writing (or orally) your feelings about music, books, painting, etc.

Create your own dictionary of new words.

Take charge of making a class diary or log. Each day make entries describing what the class has done. Read these aloud to the class at the close of each day as a method of evaluation.

Prepare a talk (in each case, show the teacher the notes from which talk will be presented) on these subjects:
    My favorite food and why
    If time were to go backwards
    If I could have three wishes
    If the whole world were made of rubber
    The most dangerous thing that ever happened to me
    The saddest thing that ever happened to me
    If I could be invisible
    My hobby
    Things that are beautiful to me and why
    The reasons we obey laws
    How to be well liked
    What I want to be when I graduate
    The time I had the most fun
    If I were a parent
    If I had a million dollars
    I I could fly
    If I could invent anything
    The time I was most embarrassed
    If I were a girl (boy)
    How to win friends and influence people

Interview the principal. Write a report telling about his life. Use these topics:
    Birthplace

Childhood experiences
Hobbies now
Hobbies when he was a student
Professional training
Things he (she) wishes for

Write a letter to the following consulate, chamber of commerce, etc. Obtain free materials for your science (social studies) unit.
(Teachers list addresses appropriate to the unit.)

-------------------------   -------------------------

-------------------------   -------------------------

-------------------------   -------------------------

Think about all the cowboy movies you can remember, and watch several in the next week. List all the things that happen regularly. What things are common to them all? For example, does the "good" man always win in the end? Prepare a report on your findings.

Write a letter to the following pen-pal project:

Friendship League Inc.
Boston, Massachusetts

Write an autobiography, telling your life from childhood to the present. Use the following outline:
Birthplace
Occupation of parents
Memory of early life: first house
                    exciting events
                    pets
First school experiences
The happiest moments in my life
Biggest disappointment
Hopes for the future
Hobbies

Write a biography of your mother or father or some interesting adult you know. Include the following information:
Birthplace
Number of brothers and sisters
Their parents' occupations
Nationality
Schooling
Exciting events in their early lives
Present occupations
Hobbies

Select the career that appeals to you most; list five qualifications you have that might appeal to a future employer.

List six careers for which you think you might be suited. Check the one for which you think you are best fitted. Tell why.

The eagle is often criticized as the symbol of the United States because it brings to mind a bird of prey, a bird which lives by killing other animals. Tell why this bird was selected as our symbol and give its history.

Write down three of your "pet peeves" along with creative suggestions as to how they might be minimized.

Pretend you have invented a new breakfast food. List six ways in which you might test it before offering it to the public.

Make a list of all the ideas you can think of to encourage motorists to drive carefully and safely.

Write your ideas on how you would get more citizens to go to the polls on election day if you were the mayor of a city.

Name all the possible uses for a common brick you can think of.

Look at a simple screwdriver (metal blade, wooden handle). Jot down all the ways screwdrivers have been improved to make them more effective instruments. Suggest three further improvements in the design of this tool.

Pretend it is a cold rainy day. Think up ten ways a child of eight could amuse himself indoors by using imagination.

Draw a picture of the nicest thing you can think of, write a story about it.

"A tenor is not a voice, it's a disease," said G. B. Shaw. Explain what he meant. Write a similar humorous statement on the subjects of woman, politician, television.

Give six steps you would take, if you were in charge of a library to make it more popular.

Write six alternative headlines for the leading article in yesterday's newspaper.

Write down the word "mother." Under it put down the first word it makes you think of. Repeat the process with the second and succeeding words until you have a list of six. Identify the law of association by which you were guided to each.

Write a classified ad offering for sale a vest-pocket exercising kit and a bed-making machine.

If you were to teach reading in the elementary schools, what would you do to make it more interesting and more important to your students?

Write five imaginary headlines that you would most like to see in tomorrow morning's newspaper.

Suggest what improvements in a bus you would make for the comfort and convenience of passengers.

Name five inventions which the world could use to advantage which have not yet been invented.

Using your own words and the encyclopedia, prepare a report on the evolution of languages; numbers.

Evaluate current comic books as to:
    Interest
    Action
    Violence content
    Does good win out over evil?
    Which types are better than others? Why?

Act as room librarian:
    Keep books in order.
    Sign them in and out.
    Display new books.
    Keep an interesting library corner.

Collect books in other languages and make a display of them.

Tell about your most exciting day.

Tell about the funniest thing you ever saw.

If you could do what you want to do for one whole day, tell what you would do and why.

What impossible thing would you like to do.

Post pictures of various pets. Make up some good advice for a mother pet to give a baby pet before it goes out into the world.

Be any one of Uncle Sam's treasures (Statue of Liberty, Declaration of Independence, The First Flag, etc.). Tell what you stand for.

Describe one miniature masterpiece of nature—one small perfect thing.

4

Varieties of Methods for Language Teaching

Method is defined in Webster's *New World Dictionary* as a way of doing anything, a process, especially a regular, orderly, definite procedure or way of teaching, investigating, etc. Definitions of method in books on education range all the way from types of school and classroom organization, such as team teaching, the Carnegie unit, and the Lancasterian system,[1] to specific ways of presenting a single structure.[2] Such confusion in the use of language is very common, and this chapter is designed to point up some of the areas of confusion, and to give the beginning teacher some criteria for choice of method.

If the definition of method as a regular, definite way of teaching is acceptable, although general, several questions need to be asked before one can decide how to teach. First, what is to be taught, second, why is it to be taught to this child at this time, and third, how can it be taught most effectively and efficiently in terms of speed and ease of learning, and time, money, and effort involved in teaching?

Learning and Experience

Learning by experience has been a popular concept in lay circles as well as educational circles for many years. What exactly does one learn by experience? Do most experiences ever occur twice in

[1] Harold T. Johnson, *Foundations of Curriculum* (Columbus, Ohio: Charles E. Merrill Publishing Co., 1968).

[2] Fe R. Dacanay and J. Donald Bowen, *Techniques and Procedures in Second Language Teaching* (Quezon City, Philippines: Phoenix Publishing House, 1963).

the same way? Is the value of the experience to be found in its potential for transfer of learning? There is a widespread notion that learning from experience is superior to learning from books, professors, or homework, as evidenced by many and varied requests for "experienced" people. Why is this true? What specifiable regularities can be found in experience?

To answer some of these questions it will be helpful to ascertain the meaning of learning. There are several different ways in which this term is used by authorities in the field of education and learning theory. Learning is used to mean an observable change in behavior. It may be caused by some observable action, and it may have only temporary significance; in any case it is in an observable interaction between man and his environment. Another definition of learning is that it is an interpretation or inference drawn from observation involving such concepts as thoughts, intentions, motives, or resolutions. Such a definition is probably based on a conception of relations existing between needs, motives, beliefs, and intentions. A third definition states that learning occurs when a general principle is applied to a specific situation.

A number of empiricists begining with Locke have stated that man learns only by experience. Simple ideas come directly from experience, and more complex ideas come indirectly from experience. If experience can be defined as any interaction between an individual and his environment, and if learning can be defined as a change in behavior not resulting from maturation or fatigue, then both going on study trips and reading books can be considered learning experiences.

Statements in the English language such as, "He certainly learned from that experience," or "He didn't learn," imply that sometimes people learn from experiences and sometimes they do not. Dewey's definition of experience negates the idea that one might not learn from experience. He states:

> When an activity is continued into the undergoing of consequences, when the change made by action is reflected back into a change made in us, the mere flux is loaded with significance. We learn something. It is not experience when a child merely sticks his finger into a flame; it is experience when the movement is connected with the pain which he undergoes in consequence.[3]

[3] John Dewey, *Democracy in Education* (New York: The Macmillan Co., 1916).

According to Robert Hutchins,[4] learning by experience is different from learning in school. He states that experience may be left to other institutions and influences, and he recommends that education should emphasize the contributions that it is supremely fitted to make. He points out that young people do not spend all their time in school, and that experience, therefore, may be wisely left to life, permitting the schools to set about their job of intellectual training.

Learning by experience is often used as part of an evaluative statement on the nature of learning, or the nature of education, in an implicitly persuasive definition. Thus used, it implies relating two sense data that are seen to be connected, explaining the general process by which knowledge comes into being, or pointing out an accompanying characteristic of experience which may or may not always be present. There seems to be a newer focus on *learning experiences* rather than *learning by experience*. This focus emphasizes experience as that into which learning leads rather than as that from which learning results. The new emphasis does not eliminate the linguistic confusion that exists in the terminology, however.

Child-Centered Learning Experiences

Other assertions in education, equally meaningless, create confusion. Yet many so-called methods are based on such assertions. "Education for life adustment" is an example of vagueness and ambiguity. What does adjustment mean? Another statement, "Teach the child, not the content," is equally ludicrous. How can one teach someone without teaching him something? The "Needs Curriculum" has had great appeal even though there is little consensus regarding the ambiguous term *need*. Need is defined as whatever one lacks or is deficient in. It is then used in the educational literature in such statements as, "Children need affection." This statement generally is not used in the context of a lack, but rather in the sense that the child desires affection periodically. Statements such as, "The class needs drill," may or may not be true, but they are probably not based on the lack of such things as drill. Statements such as "A 'C' average is needed for graduation" puts need in the context of a rule.

[4] Robert M. Hutchins, *The Higher Learning in America* (New Haven, Conn.: Yale University Press, 1956).

In addition, school requirements and social requirements are frequently not the same. If meeting needs means to assist the student to reach his goal, the idea is conclusive although largely without support. If meeting needs refers to specific motives such as "have a wagon" or "build a house," or to general motives like providing affection, status, or achievement, there are different ways of achieving such goals. The methods of achievement can be considered only after the kind of affection, status, or achievement needed has been established.

Subject Matter and Learning

Another confusing term, widely used and affecting concepts of method, is *subject matter*. Every method is dependent on what subject matter is being taught, and yet definitions of subject matter range from concrete specifics that can be perceived by the senses to subject matter such as knowledge.[5] Subject matter defined as knowledge can vary in significance and utility, and it can be taught effectively, ineffectively, or not at all, but it is still subject matter. Smith, Stanley, and Shores have defined subject matter as follows:

> The members of a social group participate in two kinds of activities: first, those such as hunting, selling, farming, manufacturing, and the like, which result in the procurement of food, clothing, shelter, and other necessities of life; second, those involving the common life of the group, such as singing, storytelling, worshipping, bartering, voting, and obeying a system of law. From these activities emerge techniques, facts, principles of interpretation, rules of conduct, and aesthetic principles comprising what the social group has learned about the world, about ways of using the world and of improving its beauty, about man himself, and about how to live together. Such knowledge, values, and techniques constitute the subject matter of the group.[6]

Such a definition imbeds relationships between knowledge, values, and techniques, and it requires a look at at least two kinds of knowledge, knowledge-about and knowledge-how. **Knowledge-about** is knowledge that something is so, and **knowledge-how** is how to do something. Although the two kinds of knowledge are related they are yet distinct, and lack of recognition of the discreet nature

---

[5] William H. Burton, "Implications for Organization of Instruction and Adjuncts," *Learning and Instruction,* 49th Yearbook (Chicago: National Society for the Study of Education, 1950), Part I, Chapter IX.

[6] B. Othanel Smith, William O. Stanley, and J. Harlan Shores, *Fundamentals of Curriculum Development* (Yonkers-on-Hudson: World Book Company, 1950).

of these two kinds of knowledge has frequently led to confusion in teaching. For example, in language development, a native speaker of English who comes from an educated family may speak English fluently and effectively without knowing any of the rules of syntax or pronunciation, and without being able to talk about his language in any fashion. On the other hand, a foreign student may know all the rules and be able to articulate them and yet not be able to speak English. In the first case the speaker knows how, in the second, the speaker knows about. The former emphasis in language teaching, predicting that large doses of grammar would improve speech or writing, did not take these differences into account. New methods in teaching must be cognizant of such distinctions.

Knowledge-about depends on language and involves the process of knowing or perceiving. It might, therefore, be called cognitive language. Knowledge-how does not require the verbal process involved in cognitive knowledge and perception, and therefore it may be considered noncognitive. Although knowing how can be learned through imitation and without knowing about, knowing about greatly enhances the learning of knowing how. For example, in learning to speak a second language the child needs a great deal of practice and a good model for learning how. When these are supplemented with a clear presentation of the problem to be studied, together with a contrastive analysis of the sound or structure in both the native and target languages, learning is greatly facilitated.

Teachers are concerned primarily with the dissemination of knowledge. Materials are brought into the classroom and a variety of experiences are provided to enhance knowledge, because different experiences result in different knowledge. Such knowledge is sometimes expressed in terms of factual statements and sometimes as valuative statements about the knowledge known as attitudes. Many teachers believe that knowledge is best acquired through experiences that involve the child physically, as well as mentally and emotionally, so they provide a wide variety of activities for the child. Certainly children who are actively involved in learning experiences of any kind seem to be happier and have fewer behavior problems in the classroom than children who do not participate, for one reason or another.

Some educators object to the concept of subject matter as cognitive knowledge, because they claim that it results in teaching that places a premium on memorization, in passive learning, and on reading, rather than discovery. Such relationships between the concept of subject matter as knowledge and particular methods of teaching are not necessarily dependent. A teacher can use unsound methods, or sound ones, to teach knowledge-about or knowledge-how, but the unsound methods result from either the lack of sufficient knowledge to do otherwise or the teacher's own lack of skill to use the knowledge he has to good advantage.

Methods for Teaching Language Arts

Discussion and controversy about methods have been part of the educational scene for many years. A great deal of educational research has been devoted to evaluating the effectiveness of one teaching method as compared with another, yet numerous experiments to determine the value of certain methods have produced only inconclusive results. Unquestionably, inadequate control of experimental conditions and the complexity of the phenomena being tested have affected the results, but it does seem that much of the controversy is not relevant to the real problems of learning. Almost any method is justifiable if it considers the expenditure of time and energy involved on the part of both students and teacher, the availability of aids, and the interests and resources of the students and teacher, and if it remains faithful to the desired objective. As long as methods of language teaching do not falsify or betray objectives, they can vary according to the size, age, interests, and abilities of the class, its previous training, the materials available, the training and ability of the teacher, and other details that are peculiar to a given situation. The teacher's responsibility, then, is to be sure that the objectives are clear and valid for the students, that materials are adapted and used to facilitate the achievement of the goals, and that he is utilizing all available information about the learning progress of his students.

The following methods have been used and are being used for teaching the various aspects of language in the public schools:

1. The unit method crosses subject matter lines to integrate learning experiences. The plan requires more time than the usual class periods and uses a variety of activities, experiences, and learning approaches. The content of the unit is selected to contribute to the meaningful whole which will result from the various areas studied.

This approach emphasizes the use of language, or the knowledge-how, and it utilizes knowledge-about.

2. The problem-centered method, in which the teacher arranges a situation in such a manner that the children can discover and define the problem, provides teacher and pupils an opportunity to decide together possible approaches to the solution of the problem. Some of these approaches will be discarded on the basis of information already available; others will be tried and evaluated. Again, knowledge-how is emphasized and knowledge-about is brought to bear as needed.

3. In the broad concept plan, specific content and activities are selected and organized as a unit of study that will extend over several weeks and result in broad concepts, generalizations, or understandings. This approach emphasizes knowledge-about.

4. The inquiry method based on observation of data, discovery of elements, generalizations, testing of generalizations, and modifying generalizations is similar to the problem-solving and discovery methods, although it uses a variety of different techniques. All of these methods emphasize knowledge-how, and knowledge-about is utilized as it contributes to an understanding of the process.

5. The generative-transformational method for understanding language, used in modern English grammar to teach the writing system of English, presents the concepts found in the writing of professionals. Knowledge-about morphology, phonology, and syntax is taught. This method of teaching English grammar is used in recent texts, such as the Roberts English Series,[7] and is designed to enhance and extend knowledge-how through knowledge-about.

6. Many methods have been suggested for teaching the basic word lists that are part of most spelling programs. *The test-study method* recommends giving the children a test to see what words they know before assigning them words to study. *The study-test method* presents the new words, provides opportunity for the use of the new words, tests the students, utilizes the words in further practice, and tests again. Variations of these methods are found, together with recommendations for drills and games. A new method

[7] Paul Roberts, *The Roberts English Series: A Linguistics Program,* Teacher's Edition, grades 3–9 (New York: Harcourt, Brace & World, Inc., 1966).

recommends teaching words in linguistic patterns that demonstrate the relationships of words and regularity of rules. Thus it helps children to discover and generalize the rules of sound and spelling which depend on the syntactic as well as the phonological component of grammar, e.g., the spelling of plurals and other inflectional changes, additions, and deletions, and derivational changes such as adding prefixes and suffixes. These methods are primarily concerned with knowledge-about to establish spelling as a tool for writing.

7. The methods for teaching the mechanics of writing, handwriting, spelling, capitalization, and punctuation vary, but they all utilize the concepts of show, practice, and evaluate. The elements involved in composition can be taught both directly and inductively, and the method selected will depend on the situation. (See Chapter 11 for specific suggestions.) One method for teaching rhetoric at the upper grade levels combines grammar and compositions as follows:

(a) Have the students see and construct sentences lacking the element to be taught.

(b) Add to these sentences the new element in such a way as to make clear what has been added.

(c) Lead students to recognize what has happened to the meaning or to the structure of the sentence as a result of the addition.

(d) Have students construct many sentences using the new element.

(e) When use of the new element is familiar, when it can be recognized, and when students can use it accurately, teach its name and practice using it.

(f) Test students' grasp of the new element by having them write sentences using the named element in its various functions.[8]

8. The group method, providing children the opportunity to work in small groups, makes it possible for the teacher to involve every child in experiments, discussion, problem solving, and other learning experiences. Group process is the means by which the individual can participate with satisfaction to himself in social planning and control, and feel that his efforts are not lost or submerged by forces too great for him to cope with as an individual. The group method, the basic method of democratic socialization, is the framework in

---

[8] Philip H. Cook, "Putting Grammar To Work: The Generative Grammar in the Generative Rhetoric," *English Journal*, vol. 57, no. 8 (November, 1968).

which the individual can improve himself as a contributing member of society.

Although the group process contributes to providing for individual differences, offers an ideal learning situation for developing citizenship qualities needed in a democracy, and stimulates language development, it is rarely used in the classroom. For this reason the Teacher's Aid at the end of this chapter gives specific principles and directions for group process. The teacher will recognize many of the basic principles of sensitivity training included. The major emphasis in group process, however, is understanding, appreciation, and respect for others while retaining and developing the self-concept, acquired together with skills, attitudes, knowledge, and appreciation through communication with the inner self and the physical and esthetic environment, in addition to relationships with other people.

Methods for Teaching Reading

There are a number of methods for teaching reading in use in the public schools today:

1. Individualized reading, although frequently called a method, uses so many different procedures that it is difficult to describe as a method. It proposes to allow the child to read at his own level the books he likes best and to provide him an opportunity to make steady progress without experiencing failure. The value of this method as a total reading program is largely dependent on the ability of the teacher and the maturity of the children. All reading programs include individualized experiences for children.

2. The phonic method is a phonovisual approach to looking at letters and learning the sounds that the letters symbolize. This method is usually used in conjunction with other methods.

3. The basal reader or controlled vocabulary method attempts to provide sequential development in reading from reading readiness through skill development to understanding and interpreting literature, reading for research purposes, and individualized reading for personal growth and enjoyment. The basal reader method attempts to help the child develop a sight vocabulary and attack words independently through the use of phonic, structural, and contextual clues.

4. The linguistic method seems to be an attempt to move naturally from known sounds to the symbols for the sounds. Reading is thought of as turning symbols back into speech. When symbols are patterned so that children can discover relationships, reading is facilitated. This method has real promise for the improvement of reading instruction, although many so-called linguistic readers offer little in the way of content or interest to children. The Dade County Linguistic Readers are a notable exception and provide interesting content as well as linguistically sound organization.[9]

5. The Initial Teaching Alphabet (ITA) *, contributed by Sir James Pitman of England, consists of forty-four graphemes, or symbols for sounds. The ITA is not phonemic, does not have a one-to-one correspondence between the sounds and letters of English, but it does avoid many of the problems of the twenty-six letter English alphabet. The first symbol, æ, represents the long *a* because the regular spelling of the long *a* in English is VCe (vowel, consonant, *e*) as in *made*. According to Pitman, when the child reads a word like *made* he must read to the final *e* and then return to the vowel before he can pronounce it. If the vowels are together, as in æ, such reverse action is not necessary. He follows through with the same idea in all the symbols for the long vowels, ee, ie, œ, and ue.

Another symbol that differs from traditional orthography and looks like a backwards z (ƨ) is used to represent the /z/ sound of noun plurals and other /z/ pronunciations of the spelling *s*. The ƨ can be converted with ease to the manuscript *s* when the transition is made to traditional orthography.

The voiced and voiceless /th/ sounds are symbolized by th for the voiceless sound as in *thin* and th for the voiced sound as in *the*.

The consonant blend /sh/ is represented by ſh, /ch/ by ch, and the /ng/ sound is represented with an *n* with a small g beneath it ŋ to correlate it with the later traditional spelling of the sound. Two other different symbols are the ω for the vowel sound of *book* and the ꝏ that symbolizes the vowel sound in *spoon*.

The effectiveness of ITA for beginning readers is currently under investigation, and although there are many proponents for the

* From i.t.a. Bulletin, Volume 3, No. 3 (Spring, 1966). New York: Initial Teaching Alphabet Publications, Inc. Reprinted with permission.

[9] Pauline M. Rojas, director, *Miami Linguistic Readers*. Miami Ford Foundation Project (Boston: D. C. Heath & Co., 1966).

method, questions regarding its value for all children as an initial step, and the long-range value in terms of improved reading and writing, have not yet been answered.

6. Programmed instruction provides a developmental program for children ranging from visual discrimination to the exploration of literature. The materials are used by children who work at their own rate of speed with little help from the teacher. Responses are checked immediately, and programs designed to cover all of the points in the developmental sequence are presented in small units to ensure the success of the pupils. Some teachers resist programmed instruction because of its emphasis on factual knowledge, and some students seem less motivated when they are required to work independently. Nevertheless, programmed learning provides valuable learning and can be used in conjunction with other methods.

7. The language experience method of Lee and Allen [10] combines oral and written language with reading. Children move from a common experience, such as taking a study trip, doing experiments, or viewing a film or picture to a class discussion. The teacher records the utterances of the pupils, and the teacher and pupils read what has been recorded and discuss the words. The information is then duplicated and used for individual group reading lessons. Children can then move on to copy the exercise, add sentences, or write their own ideas. Linguistic knowledge emphasizes the fact that reading should follow listening and speaking, and that children should be taught to read patterns that they have already met in their use of the language. The content of such reading material has both meaning and interest for children.

Inductive and Deductive Methods

Two other teaching methods that receive a great deal of attention in the literature are the inductive method and the deductive method. The discussions of educators regarding the merits of inductive versus deductive methods create the illusion that they involve two different types of learning. However, deductive and inductive processes represent two ways of arranging conditions to make necessary discriminations among stimuli. **Inductive learning** is the term used for the kind of learning that takes place as a result of interaction with a variety of experiences, all of which have some common conceptual element, or which involve a common principle. As the learner is able to identify the concept or discover the principle, he is learning. This kind of learning is used in the inquiry and discovery methods. **Deductive learning** occurs when, after having been given the identifying elements of the concept or element to be learned, the learner identifies the element and applies the principle as he uses his newly acquired knowledge.

The relative effectiveness of inductive and deductive methods obviously depends on a number of variables, such as the complexity of the concept, the capacity and experience of the learner, and the criteria used to judge the results of learning. Many objectives can be accomplished effectively and with great efficiency and speed using the deductive method. Because studies demonstrate that motiva-

---

[10] Dorriss M. Lee and R. V. Allen, *Learning to Read Through Experience*, 2 ed. (New York: Appleton-Century-Crofts, 1963).

tion and retention are frequently higher when students learn inductively, complex concepts and principles that involve periods of time and a fair amount of effort will probably be most effectively handled with an inductive arrangement. Studies also show that some children learn very slowly through an inductive approach, while others fail completely to grasp the concept or are unable to define it with any degree of precision. The inductive method is presently receiving widespread acclaim,[11] but the preceding evidence indicates that no matter how effective it is, a single method cannot achieve the great variety of educational objectives connected with language learning, nor can a single method provide for the individual and trait differences to be found in children.

Before attempting to select methods for teaching, the beginning teacher might find it profitable to analyze the behavior of teachers and pupils as they interact in the learning environment. Teachers locate, make, organize, and arrange materials for learning experiences, and present activities and lessons to achieve specific language objectives. They instruct by giving directions, defining, classifying, explaining, comparing and contrasting, making inferences about what is known and not known, evaluating, and identifying. Teachers interact with children as they state rules and beliefs, share knowledge, provide specific suggestions to help the child improve his performance of motor skills such as handwriting, and reinforce learning. Teachers admonish children by praising, correcting, and commending. Teachers act as a model for language when they show rather than tell the pupil how something is done, and teachers express attitudes toward language and toward learning through bodily posture, facial expressions, expressions of the eyes, and tone of voice, as well as through the words they use.

As pupils make and use materials, define, classify, explain, and perform other of the same kinds of behaviors that the teachers do, they are demonstrating their participation level in the instruction. Teachers will be in a position to analyze and select methods of instruction as a result of looking at actual instructional operations in the classroom and evaluating them in light of the physical, psychological, and emotional reactions of the children who are experiencing them.

[11] Neil Postman and Charles Weingartner, *Linguistics, A Revolution in Teaching* (New York: Dell Publishing Co., Inc., 1967).

In summary, methods must be appropriate to objectives, and the main objective of language learning is self-discovery, which occurs as the individual develops through interaction with his environment and communication with other human beings.

QUESTIONS FOR STUDY

1. Examine methods used for teaching reading in the elementary school and grade of your choice. What methods are being used?
2. What are the language objectives for your grade level? What language abilities do these children now have? What knowledge and skills do they still need to acquire?
3. What is the language curriculum of your school? How was it determined? How are the texts used? What methods are used for teaching listening, speaking, writing (including handwriting and spelling)?

SUGGESTIONS FOR FURTHER READING

Brooks, Nelson, *Language and Language Learning*, 2d ed. (New York: Harcourt, Brace & World, Inc., 1964).

Johnson, Harold T., *Foundations of Curriculum* (Columbus, Ohio: Charles E. Merrill Publishing Co., 1968).

Jones, J. Charles, *Learning* (New York: Harcourt, Brace & World, Inc., 1967).

Lado, Robert, *Language Teaching: A Scientific Approach* (New York: McGraw-Hill Book Co., 1964).

Moffett, James, *A Student-Centered Language Arts Curriculum Grades K–6* (Boston: Houghton Mifflin Co., 1968).

Postman, Neil, and Weingartner, Charles, *Linguistics: A Revolution in Teaching* (New York: Dell Publishing Co., Inc., 1967).

Smith, B. Othanel, and Ennis, Robert H., eds., *Language and Concepts in Education* (Chicago: Rand McNally & Co., 1965).

Smith, Nila Benton, *Reading Instruction for Today's Children* (Englewood Cliffs, N.J.: Prentice-Hall, Inc., 1963).

Sowards, G. Wesley, and Scoby, Mary-Margaret, *The Changing Curriculum and the Elementary Teacher*, 2d ed. (San Francisco: Wadsworth Publishing Co., Inc., 1968).

Tiedt, Iris M., and Tiedt, Sidney W., *Contemporary English in the Elementary School* (Englewood Cliffs, N.J.: Prentice-Hall, Inc., 1967).

TEACHER'S AID

Working in small groups provides elementary school children with a great variety of learning experiences. Yet elementary school teachers have become so disenchanted with what they call "committee work" that little small group activity is carried on in elementary school classrooms. In many instances children were formerly placed in small groups to do research reading, to find the answer to specific individual questions, or to carry out individual activities. Such activities, carried out by individuals, serve no group purpose, and children organized into small groups for these activities became confused, wasted time, or used the time to visit with each other or to roam about seeing what someone else was doing. Control of the children was difficult under these circumstances, and teachers abolished small group work.

In spite of the misunderstanding of group process, the opportunity to work in small groups provides the children a chance to learn to communicate with each other in important ways. If a discussion is being carried on in a classroom group of thirty-five children, the majority of the children will not contribute. If circumstances were such that each child actually did contribute, and if he spoke for one minute, he still would have thirty-four minutes of listening. This kind of interaction is not sufficient for elementary school children. If the same class is divided into six groups of six children (one group will have five), the children will have many opportunities to share ideas, and a more complete discussion can take place in much less time.

The following activities are suitable for small group work in the elementary classroom:

1. Organizing questions and problems for study
2. Defining problems
3. Deciding possible methods of attacking problems
4. Assigning individual responsibilities to gather data
5. Evaluating data secured by individuals
6. Discussing a story or other information read by the entire group
7. Carrying out an experiment, discussing results
8. Evaluating classroom and playground behavior
9. Establishing behavioral goals

Research activities can be carried on by individuals, pursued in small groups, or presented to the entire class. The method used should be determined by the purpose of the activity. If a child is reading to find information, there is no need for him to be in a group. After he has located the information, recording what seems to be important to him, he may wish to discuss the relevancy of the information to the larger problem with the rest of the group, or he may want to find out whether the sources used by other children in the group yielded the same information or conflicting data. The following activities are recommended research activities for the elementary classroom:

1. Research reading (individual, guided)
2. Stories or talks using pictures, realia, maps, charts
3. Films, filmstrips, records
4. Study trips
5. Guest speakers
6. Experiments
7. Special lessons to teach children to locate, document, and use material.

Formation of groups requires careful planning. For the small group, five to seven seems to be the ideal number, providing enough people to contribute many ideas, yet giving everyone adequate opportunity for participation. (When a group has eight people, it frequently breaks into two groups of four.) With the purpose of the group work in mind, the teacher will want to consider (1) the balance between boys and girls, (2) the balance of good and poor readers, (3) particular abilities and interests of the children in the group, and (4) personality adjustment.

Selection of group. Children should be allowed to choose the group in which they would like to work, either on the basis of selecting the area of greatest interest or the people with whom they would most like to work. If the teacher allows each child to make his first, second, and third choices, he will ordinarily be placed in the group of his first choice, and at least his second choice.

When given a choice, children usually prefer to select groups on the basis of friends for the first group experience. Doubtless this gives them a feeling of security as they embark upon a new venture. After the first group experience, they are ready to base their choice on interest in content, and this should be strongly encouraged.

Group Standards. As previously stated, group work can be either a waste of time or an extremely gratifying experience for children, depending primarily on the planning and organizational skill of the teacher. Every group needs a leader. The leader needs to understand the following basic principles:

1. That each individual has a contribution to make, even though human potentialities vary.
2. That a diversity of interests, backgrounds, points of view, temperaments, and ways of working exist within the group, but that the group can agree and work on a common problem which *they* set up and wish to solve.
3. That the group needs the opportunity to set its goals, or to revise and reset them, rather than to have leader-set goals imposed on them.

The leader's responsibilities can be summarized as follows:

1. To provide for continuity in the attack on the problem, through such procedures as the following:

   (a) Making sure the members of the group understand the problem.
   (b) Frequently summarizing the important points.
   (c) Coordinating the efforts of the group.
   (d) Allowing sufficient time for pooling facts and harmonizing conflicting ideas of values.
   (e) Restating the main problem at times of confusion.

2. To enable the group discussion to progress through:

   (a) Giving adequate opportunities for participation.
   (b) Avoiding member-to-leader participation only, permitting member-to-member participation when the group is ready (encourage occasional "buzz" sessions and brainstorming).
   (c) Preventing a few members from taking too much time and trying to provide for opportunities for each member to contribute.
   (d) Preventing "plateaus" in group thinking in contrast to progressing, the plateaus often being marked by a series of quotations of experience, or orations on commonly accepted topics.
   (e) Thinking the problem through before the meeting.
   (f) Making sure that different points of view concerning the problem are presented and sympathetically understood, if necessary stating some points of view himself.
   (g) Guiding the discussion away from mere contention through humor and summarizing both points of view.

After children understand the roles and functions of leadership, having been taught by precept and example (watching the teacher who is the leader of the classroom group), and through discussion using charts, films, film-strips, they should set up their own standards for selecting a chairman. For example,

> A good chairman—
> respects each individual,
> organizes and plans work well,
> prepares carefully for group meetings.

Such standards should be as brief as possible, positive, and discussed thoroughly so that every child understands the requirements. After setting up standards, the groups choose their own chairmen.

Group participants also have specific obligations, and the following principles will contribute to the success of the group endeavor:

1. Growth takes place at different rates, and some members of the group will be slow to grasp ideas and draw relationships, while others will be quick.
2. The group must move toward their goals as rapidly as possible, but slowly enough to keep people from feeling insecure and losing identification with the problem.

Specific obligations of group members include:

1. Distinguishing between the intent of the person speaking and what he says or the way he says it.
2. Letting the shy child, or the more slow-spoken, have the floor and listening to his contribution, and asking questions to encourage the child to explain further when misunderstanding or disagreement arises. Many children quickly reject new or unusual ideas. This in turn discourages the sensitive child. The other children owe the child with the different idea courtesy and respect; they need to probe and to try to understand what he is saying. The child with the unusual idea needs to be patient with the other children and try to relate what he is saying to something they can understand. These problems in communication are crucial; if children can begin at an early age to respect each individual, to look for his qualities of worth, to accept differences as valuable, making it possible for individuals to contribute to each other's needs, to understand that basically humans are far more alike than they are different, to appreciate and understand each other's feelings, they will begin to achieve some important democratic goals.
3. Listening to the contribution of others and seeking in his own mind to relate what is being said to the problem. Much time is lost because members fail to listen.
4. Contributing to the group, realizing that his idea together with the ideas of other members will eventually add up to something of value.
5. Stating points briefly and clearly.
6. Keeping an open mind, being willing to consider every aspect of the problem.
7. Hearing from all group members before evaluating ideas and suggestions.

Perhaps the greatest hazard to group process is the feeling that it takes too long. It does take a long time, but if it is carefully structured, and the children are achieving their educational goals, it is well worth the time spent. The teacher must evaluate what the children would be doing instead of this activity, and evaluate the objectives of the group. If the same objectives can be achieved as effectively in less time in some other way, then indeed they should be. Also, emotional factors such as face-saving, defense, egotistic display, reacting to personalities rather than ideas and contributions can trap the participants. The leader must be careful to avoid the spotlight, giving too many opinions or suggestions, or commenting after each contribution, and he must encourage the participants to direct and control the meeting.

The responsibilities of the participants should be enumerated and discussed, and standards for group work set up by the children. For example,

> During group work each individual will—
>> speak one at a time,
>>
>> keep his voice low,
>>
>> stick to the topic,
>>
>> listen and ask questions,
>>
>> use materials wisely,
>>
>> contribute.

To aid in beginning group work, the teacher will want to structure the work period carefully. There should be a preplanning time for the children, another period set aside for taking care of the business at hand, a time for cleaning up, and a time for evaluation. The amount of time spent on each of these facets of work will vary according to the activity. When children first get together in groups, the preplanning stage will take some time. The children will have to define their problems, review their objectives, decide how to attack their problems, decide what materials they will need, plan how and when to get the materials, and list areas of need, whether these are materials, books, or skills such as learning to use reference books, how to get information from other sources, how to organize and present information to the class, how to use information to solve their problems.

As problems are defined and goals made explicit, the children will be ready to spend more time doing research and using the data gathered. If children are using a variety of materials to utilize their data—charts, maps, dioramas, roller movies, etc.—or if they are using many materials to gather information, such as by doing experiments, they will need more time for clean-up at the end of the period. Each work period should be followed with an evaluation period, so that the children can discuss what they were able to accomplish, where they had difficulty, and what they will do differently the next time they meet.

The work habits that the child develops during group work are extremely important. The teacher can evaluate the group experience by asking the questions listed at the top of the next page.

1. Are the children learning to locate and use relevant information?
2. Do the children finish what they start? Are they able to carry through to reasonable and satisfying conclusions?
3. Are the children accepting responsibility for their own goals and standards?
4. Are the children developing in their ability to use and care for materials? What are the standards of neatness, orderliness, cleanliness? Are the children accepting responsibility for cleaning up after themselves?

In summary, to be effective group work [12] must contribute to the acquisition and use of knowledge, the development of specific language skills, listening, speaking, reading, writing, organizing ideas, using the forms and conventions of the language (capitalization, punctuation, spelling, sentence structure, paragraphing, handwriting, personal and business letter forms), and expressing ideas in a variety of ways, such as panel discussions, dramatizations, chalk talks, storytelling, reports, charts, maps, pictures, poems, songs, instrumental music, and modern dance. Group work should also teach pupils good behavior as they learn to accept and respect each other, to plan and direct their own work, to evaluate their actions, and to accept the responsibility for what they do.

[12] For further background see Smith, Louis M., "Group Processes in Elementary and Secondary Schools," *What Research Says to The Teacher*, American Educational Research Association of the N.E.A. Bulletin no. 19 (Washington, D.C., December, 1959).

5

Developing Competency
in Listening

Schools now realize that the child needs to develop certain listening and speaking skills in the early school years, as well as to be taught to read and write. Formerly, the experience and training in oral communication that the child received in the family and in the general social environment was considered sufficient. Reading and writing prepared the child for the academic phases of school life as well as for increased self-reliance, and they were considered to be the principal task of the primary grades. Other linguistic competencies were frequently pushed aside in the school curriculum.

Unfortunately, in some schools reading and writing are still considered ends in themselves at the primary level, and the child is driven and pushed relentlessly while a concentrated frontal attack is made on his reading deficiencies as he struggles forward. For many students little time is available for the teaching of art, music, science, social studies, or providing oral language experiences during the first three or four years of school.

While it is indeed true that reading and writing are essential to the child's further learning, overemphasis during the early years can be as frustrating and hopeless for the teacher as it is damaging to the child.

Fortunately there have been signs in the past decade that the schools are achieving a balanced view concerning language development. Reading and writing retain a key position, but listening and speaking are considered basic in language development. Educational objectives, therefore, include oral-aural skills, and the new programs emphasize the interrelatedness of language skills and demand greater efficiency in skill development.[1]

Although the total act of receiving auditory communication is usually referred to as "listening," there are in fact three distinguishable stages involved: hearing, listening, and auding.[2] **Hearing** is used to designate the process by which speech sounds in the form of sound waves are received and modified by the ear. **Listening** refers to the process of becoming aware of sound sequences, identifying the sounds, recognizing sound sequences through the avenues of auditory analysis, mental reorganization, and association of meaning. **Auding** is the term used to designate the process by which the continuous flow of words is translated into meaning. It involves indexing, making comparisons, noting sequence, forming sensory impressions, and appreciating.

Factors Influencing Hearing

Auditory Acuity. The physical response of the ear to sound vibrations is called auditory acuity. This may be defined as the ability to respond to various frequencies (tones) at various intensities (levels of loudness). The child who is unable to respond to the frequencies which furnish the majority of word cues lacks necessary auditory acuity, and is said to have a hearing loss, and thus requires further observation and evaluation.

Although hearing losses are usually measured with an audiometer, the alert classroom teacher can notice symptoms which would indicate a hearing loss severe enough to inhibit learning. For example, is there a child who typically speaks too loudly or too softly? Poor articulation may be a clue that a child does not hear sounds correctly. Watch the child who rarely pronounces words distinctly or accurately, such as the child who adds sounds to words. In addition, children who are hesitant in their response to phonic exercises may be having difficulty hearing. Of course, children for whom English is a second language, or children from disadvantaged backgrounds frequently have difficulty in distinguishing sounds, pro-

[1] Paul S. Anderson, *Language Skills in Elementary Education* (New York: The Macmillan Co., 1964), pp. 27–42.

[2] Stanford E. Taylor, "Listening," *What Research Says to the Teacher*, American Educational Research Association of the N.E.A. Bulletin no. 29 (Washington, D.C., April, 1964), p. 8.

nouncing words, and responding to phonic clues, although their auditory acuity is excellent.

The child who leans forward when spoken to or cups a hand behind an ear to increase the intensity of the speaker's voice, and the child who has difficulty matching a tone or carrying a tune may have hearing losses, and each requires further attention.

Masking. Another condition which influences hearing occurs when the message being listened to becomes less audible because of the superimposition of other sounds. This condition is known as masking. Research indicates that sounds of the same frequency can alter one another.[3] In the classroom this means that background noise and nearby conversation can have the effect of masking the voice being listened to. In one study, sound composed of all frequencies was superimposed at various levels of loudness over sentences read aloud. Retention was measured, and it was found that as the noise level increased, the recall of content decreased. The conclusion that children with some hearing loss and those with low levels of auditory discrimination are adversely affected by masking in noisy classrooms or group discussion situations seems reasonable in light of the evidence available.[4] This does not mean that classrooms must be silent at all times. It does mean that for the sake of the children who are listening, masking problems should be minimized as much as possible during such activities as the giving of directions and explanations and the reading or telling of stories or poems.

Auditory Fatigue. Temporary hearing loss may be caused by continuous or repeated exposure to sounds of certain frequencies. This condition, which may adversely affect hearing, is labeled auditory fatigue. Because sounds within the speech range are the most likely to produce auditory fatigue, the teacher must be on guard against a monotonous tone or a droning voice.

Research studies with adults have shown that enduring hearing losses can result when a person is exposed to noise for prolonged periods of time.[5] On the basis of this evidence one can hypothesize that the daily noise level experienced by children living in urban communities negatively affects their hearing ability.

[3] *Ibid.*, p. 8.
[4] *Ibid.*, p. 8.
[5] *Ibid.*, p. 9.

Binaural Hearing.   The listener's ability to place a sound source or judge its distance and direction is based on the intensity of the sound arriving at each ear and on the difference in the time it takes for the sound to reach each ear. Binaural hearing enables the listener to keep separate two or more sound sources, directing his attention to one source, suppressing the others, and thus keeping his message straight. Binaural hearing also produces increased volume.

It is helpful for the teacher to provide situations in which the listener is being exposed to only one sound source, because the intelligibility of the aural message usually increases as the intensity of the sound grows. However, when masking noises are present or when fatigue elements are prevalent, intensifying the sound only results in additional masking, more fatigue, and less intelligibility.

Factors Influencing Listening

Attention and Concentration.   Listening is the bringing to bear of attention and concentration on an auditory stimulus. Attention is the directing of awareness, and concentration can be thought of as a sustaining of attention. Although this clarification of information is helpful to the teacher, the primary problem remains: How does the teacher get the child to pay attention and to concentrate? Perhaps the first step is to become aware of the factors which enable a person to direct awareness and to sustain attention:

1. The general physical and mental condition of the listener is of basic importance. If a child is emotionally upset and greatly concerned about a problem he will most certainly be unable to concentrate on something which in no way relates to his concern. If the child is undernourished or ill, he will in all probability be unable to concentrate on some facet of information which has nothing to do with solving his basic needs.

2. The attitude of the listener also affects his listening ability. If he dislikes the point of view of the speaker, or if he is prejudiced in some way against the speaker, he will either refuse to listen or listen only for material to further feed his prejudice. Children must understand the purpose and intent of the listening experience if it is to have value.

3. Personality traits are also involved in success in listening. If the listener is too concerned with himself and his own ideas, he may be unable to listen for fear that he might forget what he has to contribute.

4. The content of the message is an important factor to be considered in the listening process. Information input overload describes a condition in which the message is too difficult for the listener to assimilate or manipulate ideas. When this occurs attention wanes, or the listener takes refuge in selective listening to escape the pressure of the overload. If the message is too simple, the listener may take refuge in mental excursions.

5. The speaker can be an important factor in listening. Studies have demonstrated that it does make a difference whether a speaker is interesting or uninteresting, liked or disliked, animated or expressionless, whether he holds his audience by varying his style or whether he is monotonous.[6]

6. The listening environment plays an important part in listening. If the temperature is uncomfortable, the acoustics poor, or if too many visual or auditory distractions are present, attention will suffer.

7. The learned ability to focus attention. This factor has been left for this position because the teacher is almost completely responsible for this one. It involves the ability to identify and recognize sounds, to use auditory analysis and mental reorganization. The child must learn these important listening skills:

(a) **Auditory analysis** involves the awareness of the characteristics of sound. The listener relies on auditory discrimination, comparing the sounds he hears with those with which he is familiar. During auditory analysis, the listener notes likenesses and differences, responds to changes in frequency, intensity, and rhythm, and notes the manner in which these changes take place. It is sometimes necessary for the listener to readjust his thinking when he anticipates one word, only half hears it, and corrects his first impression when the context which follows makes the meaning of the partially heard word clear.

[6] *Ibid.*, p. 10.

(b) **Mental reorganization,** a process used to aid retention, involves grouping, recoding, or mentally rehearsing a sound sequence. Words identified and recognized because of their meanings require experience, background, and the ability to use aural context clues on the part of the listener. Each of these skills can be taught. One problem relating to word association involves unrelated associations, which can distract or alter communication. The listener may react emotionally or completely misinterpret a message because of the presence of a word or phrase which calls forth an unintended meaning.

Factors Influencing Auding

Thinking skills used during the auding act are similar to those employed during reading, writing, and speaking. The first of these skills is *indexing*. During this process the listener assigns relative values to information. He listens for main ideas and supporting details, separates relevant information from irrelevant information, and creates a mental outline, ranking the information he hears according to its importance.

The second factor which influences auding also involves a skill which can be taught. The skill of *making comparisons* allows the listener to note similarities and differences, to learn about something new, to relate the new to something already known, and to see additional relationships through categorizing information.

Third, *noting sequence* will enable the listener to arrange material according to time, space, position, or degree. Noting sequence provides the listener the opportunity to arrange pieces of information into a larger framework, thus aiding retention and making possible the maximum utilization of information.

When the listener reacts with his senses—taste, touch, smell, sight, and hearing—he is *forming* sensory impressions. The ability to form sensory impressions makes it possible for the listener to translate the words which he hears into sensory images. For example, as the listener hears words, he can actually taste tastes or smell smells. This ability greatly enhances appreciation. Listening to music, sermons, speeches, poetry, or other content designed to activate the feelings of the listener requires appreciation. Appreciative listening demands a response on the part of the listener.

Listening is an intake or receptive process of communication. The listener frequently finds himself faced with situations over which he has no control. For example, he has no control over the rate of speed used by the speaker or over the vocabulary used. The teacher must be careful to speak slowly enough to be understood and to use familiar vocabulary or teach meanings of new vocabulary. During reading, also an intake process, the reader can find his own best speed, can take time to find the meanings of words which are new to him, and reread a passage if necessary to clarify meaning. Words, on the other hand, are spoken but once; the listener hears them then or not at all. This means that listening is an extremely difficult task and that the skills involved must be highly developed. The importance of teaching children how to listen cannot be over-stressed.

Kinds and Levels of Listening

Research evidence indicates that listening skills can be taught and that listening ability does improve substantially when specific instruction is provided.[7] What, then, can teachers do to provide adequate development of listening skills?

First, teachers need to be aware of the various kinds of listening that will go on during a typical day in the classroom.

1. Casual listening includes conversational listening, listening courteously, and secondary listening. Conversational and courteous listening takes place as the children talk to each other during recess time and when they come into the classroom in the morning and get ready for the day. Casual listening also takes place during conversations as children carry out small-group activities, during sharing time when children share possessions and ideas, and during the sessions when the teacher and the children work while background music is being played, or as the teacher works with one group while the other children work independently.

2. Creative listening involves an imaginative reconstruction of the pleasures of sound, vision, motion, or feelings suggested by whatever the listener is hearing. This might involve music, drama, poetry, or any other form of literature. Creative listening is appreciational or aesthetic listening at its highest level.

[7] Ibid., p. 18.

3. Exploratory listening, which may occur during reporting sessions, explanations, and discussions, alerts the mind to areas of interest. This kind of listening should promote questions.

4. Intent listening is concentrative and critical in nature. During an activity which requires intent listening, one can expect to elicit specific items of information and to watch for inaccuracies, lack of authenticity, and bias. Intent listening is involved when children listen to directions and reports.

Ruth Strickland has organized the levels of listening into seven developmental categories.[8] The first listening stage involves little conscious effort to listen except as the child is directly concerned with what is being presented. The child moves from this stage to one in which he listens intentionally, but superficially. During this second stage he is easily distracted by people and things in the environment. The third stage of listening involves a kind of half-listening, while holding fast to one's own ideas and waiting to insert them at the first opportunity. Fourth, the listener listens passively with apparent absorption, but with little reaction. The fifth stage moves into a higher level of listening which includes forming associations and responding with items from one's own experience. The sixth stage adds reacting to what is being presented to the previous experience. In this stage the listener expresses some reaction through questions and comments. The seventh stage, which involves listening with evidence of genuine mental and emotional participation and a final meeting of the minds, is of course the ultimate goal in listening, involving hearing, listening, and auding as previously discussed.

Suggestions for Developing Effective Listening

The teacher can do much to provide a classroom atmosphere which is conducive to listening. Such classrooms will be relaxed, comfortable, and reasonably quiet during the listening experiences. Each child must feel secure and confident that when he speaks others will listen courteously to his contributions. Children need not agree with each other or with the teacher, but they must be

[8] Ruth Strickland, *English Is Our Language: Guide for Teaching Grades I and II* (Boston: D. C. Heath & Co., 1950), p. 114.

taught to listen respectfully and consider points of view other than their own.

Young children usually sit close to the speaker in an informal arrangement for listening. Children may be encouraged to get up and move quietly, without disturbing others, at any time if they cannot hear. Both room and outside noise should be minimized whenever possible.

Teachers may take advantage of all of the opportunities for listening which arise throughout the school day. These are to be found during periods of talking, conversing, sharing, planning, discussing, reporting, explaining, evaluating, solving problems, and expressing creative thinking. This does not mean that listening will be an incidental experience. The mere opportunity to listen does not teach a child to listen effectively. Carefully planned instruction is essential to develop listening, but regular classroom experiences can become the vehicles of listening instruction.

Children should be led to expect meaning and to ask questions about what they hear.

Long periods of listening may be broken with opportunities for the children to participate, question, comment, or write.

The subject matter being listened to and the occasion for listening will vary with the maturity of the children. Older boys and girls can be guided to evaluate what they hear in terms of the choice of words used, facial expressions, and voice inflections.

Pupils frequently enjoy reproducing what they have heard. Such activities as outlines, summaries, explanations, and dramatizations can be used for this purpose.

Different purposes for listening involve different levels of listening. Children should be aware of the purposes for which they are listening. They need to establish specific listening goals for each of the listening activities which they will experience. These goals should be positive and few enough so that children can remember and achieve them. The following examples provide objectives for the various kinds and levels of listening. Before such goals could become the goals of children, the terminology used would need to be thoroughly discussed and perhaps modified, as children set them up for themselves. Questions such as "What do we mean by 'think about what the speaker is saying'?"; "How does one respond to what a speaker is saying?"; and "What does it mean to listen imaginatively?" would certainly have to precede the use of such goals. Also, the teacher must remember that usually one or two of these goals will be stressed during a listening experience.

LISTENING GOALS

We Listen Courteously.

We look at the person speaking.
We respond to what he is saying.
We wait for a turn to respond.
We let our neighbors listen.

We Listen Intently.

We listen to recognize something new, to alert our minds to ideas and areas of interest.
We listen to get specific items of information, word usage, detail, sequence, and ideas.
We listen to find answers to questions, to get information, or to develop concepts.
We listen for accuracy and authenticity.

We Listen Creatively.

We reconstruct the pleasures of sound, sight, smell, taste, and feeling.
We listen imaginatively.
We listen for motion, for mood, for specific sounds or sound combinations.
We listen for the feeling we get from poetry or music (and extension of mood).

Listening Situations

There are many listening situations in life experiences:

1. Conversation requires listening as much as—perhaps more than —any other language experience. Young children are more inclined to talk than to listen to the ideas of other children. Teachers should therefore begin to help children in their first years in school to learn to listen, providing many experiences requiring conversation. Natural situations for informal conversation, that aid children in developing courteous listening, can occur when children come into the classroom in the morning, at the midmorning lunch period, at noontime, on the playground, and at other times during the day.

2. Telephone conversations call for intent as well as courteous listening. While these conversations ordinarily occur outside of school, there are occasions when children may need to make calls while at school. Standards of listening to telephone conversations may well be set up by the class, and simulated practice provided.

3. Discussion and planning periods necessitate purposeful listening before children can come to a common agreement. If the development of ideas is to be followed, and needless questions and repetition are to be avoided, active listening is essential. Reports given by committees or by individuals for the purpose of sharing information, necessitate concentrated listening for understanding and interpretation.

4. Announcements in classroom or assembly call for understanding of the who, where, and when involved; hence, intense listening is needed. Explanations and directions given in connection with classwork, games, or exhibits are a form of announcement, and they also require concentrated attention.

5. Oral reading situations, during which children desire to give information to prove or disprove a point, or practice a selection for self-improvement, require pupils and teachers to listen critically.

6. Dramatic activities such as puppet shows, plays, and choral speaking, require skill in listening on the part of the audience. Reading and telling stories, book reviews, "show and tell" periods, and felt-board demonstrations all involve careful listening.

7. Music activities, vocal and instrumental, including listening to harmony, rhythm, and to "what the music says," aid the development of listening skills. Likewise listening to interesting outdoor sounds, such as the songs of birds, the sounds of the wind and the rain, and the calls of animals and insects, develops discrimination in listening.

8. Recordings and transcriptions of various kinds—including those made by the children, radio and television programs, simulated or live broadcasts and television shows given by the pupils, educational sound films or commercial movies, club meetings, room and auditorium programs—all provide rich opportunities for promoting better listening habits and abilities.

Methods for Developing Skill in Listening

From the enormous amount of listening children are called upon to do in meeting life situations today, it follows that more and better learning should take place through auditory experiences than seems to be the case in many schools. Listening should be given emphasis along with other language arts skills.

Many adults have never learned to listen adequately to what others have to say. They hear only a part of what is said before they embark upon their own train of thought. As soon as the speaker has said his last word, they burst forth with their story, giving no time for comment or for laughter. These people are not really interested in what the other person is saying. For lack of ability to listen, they are losing the opportunity of learning from others or of being entertained by them.

Children sometimes assume the polite appearance of listening without really understanding what is being said. At times they may hear the sound of the human voice while their attention is on some interest foreign to the situation of the moment. In other words, children may have "ears without hearing" unless they are interested in what is going on. When a child really listens, he tends to identify himself with what he hears.

The teacher who sets out to develop and improve the listening skills and habits of his group should first take inventory of the abilities and needs of the pupils in relation to their maturity and experiental backgrounds. In studying children's problems, he should be aware of the reasons why children do not listen.

Among factors that condition listening are the following:

1. Emotional disturbances, such as tensions and worries caused by home conditions or some conflict between the pupil and the teacher or other pupil.

2. Poor environmental conditions, such as wrong seating arrangement, too high or too low temperature, inadequate ventilation, uncomfortable clothing.

3. Discussions and explanations that are too difficult for the child's level of comprehension.

4. Lack of skill in listening due to inadequate instruction.

5. Lack of purpose or incentive in listening.

6. Competitive interests and other distractions.

7. Uninteresting presentation—poor organization of ideas, or a voice that is monotonous, too high, or too low.
8. Presentation of material that is not related to the child's interest to the extent that he can identify himself with it.

Althea Berry [9] points out that some of the reasons given by children for not listening are:

"I listened but I didn't pay attention."
"I heard what I wanted to hear."
"The same words mean different things to different people."
"What's really important may not seem that way to someone else."
"Some memories of other things got in the way."

As these reasons make evident, the children's interest, mind-set, and purpose determined to a large extent their ability to listen attentively. The stronger the purpose or interest, the more heed children give to what is said. A child who has a purpose in listening will naturally understand and enjoy what he hears, provided it is on his level of maturity. For example, a second grade class was divided into four groups, with a pupil chairman in each group, after independent silent reading. Each group had read a different story selected from material suitable to their reading level. One group then planned to read their story to the rest of the class and ask them questions to check their own ability to read orally and the ability of their classmates to listen attentively. When all the groups had completed their discussion of their reading, the three groups that were to form the audience for the fourth group quickly arranged their chairs. As the readers presented their story, there was evidence of concentrated attention on the part of the audience. This seemed to help the performers to do their best. At the end of the reading, the pupils in the fourth group asked questions and were pleased to find that the others could answer all of them.

In this simple experience three definite factors made for good listening: the audience was interested in hearing the story, which was new to them, the pupils had a definite purpose in listening—to be able to answer questions—and the readers had prepared carefully for the activity in their group discussion and gave a good performance.

[9] Althea Berry, "Experiences in Listening," *Elementary English*, vol. 28, no. 3 (March, 1951), pp. 130–132.

Importance of the Physical Setting

A matter that should be given careful consideration in a reading-listening experience is the seating arrangement of the audience. The children should place their chairs so that everyone can easily see the pupils who are doing the reading. It is small wonder that children become inattentive when poorly arranged chairs or desks make it impossible for them to see the pupils who are reading or speaking to them. Furniture should be shifted to suit the occasion. For class discussion, planning periods, and all situations calling for the sharing of experiences, the seating arrangement should be such that the children can look at one another without turning. One listens more attentively and for a longer period when he can look at the face of the speaker.

For these socialized situations, the children may be given the responsibility of rearranging their chairs or desks as quickly and quietly as possible. Once they become accustomed to this procedure, they lose little time in making the shift at the beginning and at the close of the period. While this change is being made, a committee can check on the temperature and the lighting of the room. These routine matters are significant because they affect the quality of the listening. Moreover, children enjoy doing them and grow with the responsibility.

Developing Interest and Purpose in Listening

Since children listen actively in terms of their interests and purposes, they need opportunities to help plan their work. As they participate in the direction of the plans they help make, they see the need to evaluate their listening achievement by establishing standards, and they are capable of doing this under the guidance of the teacher. Factual, organizational, and judgmental questions asked by pupils and teacher are positive aids in securing intent listening. The pupils need many opportunities to raise problems and questions, and to listen critically to reports on their findings made by their classmates. Comparing notes on the ideas they gain will improve their ability to interpret and evaluate what they hear before they draw conclusions. This kind of thinking calls for attention and concentration in order to get all the facts presented.

When directions are given for a class activity, such as going on an excursion, having a fire drill, making or doing something, or playing a game, each pupil needs to listen intently if he is to do his part in the group. The pupils should be told that they will be held responsible for getting the details given. It is important to ask some of the pupils to repeat the instructions in order to check their understanding of what has been said.

Radio, Television, and Motion Pictures

Television is very popular with children and adults, according to the Nielson report of 1965,[10] which estimates that 52.6 million households in the United States (excluding Alaska and Hawaii) are equipped with one or more TV receivers.

TV studies by Paul Witty [11] point up that in the Chicago area by 1965 nearly all students had access to TV at home and that they spent on an average of twenty hours per week viewing. The favorite programs of children included variety shows, cartoons, comedies, adventure and mystery features, and science fiction programs. Parents rarely supervised the viewing, and parents and teachers seemed to accept the kinds of TV programs available to children. Nevertheless, there is still much concern on the part of both parents and teachers regarding the excessive violence depicted in programs that children see.

Many studies have been carried on to determine the relationship of aggressive behavior and TV programs which feature violence. The results of the studies are often conflicting, and at the present time the scarcity of dependable research on this topic makes it difficult to formulate valid conclusions.[12]

There is also a great deal of controversy regarding the extent to which children are helped by the various facets of mass media. Children reported that such TV programs as "Science Corner," "Parlons Francais," "Airborne Science," and "Patterns in Arithmetic" were helpful. They also cited "Password" and "Discovery" as having educational value. In situations where teachers have related class work

---

[10] *Television '65—A Nielson Report* (A. C. Nielsen Company, 1965).

[11] Paul Witty, "Children of the Television Era," *Elementary English*, vol. 44, no. 5 (May, 1967), pp. 528–535.

[12] Seymour Feshbach, "The Effects of Aggressive Content in Television Programs Upon the Aggressive Behavior of the Audience," *Television and Human Behavior*, eds., Leon Arons and Mark M. May (New York: Appleton-Century-Crofts, 1963).

to specific programs for TV viewing, the programs seem to have contributed to learning. "Disneyland" was cited by young children as a motivation for reading various books such as *Bambi* and *Snowwhite and the Seven Dwarfs*, and movies have encouraged older children to read *Mary Poppins, Tom Sawyer, Little Women, Robin Hood, Treasure Island, Heidi*, and various children's books about Hellen Keller. Studies show no significant relationship between televiewing and success in school or between televiewing and reading achievement.[13]

In spite of the greater attraction of TV, children still spend quite a lot of time listening to radio. Witty's studies [14] show seven or eight hours weekly as the average number of hours for radio listening. The studies also show that pupils in 1965 attended movies on the average of once every two weeks as compared with once a week before TV.

Undoubtedly, television, radio, and motion pictures are a powerful force in building concepts and attitudes. These media will undoubtedly be continued to be used as instructional aids. They certainly help to bring the world into the classroom and provide the child an opportunity to extend his concepts of the ever-expanding community in which he lives.

Teachers can find out what media children are utilizing outside of the classroom, through conversation and discussion, and by encouraging the children to make a log of their favorite programs and movies. As children evaluate radio and television programs and movies in and out of school, they will begin to form attitudes and standards that will help them make wise choices for further listening and viewing. A selected list of programs and movies may be put on a chart or bulletin board. A committee might be appointed to keep the list up to date.

Listening to Recordings

Listening to recordings is another activity that provides children the opportunity to extend specific listening skills. Teachers, textbook publishers, and librarians are capitalizing upon this interest for educational purposes. Tape, wire, disk, and magnetic recorders are available to schools. The value of recordings is well pointed out in

---

13 Witty, op. cit., p. 530.
14 *Ibid.*, p. 529.

a Research Bulletin of the National Conference on Research in English as follows: [15]

> *Listening.* Whether judged by the criterion of frequency or the criterion of cruciality of great social significance, listening is the most important of the language arts. Tyler terms it the number one problem; Dale, Finn, and Hoban declare the "developing of discriminating, critical, listeners—an absolute necessity for the survival of our democracy in the Atomic Age."
>
> Recordings and the recorder seem eminently suited to aid in developing listening comprehension and discrimination. Research shows that the poor listener is ordinarily an inexperienced listener. Opportunities to listen to many types of recorded programs for a wide variety of learning purposes is therefore fundamental. Pupils may be taught to formulate goals for listening; to anticipate what may be said next; to make a mental review of points that have been made; and to search for implied meanings occasionally during the listening period. These are all elements established by research as essential to effective listening. The recorder may be used to make listening materials of suitable difficulty and appropriate character from the air, or excellent exercise material may be recorded from printed sources.
>
> Discrimination in listening is achieved in the main by helping pupils to develop their own standards and giving them sufficient opportunity to make the application of these standards habitual. Again, the recorder may be used to advantage. Good and poor programs or parts of programs may be taken from the air for direct comparison, analysis, and, later, for practice in application.
>
> Developing critical listening ability, also, begins with the achievement of an awareness on the part of the pupil that he is subject to influences that warp his judgment and frustrate his understanding. . . . Finally, since the habit of listening critically should function regardless of what the purpose for listening may be, much may be accomplished by persistently encouraging pupils to evaluate all their listening experiences. The recorder would appear to be an ideal tool for providing highly valid illustrative materials of current significance in a form which permits repetition for careful analysis and free discussion.

In conclusion, since children spend so much time outside school in listening to radio, television, and movies, it is important for them to have many opportunities to enjoy the best in the classroom, so that they are able to make wise choices outside of school. Never before, in school or out, has there been such a rich opportunity for adventures in listening. But if the adventurers are to develop con-

15 "Education and the Mass Media of Communication," Bulletin of the National Conference on Research in English (Chicago: National Council of Teachers of English, 1950), p. 61.

structive and wholesome ideas for use in daily living, with power to think and to form good emotional attitudes, then more and better listening skills must be developed by the school.

QUESTIONS FOR STUDY

1. What is the relationship of listening to reading in the terms seeing, recognizing, and reading, and hearing, listening, and auding?
2. How do cultural differences influence the development of listening skills?
3. What opportunities can teachers provide for introducing specific listening skills?

SUGGESTIONS FOR FURTHER READING

Applegate, Mauree, *Easy in English* (New York: Harper & Row, Publishers, 1963).

Corbin, Richard, and Crosby, Muriel, cochairmen, *Language Programs for the Disadvantaged* (Champaign, Ill.: National Council of Teachers of English, 1965).

Duker, Sam, *Listening: Readings* (New York: Scarecrow Press, Inc., 1966).

Russell, David H., and Russell, Elizabeth, *Listening Aids Through the Grades* (New York: Columbia University Press, 1959).

TEACHER'S AID

Because listening skills are emphasized in the primary grades, many of the following suggestions are planned for primary children:

Have children make experiments with word sounds for fire engine, tugboat, airplane, horse, bear, etc., sad and happy, animal sounds, nature's forces, holidays, churchbells, whistles, etc.

Instruct children to close eyes—concentrate on what they hear. After one minute, let them tell everything they heard (paper crushing, tapping a glass, writing on board, tip-toe walking, etc.).

In "Share and Tell," have child describe interesting out-of-school experiences to classmates and bring in various objects which may be of interest to them. Assign pupils to small groups of five or six children. Pupils take turns being the leader each day. Children feel more comfortable meeting in small groups. They ask more questions and exchange more comments.

In "Sharing Time," find similar objects (such as two trucks) and let children analyze differences, bringing out critical thinking as to color, shape, purpose, numbers, feel, etc. Let one child find out similarities, another differences.

Tape record children's stories. Have child listen to his own voice and others. Good for discussion.

Clap rhythm of song well known to group and choose someone to identify the song. Correct answer qualifies child to be "it" and clap out the next song.

Read wide variety of good stories and poems, calling attention to techniques of Suess, De la Mare, etc. Tongue-tickling ways of saying things are read.

Let children tell which words sound alike.

Let children select words from poems that are read which make them hear sounds: swift, slapping, rush, swishing, boom, etc.

Place many familiar items in "treasure chest." "Giant" says, "Bring my _____, _____, _____," naming three, six or ten things in the box, and chooses someone to get items from chest. If child gets all items, he becomes "giant."

Speak two sentences using the same word with different meanings. Have children name the word and discuss how two meanings are different.

Game: "I Lost My _____." Describe something and have children guess what it is.

Have child pretend he is a certain kind of worker. Children listen to guess what worker he is. (Social studies)

Have children listen to various tones of voice: sarcasm, weariness, irritation, perplexity, anger, excitement.

Have children listen to bird calls and songs and try to identify each.

Tell "chain" stories in which each child continues story events from where previous speaker stopped.

Have children listen to several short stories. Then choose a group to plan and give a dramatization of one. Others should be able to recognize the story.

After they have listened to a set of directions only once, have children carry out a simple experiment or construct a simple crafts project. They might also write these directions.

Have the children listen to a paragraph read by the teacher to hear separate sentences. How many sentences?

Give a very simple direction to the class, such as, "Take your arithmetic book out of your desk." This is followed by a series of increasingly complex directions up to the point where the students have to go through five or six consecutive steps such as, "Take your English book out of your desk, turn to page 62, begin with question 15 and answer every other question to 25."

Have captains of teams give directions for games on playground.

Game: "Guess the Mystery Spot" by listening to the directions given.

6

Developing Competency in Oral Communication

Throughout this book the importance of oral language in language development is emphasized. Although there has been some research concerning the relationship of thought and speech, two different views are presently accepted regarding this relationship. The first states that thought and the words in which the thought is expressed are the same thing, namely, that thought consists of verbalization. The second point of view regards thought as independent of language and says that language is the vehicle of thought.[1] Whether or not thought is dependent on language, the two are unquestionably related in terms of verbal interaction with self in both oral and written expression.

Available research evidence suggests a high degree of interrelatedness among the communication skills of oral language, reading, and writing.[2] The child's ability to comprehend written material through reading and to express himself through writing appears to be directly related to his ability in speaking and listening.

Objectives of Oral Communication

There are presently two main objectives in teaching oral communication at the elementary school level. The first one emphasizes the development of the child's self-concept and self-confidence as

[1] Joseph Church, *Language and the Discovery of Reality* (New York: Random House, Inc., 1961), pp. 147–158.

[2] Walter T. Petty and Roberta J. Starkey, "Oral Language and Personal and Social Development," *Elementary English,* vol. 43, no. 4 (April, 1966), p. 386.

he grows in his ability to communicate, and the second objective emphasizes the importance of speech in the child's knowledge of his language as well as his skill in its use. Both objectives stress the need for the child to determine and express his values as a contributing member of society.

Strickland lists the following sequence of levels in speaking: [3]

1. Emphasis on freeing the individual and encouraging him to participate.

2. Emphasis on increasing recognition of responsibility to others and the development of group consciousness.

3. Emphasis on interplay of ideas and meeting of minds.

4. Emphasis on responsibility for the value and the truth of one's remarks.

5. Emphasis on the improvement of personal techniques such as voice and mannerisms.

6. Emphasis on training for leadership in the carrying on of group processes.

The primacy of oral–aural language is evident in the meaning of language as well as in its sequential development. Language symbols, oral or visual, are vehicles of meaning as it is transmitted from person to person. The sound symbol, speech, is the primary symbol, while the visual symbol, writing, is the secondary symbol. The accuracy with which meaning is transmitted is often not complete even at the primary or speech level. The experience and understanding of both the speaker and the listener are significant to accurate communication, as is the ability of the speaker to express precisely the ideas which he hopes to communicate. The same factors are involved when a writer attempts to communicate with a reader, but the hazard of having to compensate for signals given through pitch, stress, tone of voice, facial expression, and gestures is added. The difference between the intended meaning and the code of signals used to transmit it, whether oral or written, needs to be considered constantly in communication through language.

Varieties of Speech

Children come to school speaking a variety of dialects of American English. The economic and cultural level of the home is evident

---

[3] Ruth G. Strickland, *The Language Arts in the Elementary School*, 2d ed. (Boston: D. C. Heath & Co., 1957), p. 185.

in the speech of the elementary school child, as is the geographic location in which his parents acquired their language.

Because a wide range of dialects is represented by successful Americans, the teacher has no clear-cut American English dialect to use as a standard to help children attain speech that will be an asset rather than a liability in achieving the objectives of their adult lives. Examples of some of the more obvious differences in American English dialects can be found in the speech of the last six presidents of the United States. President Franklin Roosevelt's dialect was that of suburban New York, somewhat modified by his years at Harvard. President Truman's dialect was very different, with its regional Missouri influence, and a vocabulary peppered with coarse and sometimes raw words. President Eisenhower's Kansas dialect, somewhat changed by West Point and the Army, President Kennedy's educated Bostonian dialect, and President Johnson's Texas dialect were noticeably different. President Nixon seems to speak "standard English" simply because his dialect is that of the author of this book!

Teachers have a tendency to believe that their own language is the standard toward which they should direct the language of their pupils. However, research is needed on the dialects that children bring to school and on what teachers should do about such dialects. Unbelievable amounts of time and effort are wasted by teachers who try to make children say *wail* and *whale* with two different beginning sounds. True, in most western dialects *wail* begins with /w/ while *whale* begins with /hw/. However, for many children moving into western schools from the east, these words begin with the same sound, and there is no resulting difficulty in recognizing the meaning of these words. Westerners recognize the difference between *bare* and *bear* which sound precisely the same, so why do teachers worry about *wail* and *whale?*

Because there are sound patterns in regional ethnic speech which denote cultural levels, and which may handicap individuals when they leave their own regions or social groups, teachers do need to be able to recognize and modify these. To date there are not sufficient data on patterns which deviate markedly from school speech for the teacher to attempt to modify speech with any degree of assurance that the patterns need to be changed. Many regional and ethnic variations add vital and colorful dimensions to American English.

Syntactical structures do not vary as widely throughout the

United States as do phonological structures, but when variance occurs in the syntax, it seems to be a more difficult problem. Disregard for tenses, for subject-verb agreement and for subject-object forms handicaps individuals in many social groups.

Because of the high percentage of low achievement existing among children whose oral language differs from the language of school textbooks, a great deal of thought needs to be given to how sound-symbol correspondences and morphological and syntactical patterns might be presented orally to these children to ensure later success in reading and spelling.

Recognizing Differences in Children's Speech

Ruth Strickland [4] points up the importance of oral language development to meet the needs of today's society in the following statement:

> The physical mobility of our population today, the need to help minority groups gain recognition and status, and the growing economic as well as social need to help depressed people of whatever ethnic or social group to climb out of their present state of deprivation and dependency, all have implications for our work with oral language.

Before teachers will be in a position to make it possible for children to acquire language that will be an asset to them as they strive to achieve their goals, they will have to know as much as possible about the children with whom they work, the language these children use, and the language they need in order to gain respect and acceptance in their chosen walks of life. As teachers become aware of the wide range of language development within the class, they may wish to analyze the factors which have caused this range of individual differences. What language models are presented in the home? What is the degree of language interaction between the parents and the child, between the child and other children in the home? What is the value placed by the home on the importance of language development? Are there dialect differences between the home and the school? In addition to getting answers to these questions, the teacher will want to observe pupil characteristics such as auditory acuity and intellectual development.

---

[4] Ruth G. Strickland, "Needed Research in Oral Language," *Elementary English,* vol. 44, no. 3 (March, 1967), p. 259.

Speech Development and School Success

Although oral communication has been receiving emphasis in educational literature since linguistic study has pointed up the relationship between oral language skills and success in reading and writing, in practice the teaching of oral language has received little attention in the total language arts program of the school. Reading is heavily emphasized in the primary grades, and specific periods of time are also set aside for the teaching of handwriting and spelling. Although opportunity for oral language experiences is available in most elementary classrooms, no definite time or plan for teaching has been established, with the result that oral language development is incidental and for some children extremely inadequate.

Developing Speech Effectiveness

The teaching of movables and subordinating elements in improving sentence meaning has not received adequate consideration, although research has shown its relationship to comprehension in listening and silent reading.[5] Children can be taught the way in which structural meaning can be changed through word substitution by examining sentences that look alike on the surface such as "John is easy to please" and "John is eager to please." (Originally pointed up by Noam Chomsky.) They also need to be taught how basic patterns can be expanded, inverted, and transformed. Such knowledge may be taught inductively through oral language lessons, and then practiced in a number of oral language experiences such as role playing, storytelling, and small-group discussions of direct experiences.

Reading literature to children, dramatic play, and the use of experience charts may be used as vehicles to demonstrate to children how intonation in speaking and punctuation in writing are used to convey meaning. Children can also discover through the use of literature how descriptive language is used in developing story characters and settings, and how movables and subordinating elements are used to provide the listener or the reader with more precise information.

[5] Ruth G. Strickland, "The Language of Elementary School Children: Its Relationship to the Language of Reading Textbooks and the Quality of Reading of Selected Children," *Bulletin of the School of Education*, no. 38 (Bloomington: Indiana University Press, July, 1962).

Vocabulary enrichment, an important part of oral language development, is related to the child's own experience. The child needs a firm grasp of the concept he is attempting to express if his communication is to be successful. The teacher will provide concrete experiences in the classroom and study trips to teach concepts, and he will also provide experiences that will help children to discover how words convey different meanings in a variety of sentence contexts.

Perhaps one of the reasons that teachers have done so little with oral language in the classroom is the problem of large classes and little time. While the teacher is busy with one small group of children during the reading period, the other children in the classroom must be quiet so that the reading group is not disturbed. Reading, of course, takes up a great period of time, and by the time the child has had arithmetic, writing, and spelling the morning is gone!

Children can work together in small groups, however, to provide each child the opportunity to speak and listen. Such small-group activity must be carefully structured in the beginning so that the children understand what they are doing and what each chlid's responsibility is. Later the groups can be organized around the problems of the children, and as each child begins to understand his responsibility to the group, the level of sensitivity grows as well as the ability to communicate feelings and ideas. (See Teacher's Aid, Chapter 4.)

Teachers may also use tape recorders and listening posts to give children a chance to hear their own speech, and to analyze language. The extensive use of experience charts provides further use for language spoken by children and recorded by the teacher. Interviews of students by the teacher can be recorded and listened to later. Such questions as those that begin with what, where, why, when, or who did, or statements requiring students to relate, explain, comment on, discuss, give some reasons, etc., will encourage reactions and opinions.

Cultural Influences on Speech

As teachers work with children in the area of oral language, they will want to be constantly aware that language does not develop in a vacuum. The language that the child brings with him to school is part of his culture, and although the teacher and the child's classmates will have some influence on his language, such influence will be in direct proportion to their understanding of cultural differences and meanings, and their acceptance of the child who speaks differently, as well as his acceptance of them.

From the beginning the child, as a social being, has developed patterned ways of doing things and talking about them, that have facilitated the communication necessary for social living. When the child comes into contact with people who speak differently, dress differently, look different, or behave in a different manner, he has in fact moved into a different culture, even though he is still in the same basic geographic location and speaking the same language. Because the teacher does in fact teach culture when he teaches language, he must be in the position of understanding not only the outward manifestations of the culture from which the child is emerging, the dress, food, speech, and behavior, but he should also be aware of the great ideas and achievements that are peculiar to the child's cultural group. Every culture has a structured system of patterned behavior; its people have characteristic ways. The teacher must know enough about the culture of each of his students to be in a position to reject false clichés, and to be able to use authentic cultural content as an aid to understanding and motivating each child toward the learning of the new culture patterns as well as the new dialect.

When a person of one culture observes another culture, he tends to interpret what he observes as having the same significance that his own culture ascribes to the occurrence. This creates frequent misunderstanding and often hostility. The child needs to be constantly aware that every human being brings different experiential backgrounds to a particular incident, and that clarity in communication will be dependent on culturally shared and generally understood purposes and meanings, and even then ideas may not be completely conveyed. Teachers have been much too casual about the many difficulties involved in accurate oral communication between themselves and children of varied linguistic backgrounds. They have judged children from other cultures within the framework of their own culture, rather than within the ethical framework of the child's culture. This behavior may result in confusion followed by defeat and finally hostility on the part of the child.

The Concept of Oracy

British educators have instituted a program in oral language to combat the trend of doing little about teaching the ability to put one word after another in one's own speech in order to create. Oracy, a term which refers to general ability in all of the oral skills (including speaking, listening, oral reading), is a central factor in the development of personality, and it is closely related to human happiness and well-being.

Some influences on oracy include early family environment, education, social environment outside the home, mass media, and the image conceived by the larger society. Andrew Wilkinson [6] lists the following as influences on oracy in Britain:

1. Speech and personality are one. To develop oracy, basically one develops personality.
2. Language experience is crucial. The young child's use of language precedes his understanding of it.
3. The quality of language experience is crucial; quantity, though necessary, is not sufficient. The wrong language experience may result in a culturally induced backwardness.
4. Formal education, by its stress on literacy, has often been hostile to oracy. The two aspects of language development need to be synthesized.
5. The national self-image has not encouraged oracy.
6. Broadcasting has encouraged oracy by providing many models of usage. It has discouraged oracy by withholding acceptance from the majority of English accents.

To discuss oracy, one must consider the prevalent definitions of some frequently used terms. **Accent** in speech is considered to be a matter of phonology, whereas **dialect** is an affair of grammar. In dialect, standard English is universally taught and used among educated people, but accent is a mark of a particular social class. **Register** is a term used for dealing with the varieties of English used by occupational groups, and these (like dialect) tend to be largely grammatical and hardly at all phonological. **Style** refers to speech appropriate for one situation but not for another. Situations change, requiring different styles of speech, but so, too, do persons being

---

[6] Andrew M. Wilkinson, *Spoken English* (Birmingham: University of Birmingham, 1965), p. 131.

addressed. Thus according to Joos,[7] the style scale moves from frozen speech to formal, to consultative, to casual, to intimate.

According to the proponents of oracy, the educated person of the twentieth century possesses oracy, as well as literacy and numeracy (the ability to understand and manipulate numerals). The nature of the spoken language as it is actually used provides the content for language study. Classroom experiences which provide opportunity for the development of oracy include speech training, discussion, talks, panels, role playing, conversation using contrived instant speech situations, reading aloud, poetry and drama, and listening.

The Role of the Teacher

Although this entire book stresses the necessity for oral language development that permits the child to perceive his worth and develop his potential, this chapter stresses the need for teachers who are adequately trained in cultural understanding as well as language. The teacher needs a great deal more preparation in both of these areas than most teachers have typically had if elementary school language arts programs are to provide children with the knowledge and skills that will help them use the spoken word to communicate thought and express feeling accurately as they interact with others in the achievement of their individual and societal goals.

In conclusion, the elementary school pupil must not be expected to achieve skill in oral language by simply being provided some opportunities for oral language experience. Rather, the teacher needs to organize learning experiences in such a way that the child discovers the patterns of his language and is increasingly able to understand the nature of his language as well as his need for it.

QUESTIONS FOR STUDY

1. What are some oral language skills that are used at the grade level of your choice? How are these taught? How are they practiced?
2. Select and visit an elementary classroom. What are the differences in language ability in this classroom? What are the causes for the differences? How can you find out?

[7] Martin Joos, *The Five Clocks,* Publication of the Indiana University Research Center in Anthropology, Folklore, and Linguistics, no. 22 (Bloomington: Indiana University Press, 1962).

3. How much time is devoted to oral language experiences during the school day? What is done during this period of time?

SUGGESTIONS FOR FURTHER READING

Brown, Roger, and Fort, Marguerite, "Address in American English," reprinted in Hymes, Dell, *Language in Culture and Society* (New York: Harper & Row, Publishers, 1964).

Francis, W. Nelson, *The Structure of American English* (New York: The Ronald Press Co., 1958).

Hathaway, Baxter, *A Transformational Syntax—The Grammar of Modern American English* (New York: The Ronald Press Co., 1967).

Krech, David, et al., *Individual in Society* (New York: McGraw-Hill Book Co., 1962.

Petty, Walter T., ed., *Research in Oral Language*, published for the NCTE (Champaign, Ill.: National Council of Teachers of English, 1967).

Possien, Wilma M., *They All Need to Talk* (New York: Appleton-Century-Crofts, 1969).

Rycenga, John A., and Schwartz, Joseph, *Perspectives on Language: An Anthology* (New York: The Ronald Press Co., 1963).

TEACHER'S AID

The following activities have been used successfully by teachers to develop oral language in the elementary school:

Play "Policeman and Lost Child." Designate a "policeman." Let one child describe his "lost child." Policeman finds the child and delivers him to teacher. Involves telephone conversation and dramatic play; how happy everyone is that the child is found!

Provide a box of various objects and ask the child to describe each in terms of what it is like—

1. To sniff
2. To feel
3. To see
4. To hear
5. To touch

Provide a phonics chart, S in the center. Children find pictures of objects beginning with /s/, paste them on chart, and class reviews orally all pictures, paying particular attention to initial sound. Provide charts for all sounds.

Ask each child to bring a toy from home to tell about. (Plan Variety)

Assign a particular oral language activity for each day of the week— for example:

Monday—Personal experiences
Tuesday—News
Wednesday—Riddles and jokes
Thursday—Information
Friday—Free sharing

"Tell Me a Story Time." Have a child tell a story based on a colorful mounted picture teacher supplies. He includes—

1. What has already happened.
2. What is happening right now in the picture.
3. What is going to happen next.

Provide nature walks which offer opportunities for sensory stimulation and expression.

Blindfold a child. Hand him an object. Let him feel, shake, smell, taste it, then tell what it is.

Instruct children to talk on play telephone, letting them take turns using it. Have them play answering and practice holding the phone. Have adults answer. Make social calls to peers and adults. Stress telephone courtesy.

Encourage use of onomatopoeic words (words whose sounds suggest the sense), buzz, hum, and purr.

Choose general verbs or adjectives from children's work, and have children replace the general words with more specific ones.

List all the words children can think of to replace such common ones as said, walk, beautiful, tree.

Describe abstract adjectives such as glittering, chaotic, serene, etc.

Read a paragraph, omitting the topic sentence; have children supply a topic sentence, telling why theirs would be adequate.

Write a topic sentence on the chalkboard. Have each child present a paragraph orally, based on the teacher's sentence. Have the other children evaluate it after deciding on criteria for a paragraph.

7

Teaching Children
To Read

How Children Learn to Read

Although more educational research has been carried on in reading than in any other curriculum area, basic knowledge concerning how children learn to read is just beginning to emerge. Reading is recognized as a complex process involving the eyes, the brain, and motor, chemical, and emotional responses of the human body. What is known about the various physical, psychological, and other factors at work has not been unified or organized into an adequate explanation of the reading process. This knowledge gap is evidenced by the numbers of children who have difficulty in reading and adults who are poor readers.

The Bureau of Research of the United States Office of Education is currently undertaking a major program of research on the reading process. One project, headed by Dr. William J. Gephard,[1] utilizes a new planning device called the "Convergence Technique." This technique, designed for the planning and management of research, was worked out by two scientists of the National Cancer Institute for an attack on leukemia. Essentially, the technique is based on the assumption that everything happening in nature, whether planetary movements, migration of birds, or persons reading, has a discoverable order. As the plan for research approximates that order,

[1] Bulletin of the U.S. Department of Health, Education, and Welfare, Office of Education, no. HEW-U71 (Washington, D.C.: August 1, 1968).

the scope of the study narrows until all efforts converge on a final target.

A six-man team of generalists and specialists is working on the project, and the team represents medicine, biological sciences, language psychology, system analysis, general education, and research management.

Although little is yet known regarding how children learn to read, there is some knowledge based on research that can be of service to the elementary school teacher.

Principles of Reading Instruction

Of first importance is an awareness of one basic distinction between speaking and reading. In order to speak, the child must learn a vocal symbol for a concept. When the child is ready to read, he learns to associate a written symbol with his previously learned vocal symbol. Writing, then, is a symbol of speech which is in turn a symbol of reality. Writing is a primary symbol of speech but a secondary symbol of reality.

Second, the sequential nature of language has been widely recognized, and the teacher needs to be aware of the place of reading in this sequence. Language development begins with listening. As the child hears, recognizes, and finally attaches meaning to sound he becomes ready to imitate and respond, or to speak. Only after he can recognize and produce vocal symbols for needed ideas is he ready to learn the written symbols for the sounds of language. Finally, after the child is able to recognize the symbols for sounds, he is ready to learn to make them.

Although listening, speaking, reading, and writing occur in this order, they also overlap. Children continue to develop new skills in listening after they are speaking. The ability to express ideas with increasing effectiveness continues after the child is reading and writing, and of course children learn to write while their reading skill and comprehension are still in the early developmental stages.

The importance of familiar vocabulary and structure for the child in the first stages of reading cannot be overemphasized. During this time the child is learning that the symbols he sees are indeed symbols of speech. This relationship will not be discoverable if the child is asked to associate letters with words that he has never heard or used.

Reading instruction should be given only after a child has a reasonable command of the basic structures he will meet in his textbooks. He must be able to hear and speak the language with success before he is asked to move to the secondary symbols of language. Although many reading readiness programs are concerned with eye movement, vocabulary development, and physical, psychological, and social development, the language structures used by the child are not always evaluated with care. For this reason, bilingual children and children of certain socioeconomic groups who use dialects differing from the classroom language frequently have difficulty in reading.

Reading Readiness

Reading readiness is a term meaning sufficient background to ensure success as the child develops the skills and knowledge involved in the initial period of reading instruction.

The teacher is responsible for teaching many of the physical aspects of reading readiness. Eye movement from left to right and top to bottom is presented and drilled in a variety of experiences. Even when teachers show pictures during the reading of a story, they are careful to present the book to the children on their right first, moving the picture slowly to the left of the circle or classroom so that the children's eyes follow from left to right. Teachers arrange activities which teach children likenesses and differences of letters. Many children do not notice the difference between such letters as *d* and *b* until it is specifically called to their attention. From the beginning, children are helped to remember ideas and to see relationships between ideas through questions that direct attention to time sequence and cause and effect. The time when reading readiness occurs seems to be an individual matter. For years it was thought to occur for most normal children at about six years of age. For this reason reading was not introduced until the first grade of the traditional school. Great pressure was placed on most children to learn to read during this year. For all the enlightened discussion of readiness, the child who failed to learn to read during grade one was forever consigned to low reading groups in subsequent school years, with the accompanying stigma and damaged self-concept.

Linguists stress the need of learning the language before learning how it is represented by the visual symbols of traditional orthography. Although educators have long been aware of the relationships involved in the language areas, they have sometimes failed to take the child from known sounds and structures to the written symbols for them.

Motivation in Reading

Most children who come to school are anxious to learn to read. For many children, adequate backgrounds that include pleasurable experiences with books and family relationships which are both wholesome and developmental make such anxiety a healthy kind of irritation that keeps them actively pursuing the goal of reading in much the same way that a grain of sand activates the oyster until a pearl of value has been achieved.

For other children the anxiety is destructive. Pressure from teachers and parents applied to the child who is neither ready nor able to read frequently results in attitudes of hostility toward school and feelings of inadequacy and hopelessness. Such pressure, of course, destroys the child's natural desire to learn to read. No artificial motivation in the form of clever teasers to make the child want to find out how the story is climaxed or attractive gimmicks and games can ever be as effective as the child's own inherent desire to "break the code." To keep the natural motivation high, beginning reading experiences should provide each child with some opportunity for success and some degree of challenge. Experiences will of necessity vary with children. Various reading methods and materials are making possible the individualization of reading instruction. Teachers are learning that no one method is effective for all children, and because so little is known about how children learn to read, they must continue to use many techniques and encourage children to experiment with many approaches to find the most suitable for each child.

Development of Reading Skills

The reading program in the primary grades provides the children with a mastery of the mechanics of reading. The child is taught to listen for likenesses and differences of sounds as well as to discriminate visually as he identifies letters, words, and longer structures, and comprehends the meaning of what he is reading. During the intermediate grades, instruction in reading includes teaching the child to understand, interpret, and organize the material read, and to use information gathered for such purposes as solving problems, planning and carrying out some activity, reporting, evaluating, and forming judgments and opinions. During this period pupils are taught to select pertinent information from newspapers, periodicals, encyclopedias, and the dictionary, as well as their textbooks. Pupils are encouraged to think beyond facts. They are taught that unless facts are put to use they are of little value. Pupils may be taught to judge the place and importance of facts in influencing human behavior and to look consistently for the source and the cause of each fact.

For many children, the mechanics of reading are accomplished by the third or fourth year in school. Other children need continued training in word recognition through phonetic, structural, and contextual analysis as well as continued development of word, phrase, and sentence meaning. During this time the teacher must continue to use many methods of perception because children learn in different ways and have differing abilities. Some children may use one method while others may combine several methods in attacking new words. Common words that have spellings that do not follow the common spelling rules are probably most effectively taught by the look-say method. Symbols such as *t, 7,* and *Mr.* are always taught this way. Words like *the, one,* and *said* are examples of words that can probably be taught most effectively in this manner. However, because the reading process includes more than visual identification, the look-say method works for only a limited number of words. Sounds of words are as important as visual perception to the identification, meaning, and consequent growth of reading vocabulary.

Phonics and Phonetics

Any mention of sound in connection with reading immediately brings to mind two terms, frequently confused, phonics and phonetics.

These two terms are indeed similar in sound and appearance but they are very different in meaning.

Phonics is a method of reading instruction. In this approach children are asked to look at a letter and are told the sound that the letter makes. For example, the teacher writes the letter *g* on the chalkboard and pronounces it /gə/ having the children repeat the sound. A more enlightened presentation of the g might suggest that this is the first sound in *give, go,* or *get.* The problem with all of this, of course, is that g is a letter, not a sound, and that the letter symbolizes the sound /g/ in *go* and the sound /j/ in *gem.*

Phonics instruction being used in classrooms today varies from textbook to textbook, from school to school, and from teacher to teacher. It is rarely taught in isolation from reading, yet there is still a great deal of controversy regarding its value.

Phonetics is not a teaching method at all, but a scientific study of the sounds made by human beings when they speak. The study of phonetics moves from the sound to its written symbol. Whereas phonics starts with the letter and asks what sound or sounds each represents, phonetics suggests that learning should proceed from the sound to the written symbol.

When children are learning to read they are indeed learning to look at letters and relate them to previously known sounds and ideas. However, the process of spelling requires the child to turn the sounds into letters. Therefore, the concepts gleaned from phonetics seem to have great value for teaching spelling. Certain authorities are also recommending an approach to reading that begins with speech and asks what letters represent the sounds. This procedure is in keeping with the concept of moving from the known to the unknown, and it may offer a helpful supplement to children who have difficulty learning to read.

Methods of Word Recognition

The following methods of word recognition have been used by teachers to develop visual perception:

1. *Configuration.* Words have different shapes. The word grandfather has a characteristic shape that differs from the shape of baby. The word is and was seem to be more difficult because they do not have characteristic shapes.

Some authorities prefer to consider configuration a clue to the recognition of sight words rather than a method of word recognition.

2. *Unusual Letter Arrangement.* There is some evidence that pointing out such letter arrangements as the double o in *moon* and

look help the child to recognize words. However, unless there is something distinctive about the middle letters, those at the beginning and end of the word usually provide the cues to recognition.

3. *Picture Clues.* Picture clues provide helpful associations for some words. Children can match the word to the picture as an exercise to extend word meaning as well as to reinforce word recognition.

4. *Context Clues.* The meaning of a phrase or sentence can provide clues that will give the child an educated guess regarding what the new word might be. The context may draw clues from the child's own past experience, it may provide a clue through comparison or contrast, it may remind the child of a familiar or idiomatic expression, or it may be defined if the word is a familiar one in the child's listening and speaking vocabulary.

5. *Compound Words.* Children can be taught to look for a familiar word in a longer word. This will be a helpful clue for a new word like *grandfather* if the child already knows the word *father.* It will be of little help in a word like *greenhouse*, even if the child knows both *green* and *house*, because the relationship between the two words and the meaning of the compound word will not be clear to the child until specifically taught.

6. *Phonetic Analysis.* To attack a word phonetically involves using the initial consonants, the common sequences of letters, or other sound clues such as minimal pairs to identify the whole word. The word *rat* can be attacked phonetically because each letter has a consistent sound in such a relationship. *Rake* also follows the rule that a vowel between two consonants in a one syllable word has a long sound when the second consonant is followed by an *e*, and a word like *bear* takes a phonetic clue when the teacher points out orally that it rhymes with *pear*. Rhyming words provide important reading clues, and children who discover word patterns for sound-alike and look-alike words begin to break the code and feel successful in reading. This early achievement seems to be the foundation for reading success to many children.

7. *Structural Analysis.* To attack a word structurally, the child must be taught the common prefixes and suffixes. He must also be taught to recognize syllables and other word parts such as base

words and inflectional morphemes. Structural analysis is a particularly effective word attack method for intermediate and upper grade children.

Vocabulary Development in Reading

Two important criteria must be considered in the selection and sequencing of reading vocabulary. First, as previously stated, the words should be words that the pupil has already mastered in his hearing and speaking vocabulary. In addition to being known, it will help if they are words that are useful to the child in other curriculum areas such as social studies, science, and arithmetic.

Second, the words should be presented in groups that reflect the regular patterns of English. For example, many beginning reading books include such constructions as, " 'I am going home,' said Bill," whereas few children use any such structure in their speech. They say instead, "I'm going home," and the sounds of the two constructions are quite different.

As words are presented in patterns, regular forms are presented first, and irregular forms are introduced later. For example, nouns that add s to form plurals may be introduced in such a way that children can discover that words ending in voiceless consonants (such as k, t, p), other than the sibilants, keep the /s/ sound, whereas words that end in voiced consonants (such as g, d, b), except sibilants, have the /z/ sound, even though an s is added to form the plural. For example, sticks–pigs, cats–lads, maps–mobs, and words like moons, moors, hills, cows, and hives.

Irregular plurals, such as those created by vowel changes, man–men, those that require no change, sheep–sheep, those that change f to v and add es, knife–knives, and the sibilants that regularly add es, pronounced /əz/ as in churches, busses, bushes, and garages, can be introduced later. If each group is introduced as a group, children will soon be able to generalize and make up rules that will describe how the language behaves.

The examples given have been concerned with sound and spelling. Similar concern should be given to common simple sentence patterns, transformations, and phrases such as prepositional phrases, noun phrases, and verb phrases. As children learn to note similarities in forms and structures as well as words, their ability to recognize familiar words and learn new ones can be expected to increase.

Words for beginning readers show a close correlation between sound and spelling. The frequently used common words that are not phonetically spelled are taught in special drills as sight words.

Oral preparation for reading includes presenting words that the child will meet in his reading, presenting the words in the patterns that the child will meet in his reading, and giving him phonetic, structural, and contextual clues that will help him unlock both pronunciation and meaning. As soon as possible, teachers vary the speaking experience with questions and context rearrangements that keep the reading experience from being an exact duplication of the speaking experience. Wherever possible, words should be introduced in grammatical units, rather than in isolation.

If vocabulary is to be presented in a manner that is consistent with the concept that children should be confronted with only one learning problem at a time, teachers will not attempt to teach pronunciation, meaning, and written symbols all at once. Meaning is drawn from the experiences that a pupil has with a word.

In the primary grades, the child draws meaning largely from his immediate environment. The teacher provides objects, pictures, and meaningful activities from which children derive new vocabulary and clarify and extend previous concepts concerning the use of partially familiar words.

In later grades, meaning can be further extended as the child has more and varied experiences, some of which can now be taken vicariously from reading. The reader supplies overtones of meaning from his own experience when he reads. For this reason, most of the gimmicks and superficial activities suggested for the development of vocabulary are essentially ineffective.

As the child develops skill in reading, wide and varied reading resources will extend his vocabulary. Complex structures illustrate meaning and relationships heretofore undiscovered by pupils. Independent informal study provides the child an opportunity to refine shades and nuances of meaning that are appropriate to and taught in particular contexts.

The child may be given literature that uses a wide variety of English dialects and idiomatic expressions, and the meaning of these words should be taught in connection with a background of the peoples from whom such structures come. The English structures used by Robert Burns, cowboys from the western part of the United

States, and school teachers from Maine sound very different. Yet each is English and one form is not superior to another.

Concepts the elementary school child has acquired from his own experience frequently are incomplete or even incorrect when applied to new reading material. The child with an adequate background of experience is ready to be taught how to use a dictionary and an encyclopedia to clarify these concepts and supply additional facts.

As children advance in reading they begin to meet new word symbols for familiar concepts. They discover that there are many words to express the same or nearly the same idea. During this period of development children read extensively to gain new concepts, to construct new meanings from previous incomplete ideas, and to learn other ways of expressing familiar ideas. As a result vocabulary expands rapidly.

In teaching vocabulary, teachers present structural meaning as well as lexical meaning. Such instruction makes children aware of the range of meaning and the special reference signaled by parts of speech, such as nouns, verbs, and adjectives.

Vocabulary development results in the development of new ideas and concepts. Such ideas are learned from new experiences or developed and integrated from previous experiences. Developing an adequate vocabulary provides the student the rich background needed to give deeper meaning to his reading and to equip him for more advanced study.

Reading for Pleasure

Encouraging children to read extensively requires the provision of a great number of varied materials so that the child can find several books in every possible area of interest. Such reading material should be on a lower level of difficulty than the level used by the child for intensive reading. It should be possible for the child reading for pleasure to grasp the meaning of unfamiliar words from the context. There is little pleasure in reading a book that cannot be understood, or that requires constant effort as words are looked up so that the meaning can come through.

If children are taught how to deduce meaning from the structural relationship of new words with familiar words in context, they can be encouraged to read on their own. For example, in the sentence, "The nog was green and black," although *nog* is a word never before seen it is obvious that it is a noun and that it is green and black. Already there is enough information in the context that much meaning, although by no means complete meaning, has come through.

Reading for pleasure is extremely important, since it not only develops vocabulary but also broadens experience and extends concepts that could not otherwise occur in the classroom because of lack of time. Reading for pleasure and extensive reading should become synonymous terms for children. If the child really enjoys his reading, he will do as much of it as time allows. As the child reads he develops values and gains knowledge and insight into his own culture and the cultures of others. Books provide him with vicarious cultural and social experiences which help him to choose the directions his own experience will take. As the child compares and contrasts his own culture to other cultures, he develops an appreciation and knowledge of himself.

An enlightened citizenry in a democratic society requires a current knowledge of peoples of the world in their various environments, and an understanding and appreciation of the literary and artistic achievements of men throughout all ages. All of this, plus the knowledge of history and the natural, physical, and social sciences, can be acquired to a large degree from books, if good reading habits are established.

Every elementary school classroom can provide a wide variety of experiences, materials, and reading resources to kindle a child's interest and build in him an awareness of the deep need for human beings to understand and appreciate each other.

In summary, the child learning to read should be expected to know his language before he is required to learn the visual symbols of traditional orthography which represent it. He should be reading material which is introduced sequentially from the familiar to the unfamiliar and from the simple to the complex. His vocabulary should be presented in small doses in meaningful situations to hold his interest. Under his teacher's guidance he should be given sufficient drills and exercises to develop an ability to recognize words through the sharpening of visual perception and discrimination. The teacher should encourage the child to move as quickly as possible from word recognition to the reading of meaningful phrase groups. Finally, the teacher's reading should serve as a model of accuracy of pronunciation, phrasing, expression, and interpretation.

QUESTIONS FOR STUDY

1. What are the approaches to teaching reading in your school? How do such methods as the basic reader approach, individualized reading, and I.T.A. differ?
2. What emphasis is being placed on reading rate in schools? Does speed reading have any place in elementary school reading instruction?
3. What place does drill have in the reading program at the elementary school level?
4. How can the reading program be related to the spelling, handwriting, and English grammar programs?

SUGGESTIONS FOR FURTHER READING

Anderson, Paul S., *Language Skills in Elementary Education* (New York: The Macmillan Co., 1964).

Darrow, Helen F., and Howes, Virgil M., *Approaches to Individualized Reading* (New York: Appleton-Century-Crofts, 1960).

Downing, John, *Experiments With an Augmented Alphabet for Beginning Readers* (New York: Educational Records Bureau, 1962).

The First R: A Survey of Selected Current Practices in Reading Instruction (Burlingame, Calif.: The California Elementary School Administrators Association, 1966).

Fries, Charles C., *Linguistics and Reading* (New York: Holt, Rinehart & Winston, Inc., 1963).

Smith, Nila Benton, *Reading Instruction for Today's Children* (Englewood Cliffs, N.J.: Prentice-Hall, Inc., 1963).

TEACHER'S AID

Reading Drill

1. GIANTS

Flash cards are used or words can be written on the board. Start with the child sitting on the floor. For every word he knows, he progresses: sitting on floor, kneeling, sitting on chair, standing, on tip-toes, and reaching for the sky. Go on to the next child. (The child competes with himself, tries to reach for the sky every day.)

2. FAN

Teacher holds flash cards in a fan shape. Child closes eyes and chooses card. If he knows the word, he can keep it. If not, he puts it back into fan.

3. ILLUSTRATING WORDS

Flash cards or words on board. If a word lends itself to illustration, a child may select and illustrate a word during seat-work time. The class guesses the illustrated words as the illustrations are shown at the end of the period.

4. CLAPPING

Flash cards or words on board. The children clap when the teacher indicates certain words, such as words that rhyme or have the same initial sound.

5. MAILING

Child can "mail" word if he can say it. Use flash cards and improvise a mailbox.

6. THINKING OF A WORD

Write words on the board. A child silently selects word and says, "I'm thinking of a word." Children take turn coming up, pointing to a word, and saying, "Is it _____?" When a child guesses correctly he can be "it."

7. DISAPPEARING WORD

Place six words on flash cards on the chalkboard tray. Read them with the class. Have children close their eyes and remove one word. Children try to guess which one has disappeared.

8. TRAVELING AROUND THE WORLD

Flash cards or words on board. One child stands behind another who is seated. Teacher holds up a word and both children say it. The one who says it first moves on to next child. When a child succeeds in going around the entire classroom without missing, he has gone around the world.

9. TEACHER'S CHAIR

Use flash cards. Teacher starts the game by holding cards while child says them. He gets every one he says correctly. The teacher keeps the ones missed. If the child says all correctly, he sits in the teacher's chair and holds cards while next child says words, and so on. This game may be played with a small group in a circle or with the entire class, each child sitting at his own desk.

10. LUCKY CARD

Use flash cards. Introduce a new or difficult word. This is the lucky card. Then mix it in with the other cards while children hide their eyes.

Turn the pile of words over and hold up word on top of pile for child to say. Go around the group this way to see which one gets the lucky card.

11. FISHING

Use flash cards. Cards are "fish" and are placed in a container. The child goes fishing and reaches into the container and draws out a word. If he says it correctly, he can keep it. If not, he puts it back into the "pond." For variety, words can be written on fish shapes, balls, flowers, Christmas ornaments, etc., and a grab bag, a surprise box, or fish bowl, etc., can be used as a container.

8

A Linguistic Approach
to Sound and Spelling

In *A Defense of English Spelling*,[1] Sluter attempts to demonstrate the systematic nature of the English spelling system. He notes first the outrageous *ough* examples which denote six different sounds, as in the words *tough, bough, dough, through, cough,* and *hiccough,* and the fact that many poems, such as "The Harbor of Fowey" by Sir Arthur Quiller-Couch and the following verse by Lord Cromer, play on the irregularities of English spelling.[2]

> When the English tongue we speak,
> Why is *break* not rhymed with *freak?*
> Will you tell me why it's true
> We say *sew,* but likewise *Jew?*
> *Beard* sounds not the same as *heard;*
> *Cord* is different from *word;*
> *Cow* is *cow,* but *low* is *low;*
> *Shoe* is never rhymed with *foe;*
> And since *pay* is rhymed with *say,*
> Why not *paid* with *said,* I pray?
> And, in short, it seems to me
> Sounds and letters disagree.
> —Lord Cromer

[1] Sir Archibald Sluter, "A Defense of English Spelling," in *A Linguistic Reader,* ed., Graham Wilson (New York: Harper & Row, Publishers, 1967).
[2] Henry Martin, *Letters and Sounds* (London: Oxford University Press, 1942).

114

And yet, as Sir Archibald points out, the following contrived words would undoubtedly represent approximately the same sounds to any native speaker of English reading them:

gock	taff	brup	nim
kile	loke	deve	trape

Unquestionably the invented word *cright* would rhyme with *bright* or *flight*. The invented word *beigh* would be /bā/.

Rules and Exceptions in English Spelling

English spelling undoubtedly has both rules and exceptions. Good spellers somehow learn the system, the rules as well as the exceptions. They do not memorize individually the orthography of all the words they will ever need to spell and then write them correctly when the occasion demands them.

Teachers have for years been discouraged, as children have memorized lists of words for a perfect paper on Friday's spelling test, to find little or no carryover into Monday's written assignment. They believed that the difficulty lay in the fact that children were often learning to spell words for the Friday test that were used infrequently in writing, with a resulting lack of carryover for reinforcement. Indeed this was a weakness of older spelling texts, but the real problem resided in the fact that the burden of discovering the system was entirely on the child. He could learn the orthography of individual words, but these words were not organized so that he could see a pattern and discover the system.

It is true indeed that some spellings of made up words could create problems for speakers. *Brove* could rhyme with *grove, prove,* or *love,* and *thead* could rhyme with *plead* or *bread.* Would one begin *thon* with the initial consonant of *that* or *thin?* Probably the consonant of *thin* would have been chosen, because in the initial position the consonant of *that* occurs only in such words as pronouns (they), demonstratives, (this), adverbs (then), and the article *the.* Certain words in English such as *schism, quay, bourn, slough, bread, friend, many, gone, right,* and *neighbor* could not be spelled by simply being clearly heard. These and many more such as *myth* or *laugh* must be learned as exceptions, one by one.

Nevertheless, research teaches us that the vast majority of words are part of a system and can be learned as rule.[3] It is important to remember that all rules provided by linguistic analysis are descriptive rather than prescriptive. Teachers have been struggling with prescriptive rules in the study of language for years, and to no avail. Because there are so many exceptions to many of the poorly conceived prescriptive rules, many teachers decided to eliminate rules altogether, and indeed much research backed them up showing the ineffectiveness of rules in helping children to learn to spell.[4] The descriptive rule or generalization, which results from the discovery of the system of the language, must not be confused with former prescriptive teaching rules.

Sounds and Spelling

Accepting the premise that English is essentially systematic and that the system must be learned by those who desire to spell correctly, the system or rules can be taught in either of two ways. One can begin with the letters of the language and make the sounds which they clearly signify. This procedure is usually followed by the child who is learning to read. The second procedure involves beginning with the sounds and showing the letters regularly used to identify them. This procedure has more importance for the child learning to spell. Such a procedure includes teaching the conventional ways of spelling the consonant and vowel sounds, e.g., /i/ as in *fine, high,* and *my,* and it is found in the Roberts English Series.[5] This series presents a spelling program in grades three through six that provides a linguistic approach to the study of spelling. The series teaches spelling as part of the writing system, which of course it is. Teachers have sometimes fallen into the trap of considering spelling a subject, taught for a prescribed period each day, evaluated as an end in itself—a score on a list of words. This has led to the disenchantment of teachers who taught spelling conscientiously as prescribed, but who saw little result in the improvement of the written language of their students.

The Roberts Series considers the spellings of somewhat less than half of the English sounds in monosyllabic words in grade three. In the fourth grade the list of English sounds in one-syllable words is

[3] Paul R. Hanna, et al., "Needed Research in Spelling," *Elementary English,* vol. 43, no. 1 (January, 1966), p. 60.

[4] C. W. Hunnicutt and William J. Iverson, *Research in the Three R's* (New York: Harper & Row, Publishers, 1958), pp. 319–346.

[5] Paul Roberts, *The Roberts English Series: A Linguistics Program,* Teacher's Edition, grades 3–6 (New York: Harcourt, Brace & World, Inc., 1966).

nearly completed. In grade five, sounds in one-syllable words are completed, and the spelling of the reduced vowel schwa / ə / in unaccented syllables, e.g., grammar and letter, is introduced. From grade five on, sound and spelling are linked with syntax because they depend on this component of grammar.

The pronunciation of a word may depend on the word class. For example, the verb *estimate* is a familiar word and pronounced in a way that makes its spelling relatively simple (es'tə-mate'), although the / ə / sound in the middle syllable might be difficult; but *estimate* the noun, pronounced (es'tə-mit) might well result in a question concerning the accurate spelling of the last syllable. Clues to spelling are provided through the use of suffixes that establish a stress which makes spelling clear, such as in the noun *estimation*. This kind of movement is the result of a very regular system in English. By grade six the child begins to study systematically the spelling of words of Latin and Greek origin.

When one begins to describe the English sound system in relation to the spelling system, it is essential to have some means of referring to the sounds. The smallest units of sound which contrast as minimum features of utterances with different contents are called **phonemes**, e.g., the first sound in *pin* /p/ is a phoneme. Although in English it may be aspirated, (as in pen,) unaspirated, (as in spin) or unreleased, (as in nip) it is still considered a single phoneme. In Thai, however, each of these subcategories, called **allomorphs**, have meaning and are therefore different phonemes. There are several systems for transcribing phonemes. The letters of the alphabet cannot be used because there are only twenty-six letters and thirty-nine to forty-six English phonemes, depending on the linguistic source and, doubtless, on the variety of dialects included in the sample.[6]

Many linguists have worked out descriptions of sound usage, and a variety of systems are available, including the International Phonetic Alphabet and the Trager-Smith convention, which was published in 1951. The Trager-Smith phonology of English is widely used in the United States and deals effectively with the complexities of English speech. However, because the child's experience with rendering of speech sounds is with the dictionary, phono-

[6] H. A. Gleason, *An Introduction to Descriptive Linguistics* (New York: Holt, Rinehart & Winston, Inc., 1961). Page 9 specifies forty-six phonemes. Paul Roberts, *The Roberts English Series*, Teacher's Edition, grade 3 (New York: Harcourt, Brace, & World, Inc., 1968). Thirty-nine sounds are specified.

logical transcriptions for children go along with the more general practices of dictionaries, with only a few modifications. For example, dictionaries show two letters *sh* for the first sound in *shall*. A phonemic transcription for children ties the two letters together as a reminder of the single sound and places them between slant lines to indicate sound rather than letters /ʃh/.[7]

Table 1 (page 121) shows the Roberts symbols for English consonants.[8] American students who speak English as a native language certainly do not need to be taught how to produce the sounds. However, they can be taught something of how some of the sounds are made and some of the distinctive features of sound such as the /s/ on the end of *cats* which makes *cat* plural. The *s* which makes *cat* plural is called a morpheme. A morpheme is the smallest unit of meaning within a word. It may be a single letter such as the *s* in *cats*, or it may be a multisyllable word such as *California*. Many morphemes are words, but all words are not morphemes. Morphemes may be inflectional, and they may be derivational.

Inflectional morphemes make words plural, possessive, comparative, and superlative and show past and present tense. They also include the *ing* and *ed* of verbs in their participle forms. For example, the plural morpheme is made by adding *s* to *cat*, by changing the vowel *a* to *e* in *men*, by no change (sheep–sheep), by adding *en* (oxen), and by changing a voiceless consonant to voiced and adding the sound /z/ or /əz/ (path–paths, house–houses). Adjectives can show changes in meaning to indicate comparison by adding *er* (loud–louder) and to demonstrate a superlative form by adding *est* (loudest). Verbs have two present tense morphemes, the base word or simple form (run) and the third person singular or *s* form (runs). *Be* has three present tense forms *am, is,* and *are*. The past tense morpheme is *ed* for regular verbs (walked) and can also be demonstrated by a vowel change (ran); by no change (hit); by a change of the base verb form from /d/ to /t/ (build, built); by a change of vowel sound plus the addition of /t/ (mean, meant; teach, taught); and the addition of /d/ plus a vowel sound change (sell–sold). The *ing* form is always introduced with *be* in kernel sentences, and the participle in such sentences always accompanies a

[7] Paul Roberts, *The Roberts English Series: A Linguistics Program*, Teacher's Edition, grade 3 (New York: Harcourt, Brace & World, Inc., 1968), p. 6.

[8] Edith Trager, material prepared for Santa Clara Unified School District Workshop, 1967.

form of *have*. A kernel sentence has two parts, a noun phrase and a verb phrase. This type of sentence will be discussed at length later in the text.

Table 2 shows the traditional name conventions and the Robert's symbols for the vowel sounds of English as well as key words to help in the pronunciation of the sounds (page 122).

Derivational morphemes include prefixes and suffixes that change individual words from one class to another or change meaning within the class. e.g., brother (noun), brotherly (adjective), happy (adjective), and unhappy (adjective). The morpheme *er* added to a verb changes the word to a noun, i.e, *sing* plus *er* becomes *singer*. Add the morpheme *ly* to the noun *friend* and the result is an adjective *friendly*. The adjective *loud* plus *ly* becomes an adverb *loudly*, and of course there are many other derivational morphemes including the frequently used *ex, un, be, re, en, ful, ence, ment, ness,* and *cy*.

Adjectives such as *peaceable* and *lovable* made from nouns plus *able*, and verbs that add *ible* in English, such as permit, reduce, and resist (permissible, reducible, and resistible) create spelling problems for children. But these additions and changes follow regular patterns which can be learned.

Tables 3 and 4 respectively show the consonant and vowel sounds of English and their common spellings.[9]

Applying Linguistics to Spelling

A research study directed by Paul R. Hanna, Lee L. Jacks Professor of Child Education at Stanford University, and supported by the Cooperative Research of the U.S. Office of Education, provides evidence that makes possible a new spelling program for children.[10]

As a result of new research into linguistics as well as into teaching-learning theories, a modern spelling program begins following the child's possession of a large oral–aural vocabulary. The average first grade child has an estimated understanding and speaking vocabulary of from 5,000 to 10,000 words. The child must be taught

[9] Paul Roberts, *Suggested Experiences in English for Grades 1 and 2 Preparatory to The Roberts English Series* (New York: Harcourt, Brace & World, Inc., 1966), pp. 9–11.

[10] Paul R. Hanna and Jean S. Hanna, "Applications of Linguistics and Psychological Cues to the Spelling Course of Study," *Elementary English*, vol. 42, no. 7 (November, 1965), p. 753.

to break his words into component sounds, then to select and write appropriate graphemes for the sounds he says and hears. Later he can learn the various standard American spellings for these sounds. Through careful teaching, the child can discover the influence of position, stress, and context on particular graphemes when there seem to be several options. As he is guided beyond phonological analyses to a thoughtful examination of the morphological elements that affect spelling, compounding words, prefixes, suffixes, and inflectional derivations, the child's ability to spell accurately should increase.

Teachers using the new spelling program will also be concerned with teaching the child to use all elements of his sensorimotor equipment, ear-voice-eye-hand, to reinforce each other in establishing spelling in his neural system and help him build spelling power that will result in a writing vocabulary adequate for all of his writing needs.

In summary, the spelling system of English requires more effort to learn than the spelling system of Spanish or Italian or Turkish. Nevertheless, English spelling has a system, and the specter of the exception must not frighten teachers and students away from the rule. If there is no rule then everything is an exception, and each word must be learned as a separate item, unrelated to any other. This, of course, would be a defeating task for most human memories, but fortunately research has demonstrated the fallacy of such thinking and the overwhelming regularity of the English spelling system.[11]

If one is to learn the spelling system of English he must learn the common spellings of the phonemes and morphemes of English and the rules for their application. These rules are descriptive of how English behaves; they do not suggest that this is how the language should behave. For example, in the spelling of English words that begin with initial /k/ the words are spelled with *k* when letters *i* or *e* follow, and with *c* in all other cases. This, of course, does not apply to the words which are Greek borrowings such as *chaos*, *character*, and *chorus*. Nor does it apply to the initial cluster /kw/, spelled *qu*, as in *queen* and *quip*. The exception *quay* (kē) is a rare word borrowed from the French and is not included in this rule.

---

[11] Hanna and Hanna, *op. cit.*, p. 61.

TABLE 1

English Consonant Phonemes

	Labials (Lips)		Dentals (Teeth)		Palatals (Palate)	Velars (Velum)
Stops (Affricates) Vl °	p			t	ch	k
Vd †	b			d	j	g
Fricatives Vl		f	th	s	sh	
Vd		v	~~th~~	z	zh	—
Nasals	m			n	—	ng
Resonants	w		(r)	l	y	h
	Bilabials	Labiodentals	Interdentals	Alveolars		

° Voiceless. † Voiced.

Explanation of Table 1

Labials, dentals, palatals, and velars are *points of articulation,* while stops, fricatives, nasals, and resonants denote the *manner of articulation.* If it is possible to visualize the diagram inside a mouth with the lips, teeth, hard palate, soft palate, and velum, one can see that the air is stopped at the lips for the /p/ and /b/, that it is forced between the upper teeth and lower lip for the /f/ and /v/, and that it goes through the nasal passage for /m/ since both lips are closed.

The labial stops /p/ and /b/ are formed identically except that /p/ is voiceless (vl) and /b/ is voiced (vd). Say the words *pin* and *bin.* They are the same except for the contrast of voiceless /p/ and voiced /b/.

Bilabial means that both lips are involved in making the sound. Labiodental means that the air is forced between the lower lip and the upper teeth; An interdental sound is made with the tongue between the upper and lower teeth, and an alveolar sound is made

Explanation of Table 1—Continued

with the tongue on the alveolar ridge directly behind the upper teeth. The palatals /ch/ and /j/ are often called affricates because they include both stops and fricatives in their formation. To make /ch/ the tongue is placed in position for the voiceless alveolar stop /t/ and then the air moves on through with the voiceless palatal fricative /sh/. The /j/ sound is made in precisely the same way except that it begins with the voiced alveolar stop /d/ and moves on to the voiced palatal fricative /zh/.

The resonants are a conglomeration in a very broad category. The sounds of /w/ and /y/ are called glides and semi-vowels by some linguists, /r/ is made in a great variety of ways, /h/ is a glottal fricative, meaning that the air is released from the glottis, and /l/ is alveolar.

TABLE 2

English Vowel Phonemes

Traditional Name	Robert's Symbol	Key Word
Short Vowels (Simple Nuclei)		
Short A	a	pat
Short E	e	pet
Short I	i	pit
Short O	o	pot
Short U	u,	putt, fur
Short OO	oo	put, good
The AU-sound	au	pause
Long Vowels and Dipthongs (Complex Nuclei)		
Long A	ā	bait
Long E	ē	beet
Long I	ī	bite
Long O	ō	boat
Long U	ū	boot
OY sound	oi	boy
OU sound	ou	bough

TABLE 3

Consonant Sounds and Their Common Spellings

Sound	At the Beginning		At the End	
/p/	p: pie		p: rip	pe: ripe
/t/	t: ten		t: pet	te: date
/k/	k: kit	c: cold	ck: lick	ke: like
/ch/	ch: chin		tch: witch	ch: reach
/b/	b: bed		b: tub	be: tube
/d/	d: do		d: rid	de: ride
/g/	g: get		g: beg	gue: league
/j/	j: jet	g: gentle	dge: budge	ge: cage
/f/	f: fun;	ph: phrase	f: beef	fe: life;
			ff: stuff	ph: para-graph
/v/	v: very		ve: save	
/s/	s: see	c: center	ss: glass	s: bus;
			se: case	ce: rice
/z/	z: zoo		z: quiz	zz: buzz;
			se: rose	ze: sneeze
/sh/	sh: ship		sh: push	s: treasure
/zh/	j: Jacques		ge: rouge	
			s: treasure (in the middle)	
/r/	r: run	wr: wrist: rh: rhyme	r: car	re: care
/l/	l: lose		ll: pill l: fail	le: smile;
/m/	m: move		m: Sam mb: tomb	me: same
/n/	n: nose kn: know	gn: gnaw	n: pin	ne: pine
/ng/			ng: strong	nk: trunk
/th/	th: thick		th: path	
/th/	th: then		th: smooth the: bathe	
/y/	y: you	u /y–ū/: use		
/w/	w: will	o /w–u/: one; qu /k–w/: quick		
/h/	h: hat;	wh: who		

TABLE 4

Some Vowel Sounds and Their Common Spellings

Simple Vowel Sounds	/a/	/e/	/i/	/o/	/u/
Spellings and Examples	a: cat	e: red ea: dead	i: hit	o: top a: far	u: but o: son

Five Complex Vowel Sounds	/ā/	/ē/	/ī/	/ō/	/ū/
Spellings and Examples	VCe: lame ai: wait ay: pay ei: weigh	VCe: Pete ee: deed ea: heat e: he ie: chief ei: deceive	VCe: line igh: high y: try ie: die	VCe: lone oa: goat ow: slow oe: hoe o: no	VCe: June oo: root ew: knew ue: Sue o: to

Four More Vowel Sounds	/oo/	/ou/	/oi/	/au/
Spellings and Examples	oo: look u: push	ou: out ow: cow	oi: oil oy: toy	au: haul aw: saw a: ball o: long ough: fought augh: taught

QUESTIONS FOR STUDY

1. What are the relationships of sounds and letters?
2. What is a phoneme? Why are phonemes important to the study of spelling?
3. What is a morpheme? How can the study of morphemes aid in spelling English?
4. What is an inflectional morpheme? How many are there in English?
5. What is a derivational morpheme? In what way is morphological structure related to word class structure in English?

The reader may wish to discuss these questions to be sure that the concepts are clear. The following references will help clarify the ideas.

SUGGESTIONS FOR FURTHER READING

Aurbach, Joseph, et al., *Transformational Grammar: A Guide for Teachers* (Washington D.C.: English Language Services, 1968).

Hall, Robert Anderson, Jr., *Linguistics and Your Language* (Garden City, N.Y.: Doubleday & Co., Inc., 1960).

Hockett, Charles Francis, *A Course in Modern Linguistics* (New York: The Macmillan Co., 1958).

Jackobson, Roman, and Halle, Morris, *Fundamentals of Language* (The Hague: Mouton and Co., 1956).

Roberts, Paul, *Modern Grammar* (New York: Harcourt, Brace & World, Inc., 1967).

Roberts, Paul, *The Roberts English Series: A Linguistics Program,* Teacher's Edition grades 3–9 (New York: Harcourt, Brace & World, Inc., 1967).

TEACHER'S AID

1. Identifying Vowel Nuclei. To test their knowledge of the vowel phonemes, have the children match the vowel nuclei sounds of the thirty-four words listed below to the phonemic vowel symbols above, putting the number of the word in the space provided after the phonemic symbol. There may be several numbers in each space to the right of the phonemic representation.

short a	/a/	_____
long e	/ē/	_____
oy	/oy/	_____
long a	/ā/	_____
long i	/ī/	_____

short oo	/oo/	_____
long o	/ō/	_____
long oo	/ū/	_____
short o	/o/	_____
au	/au/	_____
short u	/u/	_____
short e	/e/	_____
long u	/ū/	_____
ou	/ou/	_____
short i	/i/	_____

1. day	10. muse	19. cite	28. ought
2. void	11. Freud	20. aisle	29. but
3. that	12. friend	21. bout	30. weigh
4. beaux	13. suit	22. boot	31. sight
5. caught	14. suite	23. bush	32. talk
6. glove	15. put	24. thy	33. who
7. plaid	16. cede	25. said	34. owe
8. they	17. pew	26. read	
9. myth	18. sew	27. hood	

Answers

short a	/a/	3, 7
long e	/ē/	14, 16, 26
oy	/oy/	2, 11
long a	/ā/	1, 8, 30
long i	/ī/	31, 19, 20, 24
short oo	/oo/	15, 23, 27
long o	/ō/	34, 4, 18
long oo	/ū/	13, 22, 33
short o	/o/	5, 28, 32
au	/au/	5, 28, 32
short u	/u/	6, 29
short e	/e/	12, 25, 26
long u	/ū/	10, 17
ou	/ou/	21
short i	/i/	9

Some dialects will produce a variance in the answers to /o/ and /au/.

2. Put the first and second lines of several rhymes on the chalkboard and let the children fill in the final word and later compare their

---

[12] Mary C. Austin and Queenie B. Mills, *The Sound of Poetry* (Boston: Allyn and Bacon, Inc., 1963).

answers with the original, e.g., *How the Flowers Grow*,[12] by Gabriel Setoun:

> This is how the flowers grow:
> I have watched them and I (know).
>
> First, above the ground is seen
> A tiny blade of purest (green).
> Reaching up and peeping forth
> East and west and south and (north).
>
> Then it shoots up day by day,
> Circling in a curious (way).
> Round a blossom, which it keeps
> Warm and cozy while it (sleeps).

3. Put a list of frequently used words with some letters missing on the chalkboard and have children fill in the blanks. For example:

s_ _ed_le	t_e_e	sc_o_l
rec_ _ve	b_ _ld_ng	fr_ _nd
the_r	com_un_ty	

4. Have children suggest synonyms and antonyms for frequently used words. Narrow the choice by putting broken lines next to the word with dashes representing letters in the answers:

Synonyms	Antonyms
same _ _ _ _ _ _ _ _ _	straight _ _ _ _ _ _ _
(identical)	
different _ _ _ _ _ _	wrong _ _ _ _ _

5. Have children make words from lists of frequently used words with their letters scrambled.
6. Put words on word cards and cut them into jigsaw puzzles. When the puzzles have been fitted together, the words can be written in a list or used in sentences.
7. Dictate poems, bits of prose, social studies excerpts, and other selections. Move from studied dictation, in which the children are allowed to study the selections ahead of time, noting spelling, punctuation, and capitalization, to unstudied dictation with selections that the children have read but have not studied.
8. Sound Poems and Jingles

/s/ sound:

> In summer the wind is soft and low:
> "S-s-s-s" I hear him blow [s sound very soft].
> But when he's bringing the winter snow,
> "SSSSSSS" I hear him go [very loud S].

Skipping is fun,
Skipping is fun,
Skipping is fun for everyone.
The more you skip,
The better you skip,
So skip, skip, skip.

/z/ sound:

Mosquito your song   Teacher: Oh have you got a zipper coat,
Z-z-z-z-z   A zipper coat, a zipper coat?
Won't last very long,   That goes z-z-z-z-z-z.
Z-z-z-z-z
For the toad in the garden   Class: Oh yes I have a zipper coat,
Z-z-z-z-z   A zipper coat, a zipper coat.
Won't beg your pardon   Oh yes I have a zipper coat,
Z-z-z-z-z   That goes z-z-z-z-z-zip!
But will swallow you down
Z-z-z-z-z
And not make a frown.
Z-z-z-z-z [these /z/ sounds
to be made very softly].

Whenever I hear up in the sky,
Z-Z-Z-Z-Z-Z-Z-Z-Z-Z-Z-Z-Z-Z-Z
I know that a plane is passing by.
Z-Z-Z-Z-Z-Z-Z-Z-Z-Z-Z-Z-Z-Z-Z

/sh/ sound:

The little yellow duck is taking a nap.
Sh, everybody, just tip-toe, don't walk.
He's all tired out and he needs his rest,
Sh, everybody, just whisper, don't talk.

"Sh!" says mother,   New shoes, new shoes,
"Sh!" says father,   Red and pink and blue shoes,
Running in the hall   Buckle shoes, bow shoes,
Is a very great bother   Which shoes would you choose?
"Sh! Sh! Sh!"

/ch/ sound:

Here comes the choo-choo train,
Ch-ch, ch, ch, ch!
Down the track and back again,
Ch-ch, ch, ch, ch!
It takes you where you want to go
Ch-ch, ch, ch, ch!
Sometimes fast, sometimes slow,
Ch-ch, ch, ch, ch!

Now it's chugging up the hill,
Ch-ch, ch, ch, ch!
Now it's stopping! Now it's still!
Ch_____ch_____ch_____!

/th/ sound:

Once I saw a goose who said,
Th-th-th-!
When a child came near his shed,
Th-th-th!
Once he said this noise to me,
Th-th-th!
I ran away as fast as could be,
Th-th-th!

Finger Play for /f/ and /th/

Fee, fie, fo, fum!
See my finger [show finger],
See my thumb [show thumb]!
Fee, fie, fo, fum!

Fee, fie, fo, fum!
Finger's gone [hides finger],
So is thumb [hides thumb]!
Fee, fie, fo, fum!

Rhymes to prepare the child for listening to sounds:

Quiet Time
This is my quiet time.
My hands and feet are still.
My head is down,
My eyes are shut,
This is my quiet time.

Rag Doll
I'm a limp rag doll.
I have no bones.
My arms are limp.
My legs are limp.
My neck is limp.
I'm a limp rag doll.

9

Some Linguistic
Concepts of Grammar

Every native speaker of a language has a grammar built into him. The term **grammar**, as used in this chapter, means simply a set of rules or a system that produces the sentences of a language. It includes phonology, morphology, and syntax. The terms phoneme and morpheme have already been discussed. **Syntax** is the description of larger combinations, including words and parts of words and their arrangement in sentences. Transformational generative grammar, frequently called transformational grammar, stresses two components, the syntactic, which includes morphology, and the phonological. These components are defined in the following discussion of transformational grammar.

Transformational Grammar

Much recent study of the language is based on transformational generative grammar. In spite of many years of investigating language, very little is known about the way speakers actually produce sentences. Hence, transformationalists, one group of linguists, use modern symbolic logic to construct grammars. Recent developments in the theory of symbolic logic and in the theory of proof provide the means for constructing such a grammar.

Transformational grammar makes no claim to be a duplicate of the grammar which enables a native speaker to produce sentences. It is, however, the closest approximation to natural or intuitive grammar yet available. Transformational grammar is the term frequently used for transformational generative grammar. A **genera-**

tive grammer contains a list of symbols and a list of rules for combining the symbols in various ways to produce sentences.[1] Although the number of sentences in English is potentially infinite, all native speakers of English have some method of understanding completely novel sentences never spoken before. Rules that generate are actually generalizations about language which permit a native speaker to evaluate the grammaticality of any new sentence. Transformations are rules which rearrange various elements in sentences and combine the symbols in a variety of ways.

Transformational generative grammar contains both syntactic and phonological components. The **syntactic component** includes words and parts of words and their arrangement in sentences. It contains word classes, functions, number, and tense, prepositional phrases, relative clauses, the kind of matter conventionally considered to be the content of grammar. The **phonological component** describes the sound structure of the language and is made up of the rules for pronouncing English. This grammar, hereafter referred to as transformational grammar, is fairly well developed in America so far as its syntactic component is concerned.

Teachers are confused and even apprehensive about the various grammars that have been recommended for or used in the classroom, and rightly so. Many teachers have read journal articles or attended conferences which have been designed to whet the teacher's intellectual appetite for new directions in language, rather than to inform. Perhaps it will be useful to sort out and briefly discuss the various grammars which receive frequent reference.

Traditional Grammar

First of all, traditional grammar, although rooted in the Greek grammar of Dionysius Thrax (c. 200 B.C.), was most thoroughly detailed in the Latin grammars of Donatus (c. A.D. 400) and Priscian (c. A.D. 660). The methodology of these classical grammarians was adopted by the grammarians of the seventeenth and eighteenth centuries who attempted to describe English, French, Italian, and other "new" languages according to the Latin plan. These grammarians assumed that the structure of various languages, especially Latin, embodied universally valid canons of logic.[2]

---

[1] Paul Roberts, *English Sentences* (New York: Harcourt, Brace & World, Inc., 1962), p. 8.

Traditional grammar made no effort to discover how people learn languages, including their native language, or to explain the nature of correctness. Early English grammarians either overlooked the fact that all languages change, or else they considered change to be synonymous with corruption. They generally based their rules for English on Latin models, but they also displayed a heavy reliance on their own intuition about what was correct in their own language. Most of the modern "school grammars" used in elementary and secondary schools today are based almost exclusively on the models of the eighteenth century grammarians.[3] They are largely prescriptive and their explanations fail to help the reader figure out the essential systems. They ignore linguistic facts and rarely provide any theoretical basis for grammatical rules. Traditional grammars are largely contradictory and frequently absurd. Therefore, schoolchildren who have had problems understanding grammar have had good reason. The grammar presented to them has been frequently not understandable.[4]

Historical, Comparative, Descriptive, and Structural Grammar

Historical and comparative grammarians looked at language more closely than the early English grammarians. In the eighteenth and nineteenth centuries, philologists were busy looking for systematic correspondences in languages. At the same time, these ancestors of comparative and historical linguists were tracing the history of particular languages as far back as written records permitted. They figured out the development and relationships of the Indo-European family of languages and of other language groups.

Around 1910 attention turned increasingly to present-day languages and their structure. The descriptive and structural grammarians of the twentieth century sought to describe language as it was, not as people thought it should be. These linguists were looking for methods of describing language that were free from error and subjective judgments. During this period many traditional

---

[2] Leonard Bloomfield, *Language* (New York: Henry Holt and Co., 1933), p. 6.

[3] Owen Thomas, *Transformational Grammar and the Teacher of English* (New York: Holt, Rinehart & Winston, Inc., 1965), p. 210.

[4] Paul Roberts, *The Roberts English Series: A Linguistics Program*, Teacher's Edition, grade 4 (New York: Harcourt, Brace & World, Inc., 1966), p. 17.

ideas were shown to be untenable, and others were proposed to take their place. The achievements of the linguists were many.[5] One of the most important of their analyses involved the necessity of dividing the study of language into two parts, syntax and semantics. Semantics refers to lexical meaning, while syntax, according to modern linguists, provides a basis for the study of semantics.[6] The structural linguists placed increasing emphasis on the spoken language as opposed to the written language, and for this reason the disagreements between the traditional grammarians and the structural linguists, although often very strong, were not as violent as they might have been. Structural linguists insisted that there is no *single* standard of usage and correctness in language. They pointed out that any structure generally accepted as proper by a given speech community is correct for that community. If the community is the one that sets general national standards, then the structure is correct nationally. Logic has little to do with it. Structural linguists further pointed up the impossibility of basing definition on meaning. Roberts gives the following example:

> Suppose we consider such a meaning as "time." We might try to begin by asking how many "times" there are and then discovering the language forms that express these. Probably we would start by supposing three "times"—past, present, and future. But a brief examination of the language shows that there are many more time distinctions than three. We have present action ("I am writing"), repetitive present action ("I write every day"), durative present action ("I write for hours"), past action ("I wrote"), unspecified past action ("I have written"), future ("I may write"), near future ("I am about to write"), past near future ("I was about to write"), and many more. If we change the verb to seem or know, all the meanings shift somewhat, and the categories multiply. It is simply impossible, at least in the present state of knowledge, to catalogue ideas and then find the language forms they express. It was a serious weakness of traditional grammar that it tried to go from meaning to form. It was a great contribution of structural grammar that it went from form to meaning.[7]

Although structural grammar was much sounder than traditional grammar, it was also much narrower. Most of the followers of Bloomfield and Sapir were so concerned with describing the lan-

---

[5] Bloomfield, *op. cit.* Edward Sapir, *Language, An Introduction to the Study of Speech* (New York: Harcourt, Brace & World, Inc., 1921).

[6] Thomas, *op. cit.*, p. 13.

[7] Roberts, Teacher's Edition, grade 4, p. 18.

guage that they ignored how it operates. Structural linguists confused theory and method and set up rules which discouraged grammarians from attacking broad problems of language and language learning.

Generative Transform Grammar

In the mid 1950s a group of scholars called transformationalists reacted against structural linguists and sought to describe the operations of language.[8] This group recognized the virtue of traditional grammar, the contributions of historical, comparative, and descriptive linguists, and the need for describing the operations as well as the states of language. The transformational linguists asked, "What is the nature of language that human beings can learn it? What is the nature of human beings that they can learn language?"

To answer these questions the transformationalists pointed out that language is not memorization and reuse of a certain number of sentences. Most sentences used by people have never occurred before. Obviously then language is learned as a mechanism for generating sentences according to the nature of experience and the need for communicating. Grammar, say the transformationalists, is best understood as a small set of sentences, called kernel sentences, plus a set of rules for transforming these into more complicated structures. Given a finite number of sentences plus a finite number of rules, an infinite number of sentences can be generated, many of which have never before been produced.

In one very important sense, transformational grammar is a new way of looking at some traditional ideas concerning language. Transformational grammar is not complete. The details of grammar are changing and will continue to change. Teachers should contribute to the change by continuing to theorize about their subject matter, to develop the details of their theories, and then to test them against experience. Language teachers must continue to study and teach the "living language."

Teaching Grammar to Children

When the grammar of a language is presented to young children who speak it natively, a serious problem arises. Children come to school speaking complicated sentences. The third grade child is

[8] Noam Chomsky, *Syntactic Structures* (The Hague: Mouton and Co., 1957).

frequently writing sentences such as, "When I go home after school, my dog brings me his ball and some sticks." The gap between this sentence and the sentences whose structure could reasonably be explained to a third grade child is so great that this probably accounts for the lack of a systematic presentation of grammar. Teachers frequently believe that any explanation should be functional. However, to explain the preceding sentence would be extremely difficult. The sentence contains an introductory dependent clause with a special adverbial (home) and a special verb (go). It also contains a prepositional phrase and a personal pronoun. The main clause contains possessives, an indirect object, and a compound direct object. The sentence displays tense and number, subjects and predicates, and different types of nouns.

What is Grammatical?

A person who speaks English natively knows that one of the following sentences is grammatical and that one is not.

1. John gave his brother a ball.
2. John ball gave brother his.

The native speaker of English rejects sentence 2 because it does not conform to the system of English syntax. No native speaker of English would arrange his sentence in such a pattern. The rejection has nothing to do with anyone's explanation of the preceding sentence.

Grammaticality is not based on meaning. For example, the sentence "Nobody wanted to chinkle the boggans" is grammatically correct although quite meaningless.

The difference between grammaticality and ungrammaticality is not always so obvious. Examine the following sentences:

1. John brought the book to school.
2. John brung the book to school.
3. John to school brought book the.

Sentence 3 is unquestionably incorrect. No native speaker would use this sentence. Although both sentences 1 and 2 are used by native speakers, some question arises about the difference between the grammaticality of these sentences. Is sentence 1 more correct than sentence 2? If so, why? It is certainly not a question of clarity. Sentences 1 and 2 are equally clear; one grasps the meaning of 2 as quickly as the meaning of 1. Both are more understandable than sentence 3. The sound of the verbs also is irrelevant. Nothing in the sound of *brought* makes it better than *brung*. No rule in English requires that certain classes of verbs end in *ought* rather than *ung*. Nor does any English rule suggest that *ung* is an improper ending for a verb; in fact, *flung* is a perfectly respectable past verb form. Although "He brung the book" is frowned on, "He flung the book" is certainly accepted, at least in a grammatical sense. In summary, there is nothing in the system of the language that suggests that sentence 1 is preferable to sentence 2. Why then is sentence 1 preferred?

Paul Roberts [9] suggests that sentence 1 is more acceptable simply because it is associated with educated people, while sentence 2 is commonly connected with the uneducated. However, educated people do not say *brought* in this sentence for the reason that it is superior in any fashion to *brung*. Educated people say "John brought the book to school" and that *makes* it better.

The grammar of the educated influences language, particularly in verb forms and pronouns. This grammar has a prestige that the grammar of sentence 2 does not have. As far as language characteristics are concerned, the grammar of sentence 2 is capable of as much power, tenderness, clarity, and complexity as the grammar of sentence 1. Even so, speakers of sentence 1 display or at least feel a certain amount of contempt for speakers of sentence 2. Although this attitude is not sensible, much less charitable, it is a fact. Therefore, one who cannot manage the language forms of the educated will find many doors in contemporary society closed to him. Although sentences 1 and 2 differ only in the fact that they represent different dialects or varieties of English, the children who learn to speak with the grammar of sentence 2 should be encouraged to add the grammar of sentence 1 to their language development.

An additional important distinction needs to be made between grammaticality and ungrammaticality. Examine the following sentences:

1. Who were you talking to?
2. He wanted to really understand it.
3. I will see him tonight.

9 Roberts, Teacher's Edition, grade 4, pp. 1–9.

Sentence 1 ends with a preposition and uses *who* instead of *whom;* 2 splits an infinitive; 3 uses *will* instead of *shall* after I.

Although some books on usage warn against such sentences, it must be pointed out that they are not only (obviously) English, but also quite consistent with the system of Grammar 1 (Henry brought his mother some flowers.) and Grammar 2 (Henry brung his mother some flowers.) They are normal forms for educated speakers as well as for uneducated . . . It is no doubt true that certain styles of writing, perhaps certain occasions of speech as well, would call for the following sentences rather than the preceding ones:

1. To whom were you talking?
2. He wanted really to understand it.
3. I shall see him tonight.

One may achieve a certain formality by using the second set; he may also sound a bit standoffish and forbidding. But neither one is ungrammatical except in the most trivial sense.[10]

Significance of Language Study

Because language performs a social function, the individual is not free to speak as he likes. He is judged according to his speech and the manner in which it conforms to the accepted dialect of the community, standard English. This dialect, used by educated people and possessing the loyalty of the majority of the people, provides an entrance into a variety of linguistically marked circles. Thus, even though the dialect which the child brings to school is as useful for communicating as the accepted dialect, he needs this second dialect for social mobility. The advantages of learning and using standard English should be pointed out early in the child's school career. Elementary school teachers then will accept both the child and his language. No attempt will be made to eradicate the first dialect. Instead, a second dialect will be taught as if it were a foreign tongue. The child acquiring the second dialect becomes in a sense bilingual. Charlotte Brooks recommends [11] sharing the following ideas, fitted to the age, maturity, and ability of the child:

> I accept you and your language. (Of course this must be demon-
> strated constantly, not just stated.) Use your language when you need

[10] Roberts, Teacher's Edition, grade 4, p. 9.
[11] Charlotte K. Brooks, "Some Approaches to Teaching Standard English as a Second Language," *Elementary English*, vol. 41, no. 7 (Nov., 1964), pp. 728–733.

it for communication with your friends or family. But if you really want to be a free and successful participant in other areas of this American life, why not also learn the language spoken here, standard English?

Children who learn standard English in the home would rarely find it useful to learn another grammar. Should they then be required to study grammar? They already possess the system of language that will permit them comfortable movement in the "accepted" and "desirable" linguistically marked areas of society, and they can certainly distinguish between grammatical and ungrammatical patterns. If children have already discovered and are using the accepted patterns of the language, why then do they need a conscious understanding of the system and the way it operates?

From a practical point of view such a study of language possibly permits greater freedom and flexibility in writing. Written sentences are often more intricate and bound by convention than spoken sentences, and more mature students will probably feel much more comfortable and secure possessing the knowledge and skills essential to adequate and effective expression.

Research indicates that any formal study of grammar has heretofore had little, if any, effect on usage.[12] This may mean that the knowledge about a language has little to do with knowing a language, or it may mean that previous attempts to teach grammar and usage have been so unrelated to the specific need for such knowledge that the knowledge has been reduced to meaningless facts. The relationship between knowing a language and knowing about a language is not clear and probably varies with individuals and age groups. Therefore, there are no clear-cut, concrete guides for what should be taught, when.

If, however, one approaches the study of his language with the attitude that in so doing he is in fact studying himself and how he works, he will unquestionably find it more engrossing. Imagine possessing this incredible, complicated apparatus which enables one to produce infinite numbers of sentences, including many that have never before been expressed. Why are we so impressed with the mechanical marvels of our space age while we take for granted or are frequently even disinterested in discovering an explanation for the way in which language operates? Language is the element of

---

[12] C. W. Hunnicutt and William J. Iverson, *Research in the Three R's* (New York: Harper & Row, Publishers, 1958), pp. 318–342.

our nature that has literally set us above all the other creatures in our world, a marvel of marvels even in the space age! One should then study his language simply because he wants to understand it. For years children have been told that the study of grammar, although bitter and tedious, will one day be useful. Students have simply refused to believe such propaganda, as evidenced by their correct use of forms when filling in the blanks during formal language classes, and their immediate reversion to formerly used patterns in speaking and writing. Undoubtedly a different attitude and an entirely new motivation needs to precede the study of language. Why not study language because it is worthy of study? Seek ye first for the joy of discovering, and the practical application, if any, can be one of the things which are added unto you.

The Syntactical Component of Grammar

This brief review of grammar, including the morphemes of the language as well as word classes, functions, phrases, and clauses, will alert the teacher to new directions in the study of English grammar.

Morphemes provide structural or syntactical meaning in sentences. When a sentence is analyzed in terms of morphemes, every element of meaning is pointed out. Most discussions of morphemes include three major categories: inflected morphemes, derivational morphemes, and base words.

1. The eight inflected morphemes in English are:

plural	participles
possessive	ing
present tense	comparative
past tense	superlative

Nouns can be made plural (man—men) and possessive (man's—men's). Verbs show present and past (walk—walks—walked), and participle and ing (walked—walking) forms. Adjectives and adverbs of manner have comparative and superlative (tall—taller—tallest; slow—slower—slowest) forms.

2. Derivational morphemes are added to base words in the form of prefixes and suffixes. Frequently, although not always, a derivational morpheme changes a word from one class to another. For example, the suffix *ly* added to the noun *friend* creates the adjective *friendly*. However, *un* added to the adjective *friendly* changes the

meaning, but *unfriendly* is still an adjective. A single suffix such as *er* may be more than one morpheme. In *sing* + *er* the *er* means one who does, a derivational morpheme, whereas the *er* in *light* + *er* is the comparative inflectional morpheme.

3. Base words, the largest set of morphemes, are single units of meaning, like *morning, doctor, Omaha,* or *animal.* A word like *runners* contains three morphemes, *run* + *er* (one who does) + *s* (plural). The added *n* is simply a spelling convention and does not affect the number of meaningful units in any way.

Inflected word classes—nouns, verbs, adjectives, and adverbs of manner—are sometimes called open classes because new words are being added to these constantly.

Function words are closed classes. These include the pronouns, conjunctions, prepositions, determiners, intensifiers, modals, interjections, and adverbs of time, place, and frequency.

1. Pronouns include both personal and indefinite pronouns.
    a. The personal pronouns are *I, you, he, she, it, we,* and *they.* These, of course, have subject, object, and possessive forms.
    b. The indefinite pronouns are words such as *everything, anybody, someone,* and *no one* (see page 142).
2. Coordinating conjunctions can be remembered by thinking of the acronym FANBOYS—*for, and, nor, but, or, yet,* and *so.*
3. Prepositions are words such as *in, on, before, after,* and *under.* There is an important difference between a preposition and the same word used as a verb + particle, as for example, in "He ran *up the hill.*" and "He *ran up* the bill." These sentences look alike on the surface, but are structurally very different.
4. Determiners include:
    a. Pre-articles such as *many of, several of, one of.*
    b. Articles—*the, a, some, null.*
    c. Demonstratives—*this, that, these, those, a certain,* and *some* with secondary stress, e.g., "*Some boy* is forgetting his manners!"
    d. Possessives such as *my, his, ours, theirs, John's.*
    e. Numbers, both cardinal (*one, two, three*) and ordinal (*first, second, third*).
5. Intensifiers are words like *very, quite,* and *rather.*
6. Modals are closed word classes. In the present tense they are, *can, shall, will, may,* and *must;* in the past tense they are, *could, should, would,* and *might. Dare* and *need* are considered to be semimodals by some grammarians, because modals do not have

an *s* form and are not followed by the word *to*. Certain forms like *ought to, have to, be to,* and *be going to* do not behave like modals, although they sometimes have similar semantic meaning, e.g., *ought to* means *should; have to* means *must*.

7. Interjections are words like *"Oh!"* or expressions like *"Good grief!"* They are syntactically not part of sentences and are not inflected, and they do change frequently. For example, *"Od's bodkins!"* was an interjection during Shakespeare's time, but it is no longer used.

8. Adverbs of time are words like *now* and *then*. *Here* and *there* are adverbs of place, and *often* and *rarely* are adverbs of frequency. They are all closed word classes.

Phrases are frequently groups of two or more words that can function as a grammatical structure, e.g., *of mine, gave money*. Noun phrases and verb phrases are defined on pages 142 and 144. Prepositional phrases, frequently used in English, are simply prepositions plus noun phrases.

Clauses are constructions that contain a subject and a predicate. The predicate must contain a tense morpheme, present or past. Relative clauses are sentences with the word *who, that, which,* or *whom* occurring in place of a noun or with the word *whose* taking the place of the determiner. Subordinate clauses function as nouns, adjectives, and adverbs and can occur at the beginning, in the middle, or at the end of a sentence as sentence modifiers.

The Basic or Kernel Sentence

According to transformational grammarians, the system of English involves a finite number of kernel sentences and a finite number of possible transformations through which an infinite number of utterances can be generated.

As previously stated, in attempts to teach children how English operates, teachers have been hampered by the lack of a specific information that made possible a description of the relationships inherent in the system. It is now possible to describe both the phonological and syntactical elements of the language. For example, a basic or kernel sentence can be differentiated from a sentence which includes elements from two or more basic sentences, or one which is transformed in terms of word order for new meaning, such as a simple yes/no question transformation (e.g., "John may come," becomes "May John come?").

The elements of English sentences are expressed as rules in generative-transform grammar. It is important to remember that these rules are descriptive, not prescriptive. The first rule that is introduced to young native speakers of English is the rule expressed in the symbols S → NP + VP. In this rule S stands for kernel sentence and the arrow means *consists of*. The symbol NP stands for four possible structures in English. These include proper noun, personal pronoun, indefinite pronoun and determiner plus noun. The rule looks like this:

$$\text{NP} \rightarrow \text{proper noun}$$
$$\text{personal pronoun}$$
$$\text{indefinite pronoun}$$
$$\text{determiner} + \text{noun}$$

An explanation of this rule follows:

Proper noun → words like John
The United States
Santa Barbara

Personal pronouns → I   you   he   she   it
it   we   they

Indefinite pronouns → somebody   something   someone
anybody   anything   anyone
everybody   everything   everyone
nobody   nothing   no one

Det + noun → determiner + common noun

Det → (prearticle) + article + (demonstration) + (number)

The determiner must have an article and may or may not have the other parts, so article will be the only structure fully discussed here:

Art → definite or nondefinite
Def → (definite) the
Nondef → (nondefinite)

a   an   (a boy, an orange)
some   (plural of a, an, some boys, some oranges)
null ϕ (not used, as in *birds fly*)

Some is used as an unstressed plural of *a* in the Roberts English Series. There is some question about the difference between this usage and a deletion from the prearticle *some of* plus the definite article, which would also result in *some boys*. This is an area that continues to need explication.

Noun → count nouns
      noncount nouns

Count nouns → anything that can be counted or will take the plural form, words like *chair, dog, book*.

Noncount noun → mass → words like *sand, oil, information* . . .
      quality → words like *sarcasm, laziness, courage* . . .

The three dots used in the definitions of proper noun and common mean that there are many other words in these categories. The categories do not include functions or become involved in semantic meaning. The rules demonstrate structure only. Note that there are seven personal pronouns in English. The object forms of these pronouns represent phonological and functional changes.

There are twelve indefinite pronouns in English, and they are all previously listed. Semantic meaning should not be considered when the various pronouns are presented, since these are structural descriptions only. For example, *it* in "It's raining" is extremely indefinite, whereas "Everyone take out his book" is an instruction to a definite number of people. Because indefinite pronouns are always syntactically singular, although frequently semantically plural, confusion results in the subject-verb agreement. For example "Everyone are here" would not be used by a native speaker, but "Everyone take out their books" is frequently heard in classrooms as a direction given by teachers considered to be educated speakers of English.

Components of the Kernel Sentence

This brief description of the noun phrase, and the verb phrase which follows, can be supplemented by using any of the references listed at the end of this chapter.

$$\text{VP} \rightarrow \text{Aux} + \begin{cases} \text{Be} + \begin{cases} \text{NP} \\ \text{Adjective} \\ \text{Adverb} \end{cases} \\ \text{Verbal} \end{cases}$$

VP is the symbol for verb phrase, and every verb phrase has an auxiliary which is symbolized in this rule by Aux.

Aux → tense + (modal) + (have + part) + (be+ing)

Every auxiliary must show tense. It may have the elements shown in parentheses, but tense must be present.

Tense → present, past

As previously stated, there are only two tenses in the English language. Tense is a technical term which stands for the forms of verbs, and in English there are two, the simple present *walk* and third person singular present *walks,* and the past tense *walked.* Of course there are many times in English, including future time, but these are complex and expressed by the use of many words, for example, "Tomorrow, I will have worked here two months."

The next item in Aux is modal.

Modal → can   shall   will   may   must   (present tense)
          could   should   would   might   (past tense)

The words *dare* and *need* are sometimes used as modals in such sentences as "He need only wait" and "She dare not think about it." *Ought* is sometimes considered a modal, but in its use with *to* it cannot be transformed into a yes/no question in the way other modals can. For example, "He should go" becomes "Should he go?" but "He ought to go" cannot become "Ought to he go?" Because *ought to, have to,* and *be going to* are often used as part of the auxiliary, they are part of a special expanded rule.

Have + part → have + participle. If this structure is used in the auxiliary it must follow the modal, if there is one, and tense. *Have + part* is used with the participle form of the verb or *be* (e.g., "He may have gone.").

Be + ing → be + ing. The morpheme *ing* is added to a verb or *be* to pinpoint an action in the present moment, or to express an action continuing through the present moment, beginning before it, and continuing after it.

The items in the auxiliary must be introduced into the morpheme string in the order in which they have been presented.

The next item in the rule is *be. Be* does not behave like a verbal. It has eight forms instead of five, and it must be followed by a noun phrase, an adjective, or an adverbial of place in a kernel sentence. The following are examples:

> John is a boy scout.   (be + NP)
> John is happy.   (be + Adj)
> John is in his room.   (be + Adv-p)

The verbal includes several subcategories of verbs and is written like this:

$$
\text{verbal} \to
\begin{array}{l}
\text{Vi} \\
\text{Vt + NP} \\
\text{Vs + Adj} \\
\text{Vb + NP} \\
\text{Adj} \\
\text{V mid + NP}
\end{array}
$$

Vi → intransitive verb. The intransitive verb can stand alone or it can be followed by an adverbial of manner. An example of Vi is "John laughed," or "John laughed loudly."

Vt + NP → transitive verb + noun phrase. A transitive verb takes an object and in this pattern the NP is the object. An example of this pattern is "John threw the ball."

Vs + Adj → verb of the *seem* variety (words such as *look, appear, smell, feel*). The Vs is always followed by an adjective. An example of this pattern is "John seemed tired."

Vb + NP and Vb +Adj → verb of the *become* variety (including *remain*) plus a noun or adjective. For this pattern either an NP or Adj can be used without changing the category of the verb, for example, "John became a captain." and "John became impatient."

V-mid → middle verb. This verb, like a transitive verb, is followed by a NP. However, the NP used with V-mid is not an object, so in this respect it is like an intransitive verb which is also not followed by an object. V-mid cannot be made passive, nor can it be followed by an adverbial of manner. Examples of V-mid are *have, cost, weigh, total,* and *amount to.* "It costs a dollar." and "He has a car." are examples of sentences using mid-verbs.

In the previous discussion of S → NP + VP, the word *phrase* can be used to mean only one word, as in "John left," or a number of words, as in "The boy ate the candy." In the first sentence *John* is the NP and *left* is the VP. *John* is a proper noun and *left* is an intransitive verb, but the symbols NP and VP stand for single words.

In the second sentence *the boy* is the NP and *ate the candy* is the VP. Now NP and VP stand for groups of words.

A frequently confusing fact of transformational grammar involves the placement of suffixes in the auxiliary. Whenever an auxiliary appears in the morpheme string of a basic sentence, an affix transformation must occur before the final morpheme string becomes a kernel sentence. For example, in the sentence "John has been going to school," the following morphemes are present in the final morpheme string:

$$John + present + have + part + be + ing + go + to + school$$

To turn this K terminal string into the final morpheme string that generates the sentence, the tense and suffixes *part* and *ing* must move to the right. So we then have

$$John + have + present + be + part + go + ing + to + school$$

or "John has been going to school." This is called the affix transformation and is obligatory in the verb phrase. Even for a sentence such as "Mary sings," the morpheme string is *Mary + present + sing.* Because the present form *s* does not prefix the verb *sing*, an affix transformation must occur before the final sentence results.

This much-too-brief discussion does not take into account any of the phonological rules or transformational rules of the language, and serves only to call attention to some of the basic concepts of transformational grammar. The references at the end of the chapter can lead into a study of the syntactical areas of English, and every elementary schoolteacher will find it helpful to become familiar with the content of a transformational approach to the study of English grammar.

Teaching Standard English

Children who come to school using a dialect other than the accepted dialect of the community should, as their primary purpose in language study, acquire the effective use of the standard or accepted English in school. Only when children use the accepted dialect with facility are they ready to study the nature of their language. Some instruction concerning the nature of the language will undoubtedly help children learn a second dialect whenever necessary.

For instance, constrastive analysis of phonemic and morphological structures of the two dialects, the child's own language together with the standard or accepted language as taught in school, points up strategic differences, and directs the attention of the student to the new skills needed and the items that need practice. For example, the child who says "I brung you some flowers" needs a great deal of practice with *brought* before he can use this verb in patterns with facility and lack of self-consciousness. The opportunity for such practice can be provided in oral exercises such as the following substitution drill:

Stimulus: I brought my mother some flowers.
Response: I brought my mother some flowers.

Stimulus: father—nails
Response: I brought my father some nails.

Stimulus: teacher—books
Response: I brought my teacher some books.

Stimulus: dog—meat
Response: I brought my dog some meat.

Stimulus: friends—candy
Response: I brought my friends some candy.

It is important to remember that practice should be provided on patterns that children actually use and have need for.

Up to the present time, most of the burden of learning to read and to write the language has been put on the child. He has had to discover the rules for spelling words. From observation of many sentences, he has been expected to come to unconscious conclusions about what makes some sentences well formed and others not. In the early grades, sentence patterns in readers conform neither to the patterns that are commonly used by children nor to those that are typical in the speech or writing of educated adults.[13] The system of language is undetailed, unexplained, and, for many children, unacquired as they receive bits of rules, hints, and corrections from their teachers.

---

[13] Thomas, op. cit., p. 210. Ruth G. Strickland, "Implications of Research in Linguistics for Elementary Teaching," *Elementary English*, vol. 40, no. 2 (February, 1963).

Establishing a Philosophy

The teacher of language needs first to establish a philosophy. If the teacher conceives the act of learning English as one in which the chief burden of deducing the system falls on the child, then he will proceed like a doctor, noting certain ailments in the class, looking through the textbook for appropriate remedies, and then applying them. His role will be to correct and repair. If, on the other hand, the teacher of language sees his task as one of teaching the system of the language, then his approach will of necessity be quite different. His approach will include helping the child to gain systematic and carefully organized understanding of the structure of his language as his needs and developmental levels dictate.

What known facts concerning language and children can serve to shape the philosophy of the teacher? First, according to Thomas, every normal child, even a child in kindergarten, produces hundreds of sentences every day. The vast majority of these sentences are perfectly formed; only a very small minority are so structurally misshapen as to be unintelligible.[14] Many of the sentences created by a child of six years are entirely original, the child has not heard them before. Therefore, the normal child of six years has a built-in device for producing sentences, a grammar.

Second, the process of how a child learns a language is still a mystery. Although the problem of language acquisition is a fascinating one for both psychologists and teachers, the most recent and exhaustive theory of the problem of how language is learned has been found to be highly questionable.[15]

If language is taught simply because it is the most human and most basic of all man's accomplishments and activities, then the system of language will be presented so that children can discover the nature of their language. If, in addition, through the study of language the child becomes increasingly aware of the great number and variety of resources possessed by every speaker of every language, his self-image and his appreciation of those around him should be enhanced. Although to this writer's knowledge evidence to establish a positive relationship between language instruction and improvement in usage has not yet been produced, it seems reason-

---

[14] Thomas, *Tranformational Grammar*, p. 206.
[15] Noam Chomsky, "Review of B. F. Skinner's Verbal Behavior," *Language*, vol. 35, no. 1 (January–March, 1959), pp. 26–58.

able to hypothesize that the proper study of language could increase the child's self-confidence in speaking, reading, writing, and listening. Thus, the following *principles of language development* seem to be acceptable generalizations for the teaching of syntax at the elementary school level:

1. The child should study language rather than grammar.
2. This study should involve discovery rather than memorization.
3. The end result should be self-discovery and increasing self-confidence.
4. The study of language should proceed through sequentially ordered instruction.

QUESTIONS FOR STUDY

1. What are some characteristics of generative-transform, also called transformational, grammar? How do these relate to other studies of the grammatical structure of English?
2. What does grammatical mean? In what ways are the following sentences ungrammatical?

   (a) He have always buy good suit.
   (b) We saw some mans today.
   (c) Stand not upon the order of your going.
   (d) He looked rather a fool.
   (e) Me and Jim got throwed off the horse.
   (f) Flying low, a herd of cow's was seen.
   (g) Anyone lived in a pretty how town, with up so floating many bells down.
3. What are the components of grammar?
4. What is syntax? How does it contribute to the understanding of grammar?
5. Why should elementary school children learn about their language?

SUGGESTIONS FOR FURTHER READING

Aurbach, Joseph, et al., *Transformational Grammar: A Guide for Teachers* (Washington, D.C.: English Language Service, 1968).

Christensen, Francis, *Notes Toward a New Rhetoric* (New York: Harper & Row, Publishers, 1967).

Harsh, Wayne, *Grammar Instruction Today* (Davis, Calif.: University of California Press, 1965).

Jacobs, Roderick A., and Rosenbaum, Peter S., *Grammar I* (Boston, Mass.: Ginn and Co., 1967).

Loban, Walter, *Problems in Oral Language* (Champaign, Ill.: National Council of Teachers of English, 1966).

Office of Education Study, "The Imitation, Comprehension, and Production of English Syntax—A Developmental Study of the Language Skills of Deprived and Non-Deprived Children" (unpublished progress report for the Office of Education, 1968).

Roberts, Paul, *The Roberts English Series: A Linguistics Program,* Teacher's Edition (Grades 3–9) (New York: Harcourt, Brace & World, Inc., 1966).

Roberts, Paul, *The Roberts English Series: A Linguistics Program* (Complete Course) (New York: Harcourt, Brace & World, Inc., 1967).

TEACHER'S AID

See the example of a bulletin board on page 151.

Relevant material is added to the bulletin board as the study of the sentence progresses. Make separate tagboard cards as needed, and place them on the bulletin board. The number of cards left on the bulletin board will depend on the concepts being taught and on the size of the printing needed for the cards to be seen. (Will the cards be read by the entire classroom or a small group?) For example the structures of a phrase should be kept together and separate from the functions, each clearly labeled. After the structures and functions of the noun phrase have been studied, they can be removed from the bulletin board and placed on a chart for later review. Now the bulletin board is ready for the structures and functions of the verb phrase. Because all of this is part of the study of the kernel sentence, further defined as subject and predicate, each of which is still further analyzed as noun phrase and verb phrase, these cards should remain constant throughout the study of the parts of a sentence. To call attention to the specific part being studied, yarn or a thin strip of red paper could be attached underneath the appropriate words.

Exercise 1

Mark the word classes by writing the appropriate symbol (see symbols and test frames next page) over each word in the following sentences:

1. His.naughty little dog escaped easily.
2. The swaying branches looked ghostly in the gloom.
3. An entertaining exhibit may come to this school.
4. In five channel crossings I felt sick twice.
5. Creeping ungrammaticalness may prove quite demoralizing for our society.

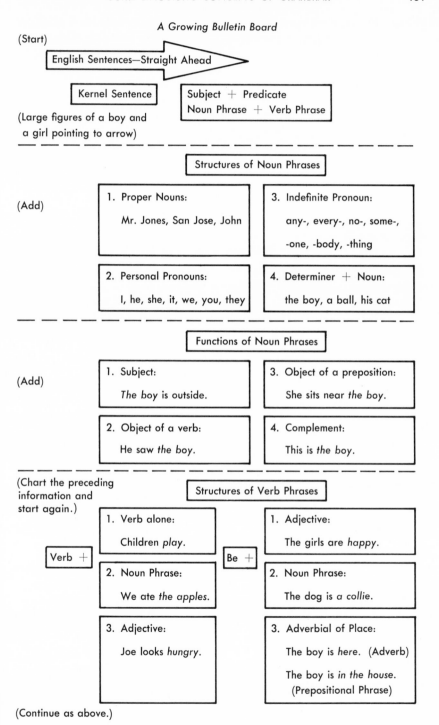

A Growing Bulletin Board

(Start)

English Sentences—Straight Ahead

Kernel Sentence   Subject + Predicate
                             Noun Phrase + Verb Phrase

(Large figures of a boy and
a girl pointing to arrow)

Structures of Noun Phrases

(Add)

1. Proper Nouns: 3. Indefinite Pronoun:

   Mr. Jones, San Jose, John   any-, every-, no-, some-,

                                 -one, -body, -thing

2. Personal Pronouns: 4. Determiner + Noun:

   I, he, she, it, we, you, they   the boy, a ball, his cat

Functions of Noun Phrases

(Add)

1. Subject: 3. Object of a preposition:

   The boy is outside.   She sits near *the boy*.

2. Object of a verb: 4. Complement:

   He saw *the boy*.   This is *the boy*.

(Chart the preceding
information and   **Structures of Verb Phrases**
start again.)

1. Verb alone: 1. Adjective:

   Children *play*.   The girls are *happy*.

Verb +   Be +

2. Noun Phrase: 2. Noun Phrase:

   We ate *the apples*.   The dog is *a collie*.

3. Adjective: 3. Adverbial of Place:

   Joe looks *hungry*.   The boy is *here*. (Adverb)

                                 The boy is *in the house*.
                                 (Prepositional Phrase)

(Continue as above.)

6. The weary old college professor in a new Cougar raced erratically across the parking lot into a ditch ordinarily used for rainwater.

Symbol

The following five exercises for the student teacher are designed to develop facility with sentence structure and can be adapted for class use.

D   Determiner (before nouns)   the, a, my, your, six, this.
N   Noun   hat, house, honesty, rice.
V   Verb (including past tense, present participle, and past participle) go, went, going, gone.
Adj   Adjective   white, good.
Adv   Adverb   quietly, here, often.
Int   Intensifier   very, rather.
Np   Pronoun in noun position   I, me, mine, she, hers.
P   Preposition (followed by nouns or pronouns)   in, of, over, through, when.
M   Modals   may, will, shall, must, can, ought.

Use test frames for:

Nouns:	He noticed two _____ s.
	His _____ was admirable.
Verbs:	Yesterday he _____ it.
	We ought to _____ (it) later.
Adjectives:	It seemed very _____.
	It was _____er than that.
	It was more _____ than that.
Adverbs:	He did it (very) _____.

Answers to Exercise 1

1.   D   Adj   Adj   N   V   Adv
2.   D   V   N   V   Adj   P   D   N
3.   D   Adj   N   M   V   P   D   N
4.   P   D   N   N   Np   V   Adj   Adv
5.   V   N   M   V   Int   Adj   P   D   N
6.   P   Adj   Adj   N   N   P   D   Adj   N   V   Adv
    P   D   V   N   P   D   N   Adv   V   P   N

Exercise 2

Change the following morpheme strings into sentences.

1. John + present + be + here
2. Ruth + past + smile
3. nobody + past + answer + the + phone
4. the + boy + plural + past + be + happy
5. the + box + present + weigh + a + ton
6. she + past + be + in + the + kitchen
7. they + present + be + neighbor + plural
8. everybody + past + work + hard
9. some + fox + plural + past + bark + on + the + hill
10. thief + plural + past + loot + the + store

Answers to Exercise 2

1. John is here.
2. Ruth smiled.
3. Nobody answered the phone.
4. The boys were happy.
5. The box weighs a ton.
6. She was in the kitchen.
7. They are neighbors.
8. Everybody worked hard.
9. Some foxes barked on the hill.
10. Thieves looted the store.

Exercise 3

Change the following sentences to morpheme strings.

1. June is here.
2. He is a soldier.
3. The animals seemed dangerous.
4. John had heard it.
5. David was watching them.
6. Gerald had eaten the fish.
7. They were shooting rabbits.
8. John had been watching them.
9. John might have been watching them.
10. Lightning may have struck the plane.

Answers to Exercise 3

1. June + present + be + here
2. he + present + be + a + soldier
3. the + animal + plural + past + seem + danger + ous
4. John + past + have + part + hear + it
5. David + past + be + ing + watch + them
6. Gerald + past + have + part + eat + the + fish
7. they + past + be + ing + shoot + rabbit + plural
8. John + past + have + part + be + ing + watch + them
9. John + past + may + have + part + be + ing + watch + them
10. lightning + present + may + have + part + strike + the + plane

Exercise 4

A. Four kinds of noun phrases are   1. proper nouns
   2. personal pronouns
   3. indefinite pronouns
   4. determiners + nouns

Circle the noun phrases in each sentence. Underneath each one, put a number to show what kind of noun phrase it is:

(1) A bell rang out clearly.   (2) Somebody should meet them.

(3) Carol likes apples.   (4) He put it in the box.

B. Copy the articles in these sentences in the blanks at the right, using φ if the article is null. Then write def or nondef to show whether the article is definite or nondefinite.

(5) Books are expensive.   _____   _____
(6) Jim cut the grass.   _____   _____
(7) We admire courage.   _____   _____
(8) Some students wandered by.   _____   _____
(9) They were walking through a wood.   _____   _____
(10) He did it with mirrors.   _____   _____

C. A noun phrase can function as   1. subject
   2. complement
   3. object of a verb
   4. object of a preposition

Circle the noun phrases, and under each one write one of the four numbers to its function.

(11) Nobody recognized him.
(12) The chipmunk stayed inside the box.
(13) Carol will be chairman.
(14) We were sorry for the mistake.
(15) Kilroy was here recently.

Answers to Exercise 4

(1) A bell
     4

(2) Somebody   them
         3   2

(3) Carol   apples
       1   4

(4) He   it   the box
     2   2   4

(5) φ   nondef

(6) the   def

(7) φ   nondef

(8) some   nondef

(9) a   nondef

(10) φ   nondef

(11) Nobody   him
       1   3

(12) The chipmunk   the box
         1   4

(13) Carol   chairman
       1   2

(14) We   the mistake
     1   4

(15) Kilroy
       1

Exercise 5

Identify the verbals in the following structures as:

(1) Vi,   (2) Vt + NP,   (3) Vs + Adj,
(4) Vb + NP or Adj,   or   (5) V-mid + NP.

_____ 1. John + Aux + help the butcher
_____ 2. the wheat + Aux + weigh a ton
_____ 3. Julia + Aux + look sick
_____ 4. he + Aux + become a minister
_____ 5. she + Aux + sing beautifully
_____ 6. his father + Aux + have a car
_____ 7. George + Aux + collect stamps zealously
_____ 8. they + Aux + appear calm
_____ 9. Mr. Montrose + Aux + repair the motor
_____ 10. it + Aux + cost a fortune
_____ 11. they + Aux + leave
_____ 12. Sylvia + Aux + remain a friend
_____ 13. the story + Aux + ring true
_____ 14. the parents + Aux + wait helplessly
_____ 15. she + Aux + seem cross
_____ 16. we + Aux + grow impatient
_____ 17. you + Aux + grow vegetables
_____ 18. the baby + Aux + grow rapidly
_____ 19. the story + Aux + sound plausible
_____ 20. she + Aux + scream in a terrified way
_____ 21. the bill + Aux + amounted to three dollars
_____ 22. the soup + Aux + smell heavenly

Answers to Exercise 5

1. 2	7. 2	13. 3	19. 3
2. 5	8. 3	14. 1	20. 1
3. 3	9. 2	15. 3	21. 5
4. 4	10. 5	16. 3	22. 3
5. 1	11. 1	17. 2	
6. 5	12. 4	18. 1	

10

Teaching Vocabulary and Etymology

The purpose of teaching vocabulary is to help the child bring meaning to and take meaning from word signs, signals, and symbols. To accomplish this goal the child must be taught many things about words and their ways as well as the words themselves. Etymology, the origin and development of words, will acquaint the child with the time dimension of language and the idea that words change their meanings and thus have histories.

Children's Vocabularies

Many studies are available which discuss the changes of the sizes of vocabularies of children entering the first grade over the years. Lorge and Chall [1] examined the reports of various investigators since the late 1800s and challenged the limitations of frequency sampling and dictionary sampling which were used. They concluded that because of the methodological errors made in the research, the vocabularies of first grade children are closer to the older estimates which reported vocabularies in the thousands than to the newer estimates which extend the estimates to the tens of thousands.

In contrast to the conclusions of Lorge and Chall, Wilbur S. Ames [2] tested 272 first grade children in ten communities in Maine

[1] Irving Lorge and Jeannie Chall, "Estimating the Size of Vocabularies of Children and Adults: An Analysis of Methodological Issues," *The Journal of Experimental Education,* vol. 32, no. 2 (Winter, 1963), pp. 147–157.

[2] Wilbur S. Ames, "The Understanding Vocabulary of First-Grade Pupils," *Elementary English,* vol. 41, no. 1 (January, 1964), pp. 64–68.

and estimated the mean understanding vocabulary at 12,456 words with a standard deviation of 2,952 words. The reliability coefficient of the test was .79, and no significant difference between the understanding vocabulary of boys and girls was found in the study.

Regardless of the estimates of the size of children's vocabularies when they enter school, the teacher is responsible for teaching children to recognize and identify words, to pronounce words, to analyze and categorize words, to read words, and finally to put words together into phrases, sentences, and paragraphs in written language. If the children come to school with well-developed vocabularies and the ability to express themselves effectively in oral communication, the teacher's task will be one of building on the foundation. If the children come from deprived areas, the teacher may well have to build a foundation upon which such children can stand to reach for success in school activities.

Vocabulary Development for the Underprivileged Child

The children of the inner city and the children of migrants—usually black, Puerto Rican, Mexican, and white children from the South—are often considered to be underprivileged when it comes to language experience.

Benjamin Bloom [3] suggests that sharp changes in background experiences for these children can result in improved educational development, and that this is indeed the business of the school.

> The absolute scale of vocabulary development and the longitudinal studies of educational achievement indicate that approximately 50% of general achievement at grade 12 (age 18) has been reached by the end of grade 3 (age 9). This suggests the great importance of the first few years of school as well as the preschool period in the developing of learning patterns and general achievement. These are the years in which general learning patterns develop most rapidly, and failure to develop appropriate achievement and learning in these years is likely to lead to continued failure or near failure throughout the remainder of the individual's school career.

There is general agreement that models of excellence in use of vocabulary or sentence structure are not readily available to underprivileged children. Also, their auditory span is less than that of middle class children, and they seem unable to sustain attention.

[3] Benjamin Bloom, *Stability and Change in Human Characteristics* (New York: John Wiley & Sons, Inc., 1964).

Such children use sentences which are short, categorical, and often incomplete, and they use a small number of words to express themselves.

The teacher, recognizing the meager vocabulary and inadequate syntax of underprivileged children, will want to provide experiences that will help them learn to name things and actions within their perceptual range. Activities such as visiting a farm, meeting the farmer and his family, exploring some of the farm buildings, learning to operate some of the equipment, riding on a tractor, looking at farm machinery, seeing real animals, and playing in the straw can give children new vocabulary as well as new ideas and attitudes that they will want to share with each other.

The deprived child often lacks the necessary perceptual experiences needed for school success. He has had little or no opportunity to see, hear, or touch the physical objects of the middle class world. He also lacks the ability to order experiences, or to put new and old ideas into varying patterns. His ability to see differences in real things may not carry over to an ability to discriminate in their representations. This, of course, is true for other children and adults as well. Most people are unable to read blueprints or wiring diagrams with accuracy unless they have been taught.

Developing Vocabulary Through Experience

The teacher thus recognizes that the major conditioning factor in vocabulary development at the concrete level is not dullness or brightness, but experience. This means that early school experiences will provide children opportunities to work with a number of materials such as wood, paper, and cloth, to paint, to cut with scissors, to eat varied foods and prepare some foods at school, to make visits, to go on study trips, and to discuss all of these activities. Children learn by active contact with things that make a difference to them. The teacher aids the child to self-discovery by providing a variety of experiences, listening to the child, helping the child to see relationships, and moving the child to next steps as growth and development indicate. Because the early vocabulary of children emphasizes nouns, rich concrete experiences which involve the child and require him to name and discuss specific things are essential to vocabulary growth. Relational and qualifying terms and complex sentences will come later.

The language that underprivileged children possess when they come to school is frequently concrete and expressive, but very different from that of the middle class children. New concrete experiences are essential to provide the foundational vocabulary for reading and school success. If underprivileged children are forced to lag along in a school program designed for middle class children, differences grow greater as the child progresses in school, and the vocabulary of the underprivileged child becomes increasingly inadequate to face learning situations. In the fourth and fifth grades the words learned by listening and speaking decrease in proportion to words learned by reading. (See Chapters 7 and 12.) At this level a number of critical words such as the conjunctions *consequently, hence,* and *therefore,* introduce a high level of abstraction that seriously handicaps the underprivileged child.

Although the disadvantaged child needs a different language program from the middle class child, rather than more of the same program, the middle class child also needs wide experience, if his vocabulary is to be developed for discriminative usage. Both groups of children need constant encouragement.

Developing Vocabulary Through Reading

Children also learn many new words in reading. Words introduced to children through the use of phonetic and structural analysis help them to attack new words in reading. As words are read many times, the reader becomes familiar with them and utilizes them in his speech. Seeing words in context helps the child to determine meaning. For example, a word such as *shook* takes on meaning in context: "He shook his hands, a quick shake, fingers down, like the fingers of a pianist above the keys" (Sinclair Lewis); "He shook with fright at the sound of the groan"; and "She shook the rug, watching the dust billow up, continuing to flail the air until the lint was gone."

Developing Vocabulary Through Etymology

In addition to experience and reading, etymology provides a vehicle for the vocabulary development of children whose language facility is adequately developed. The phenomenon of semantic shift will be of interest to many children. Semantic shift is the change in meaning which frequently occurs in the constant change of living languages. For example, *advertise* once meant to warn, and a *guest* was a stranger or an enemy. *Nice* was once a word used to describe someone who was stupid or foolish. To create an interest in words, the entire class might be encouraged to look up certain common words to discover their former meanings, and then children who show keen interest could be given special assignments to find both former meanings and related words. Such words as *school, slim, tragedy, branch, cloud, puny, glide,* and *worry* have very unusual former meanings.

Specific assignments which require the pupils to determine inductively how semantic shifts fall into patterns and how certain words have changed status over a period of time intrigue some children. For example, words like *scene, holiday,* and *affiliate* have taken on general meanings, whereas *garage, starve,* and *pill* have become specialized. The original meaning of *scene* was tent, *holiday* was one holy day, and *affiliate* meant adopt a son. The present meanings of these words are much more general. *Garage,* on the other hand, was formerly a place for protecting anything, *starve* meant to die of any cause, and *pill* was used to denote any ball.

Children may also be encouraged to discover words which have been elevated in terms of meaning over a period of years and for words whose meanings have been degraded. Historically, *shrewd* was a word meaning cursed and *chiffon* was a rag, whereas *sinister* meant simply left-handed, and *crafty* meant skillful. Words such as *steward,* which formerly meant sty-keeper or custodian of the pigs, have been elevated as well as generalized in meaning. The specialized study of various categories of words may be of interest to certain pupils and can be encouraged as enrichment exercises for individuals or groups.

Some children might be interested in looking up the origins of words, and discovering cognates such as English *book* and German *Buch.* Others might be interested in comparing a word in a variety of languages to become aware of signals that point up word relationships. For example:

English	*German*	*French*	*Italian*
horse	Pferd	cheval	cavallo
Spanish	*Rumanian*	*Greek*	*Tarascan*
caballo	cal	aloyo	jatapakua

Investigating the role of euphemisms in language helps children to discover one recognizable cause of semantic shift. Human motives to make unpleasant words more acceptable engender expressions such as *passed on* for *died, rotisserie* for *spit,* and *custodian* for *janitor.* Children can discover the use made of such euphemisms in advertising, and they can also be introduced to euphemisms in interjections, the utterances that make for colorful conversation and enlivened writing.

Using the Dictionary

Any good dictionary such as *Webster's New World Dictionary of the American Language* gives the etymology of words. Many native English speakers would be surprised to realize that only fifteen percent of the words in the dictionary are derived from Anglo Saxon or are truly native words. The origin of thirty-five percent of the words is Latin, and French has contributed approximately fifteen percent of the words. The remaining thirty-five percent of the words in the dictionary are borrowings from a variety of other languages, including Greek. These figures could lead one to believe that the use of borrowings in English is preponderant, yet in actual English prose, the usage of native words often exceeds seventy-five percent.

Borrowed Words in English

A recommended exercise to lead children to an awareness of the use of borrowings and English words in the language follows:

1 Have the students copy from twenty-five to 100 words of nonfiction from any book or journal, depending on the age and interest of the children.

2. Leave two spaces for each word.

3. Check the dictionary etymology of each word, writing the symbols to show the origin of each. Do not use the M.E. (Middle English) designation because it does not determine the origin of the word. When both Latin and Old French are given, write both. Because the goal of this exercise is to indicate the proportion of native words and borrowings used in the language, the choice between Latin and Old French is irrelevant.

TEACHING VOCABULARY AND ETYMOLOGY

4. When the analysis is complete, tally the results. If 100 words are used, the numbers of words of each origin in the passage is also the percentage.

Children can also be encouraged to make lists of recent borrowings from proper names, trade names, and other languages. Words such as *diesel* and *watt* have been borrowed from proper names; *kleenex* and *eversharp* are examples of borrowings from trade names, and *bouffant* and *chemise* are borrowings from another language. To encourage interest in this area, children can be assigned a few specific words to look up, and those who wish to do so may extend the list.

Derived Words

Many word changes result from structural alterations. With a few examples and a little support, some older children may wish to research words such as *math, auto, phone,* and *hi-fi,* which are shortened words, or words which combine two or more elements, such as windshield, sportsman, and flagpole.

Portmanteau words, which are shortened and combined words such as motel (motor + hotel), telecast (television + broadcast), and smog (smoke + fog) also fit into the category of structurally altered words, as do acronyms and words that feature reduplication and metathesis. **Acronyms** are used increasingly in today's complex world and may have special appeal for some children. Such familiar ones as RADAR, CARE, UNESCO, and NATO can be presented to all children for investigation, and those who show interest can be encouraged to extend the list. In the same manner, frequently used examples of reduplication words can be presented to arouse interest in further study. Such words as *mama, murmur,* and *alfalfa* fit into this category.

Metathesis, the transposition of the letters of a word or syllable over a period of time, provides an unusual source for investigation. The word *bird* was *bridd* in Anglo Saxon or Old English, while the word *through* was *thurgh* in Middle English. These words were pronounced differently as well as spelled in a different manner. When children and teachers become aware of these historical alterations of words, unusual spellings and pronunciations will become items of interest rather than derision.

New Words

Thousands of new words are added to the language each year. Most of these words are nouns introduced to meet the technological advances of the space age, such as *astronaut* and *transistor*, but many are also verbs, such as *phase out*. Adjectives and adverbs of manner are coined as they are needed to keep pace with the new concepts. When children begin to investigate new words they will become involved at once with slang. They should be encouraged to look up words like *dud, swell*, and *shyster* in various dictionaries so that they can discover that different definitions are found for such words. The result of such an exercise may be the compiling of a list of doubtful words, and certainly by using several dictionaries they will discover that lexicography is not yet an exact science and that dictionaries do indeed differ. This kind of investigation will help children to question such concepts as "correct" when used in terms of language usage.

The Study of Lexicography

After children have been exposed to issues such as status labels and differences in dictionaries, some may become interested in how dictionaries are made. The history of lexicography can help the older child understand not only what a dictionary is, but what people think it should be. Should dictionaries be descriptive and record the languague as it is used in speech and writing by educated people? Or should the dictionary be prescriptive, present the language as it should be used? Most recent dictionaries seem to be compromises, recording as faithfully as possible the language being used, but also inserting editorial advice regarding the usage of certain items.

Because language is changing with great rapidity in the space age, and because there is a diversity of educated dialects in America, American lexicographers are hesitant to give advice about usage. The editors of *Webster's Third New International Dictionary* have been criticized for their attempts to record contemporary American language with a minimum of prescription. According to critics, a dictionary is traditionally an authority on correctness, and the language will be corrupted rather than stabilized when words are included just because they are used widely. According to such critics, the word *finalize* is suspect even if it is used by the President of the United States!

Children should be encouraged to discover for themselves how dictionaries are developed and how attitudes vary. Certain children might be assigned to read appropriate selections from the introductory materials of the dictionaries to see what the lexicographers consider to be the rule of the dictionary, how they dealt with American and English dialects, and other relevant data concerning the language.

Older children will find their understanding of language greatly enhanced as they learn how it has been recorded in and affected by dictionaries. Samuel Johnson's Preface to his *Dictionary of the English Language*,[4] written in 1755, discusses problems of lexicography that still exist today. Johnson, who spent seven years compiling a dictionary for the purpose of "fixing and purifying the language," realized that he could not completely achieve such a goal even at that time. He suggested that the increase of knowledge resulting in new words, and the variables involved in speaking a living language as words shift their relationships, made such stabilization impossible.

Students through the study of etymology and lexicography can increase their interest in words and the ways in which words are used, and they can become increasingly aware of the humanity found in dictionaries. As children become more aware of the wealth of information about common as well as uncommon words found in dictionaries, and of the faults as well as the strengths of dictionaries, they will doubtless be more motivated to use dictionaries to develop their vocabularies and increase their understanding of etymology rather than simply as a reference for meaning and spelling.

Affixes in English

Words created by affixes and combinations of word elements are responsible for the large vocabulary of English. After children have investigated the words *affix, prefix,* and *suffix* they can be led to see relationships between the three and to study the many words which are formed by attaching affixes to base words.

Because the English vocabulary relies heavily upon derivative

---

[4] Leonard F. Dean and Kenneth G. Wilson, *Essays on Language and Usage* (London: Oxford University Press, 1959).

words for the expression of ideas, special exercises designed to help children discover words that begin with such prefixes as *un, ex,* and *sub,* and end with the suffixes *able, like,* and *ment* can extend vocabularies with ease and speed. Such exercises not only set the concepts of prefixes and suffixes, but also help children to become aware of the great number of words in English which are formed in this manner, for example:

1. Have the children list all the words they know using a specific suffix such as *able.* Keep a list and add to it as additional words are discovered in listening or reading, e.g., *suitable, usable, salable, singable,* etc.

2. Repeat the same exercise using prefixes. Use the dictionary to help.

3. Give the children a specific set of words such as *air, road, port, bed,* and *rail,* instructing them to combine these words in as many ways as possible and, then, to combine them with other words to create new words, e.g., *airport, airplane, railroad, roadbed,* etc.

4. Recommend to some children that they study word combinations of long ago, recently combined words, and unusual combinations.

Elementary schoolchildren can enlarge their vocabularies and their understanding of words as they study English spelling, English idioms, English structure, and English syntax.

Selecting and Using Words

It is possible that abstract language is valued too highly in the American culture and that as a result simple, expressive, meaningful language that includes the powerful, dynamic nature of experience is frequently lacking. Sophistication and pride in knowledge have sometimes colored gray the former stark simple beauty of black and white, as abstractions have replaced honest thought and true meaning. Most children have a way of expressing the truth simply and forcefully. Such expression should be encouraged as the ability to use greater numbers and varieties of words increases.

As children develop more effective and precise vocabularies, they should also be taught their responsibilities to use words to express truth rather than to deceive or manipulate. This concept will not result if children are constantly encouraged to improve their vocabularies when they have nothing to say. It does seem that sometimes people expend effort on crossword puzzles and other techniques for improving vocabularies, only to cloud issues and confuse thought with verbiage!

In summary, the emphasis on vocabulary building will be in direct relationship to the child's need for words to complete his perceptions of himself, his experience, and his environment. When the experience is direct and tangible, the child will need descriptive, expressive, and direct language. As experiences become increasingly abstract and symbolic, the child needs symbols and signs to express his indirect knowledge of the world. He needs to know the difference between the two kinds of experiences as well as the differences in language usage. Teachers, then, will not use gimmicks for vocabulary development, but a great variety of experiences for growth in ideas and expressions.

QUESTIONS FOR STUDY

1. To what branch of the Indo-European family of languages do Icelandic, Swedish, Danish, Norwegian, German, Dutch, Flemish and English belong?
2. From what languages did the following English words come?

choir	umbrella	tea
ugly	slogan	street
moose	kindergarten	bungalow

3. Where do the affixes *ex, re, able,* and *ment* come from?
4. What language clues tell us that Indo-Europeans lived in a temperate climate?
5. Name the English-speaking countries in the world today.
6. In what way is the concept of standard English different in America from what it is in England?

SUGGESTIONS FOR FURTHER READING

Carroll, John, "Words, Meanings and Concepts," *Harvard Educational Review,* vol. 34, no. 2 (Spring, 1964), pp. 178–201.

Deutsch, Martin, "Minority Groups and Class Status as Related to Social and Personality Factors in Scholastic Achievement," *Society of Applied Anthropology,* Monograph #2 (Ithaca, N.Y.: Cornell University Press, 1960).

Fries, Charles C., *Linguistics and Reading* (New York: Holt, Rinehart & Winston, Inc., 1963).

Gleason, H. A., *An Introduction to Descriptive Linguistics,* rev. ed. (New York: Holt, Rinehart & Winston, Inc., 1961).

Lefevre, Carl A., *Linguistics and the Teaching of Reading* (New York: McGraw-Hill Book Co., 1964).

Roberts, Paul, *The Roberts English Series, A Linguistics Program*, Complete Course (New York: Harcourt, Brace & World, Inc., 1967).

TEACHER'S AID

1. Read the selection "How Words Are Made," from *Words and Their Ways in English Speech*, by James Bradstreet Greenough and George Lyman Kittredge (Boston: Beacon Press, 1965) to find out some ways in which English adds and changes meaning.

2. H. L. Mencken describes the chief ways in which American places have been named in his book *The American Language*, 3d ed. (New York: A. A. Knopf, 1923). He says that there are eight classes of American place-names:

   (a) Personal names, chiefly the surnames of pioneers or of national heroes, e.g., Washington.

   (b) Names transferred from other older places in the eastern States or in Europe, e.g., Syracuse.

   (c) Indian names, e.g., Manhattan.

   (d) Dutch, Spanish, French, German, and Scandinavian names, many names for each language.

   (e) Biblical and mythological names, e.g., Beulah.

   (f) Names descriptive of localities, e.g., Council Bluffs.

   (g) Purely fanciful names, e.g., Tombstone, Arizona, and Social Circle, Georgia.

   Tell which class is represented in each of the following names: Pittsburgh, New York, Marysville, Philadelphia, Tacoma, Brooklyn, Alhambra, Jordan, Jones Gulch, and Sleepy Eye, Minnesota.

3. In the novel *Huckleberry Finn*, Mark Twain develops one feature of Huck's dialect that omits *ly* from adverbs of manner. Make a list of ten phrases, each containing an adverb of manner that would have *ly* in standard English. Write the standard English next to the word. How were the adverbs of manner formed in standard English?

11

Teaching the Writing System of English

The Developmental Nature of Language

The four facets of language, listening, speaking, reading, and writing, are developmental in nature. In early infancy children listen and respond to sound. As the wailing child hears his mother's footsteps approaching, he often stops crying to be sure that the comfort he seeks is indeed near. Mother's soothing voice reassures, and as the child grows he becomes increasingly aware of the sounds around him and their meaning. The child begins to speak some time after he has been able to hear words and attach meaning to their utterance. Listening and speaking skills continue to develop until the child reaches school age.

Most children come to school today with more varied and extensive backgrounds than ever before. Because of the great number and variety of children's books available, the presence of television in homes, and the increasing opportunity for varied experiences for children, many children have extensive vocabularies and are able to use hundreds of sentences accurately. Some are even able to read. The resulting sophistication in increased knowledge of facts and comprehension and interpretation of experiences places new burdens on the school.

Such language maturity on the part of some children stresses as never before the special needs of culturally disadvantaged and socially maladjusted children. The primary grades used to be chiefly concerned with teaching children to read and write. The child was taught to recognize symbols for sounds and attach meaning to them before he was expected to make the symbols himself. Although reading and writing follow listening and speaking in language development, all four language activities occur simultaneously after the initial introductory period. The child is not expected to be able to read extensively before he is taught to write, and indeed, many newer programs for primary grades are relating reading and writing in an almost reverse plan, with the philosophy being, "What I can write I can read." Actually this practice has been in use many years in the primary school in the form of experience charts. Experiences which are followed up with a period of discussion provide listening and speaking activities as children ask and answer questions. The teacher then becomes a scribe, writing the summary of the experience dictated by the children. After the chart is completed, the child reads what has been written.

In the primary grades much time is now being devoted to listening and speaking as well as to reading and writing, and the interrelationships between these language areas are utilized for improved language learning. Special provisions are being made to extend the experiential background of children from the ghettos and transient farm life, and of others who need a base for competency in language usage and for whom English is frequently not the mother tongue. Efforts are frequently made to teach English as a second language for such children.

Special experiences are also provided for children whose language development is accelerated. Such children get beginning reading activities in kindergarten, and they are given other school experiences which extend their ability to use language to express their own ideas and their interpretations of their experiences.

Developmental Steps Toward Writing

Recognizing writing as the capstone of language experience does not negate the importance of the listening and speaking activities which provide the content for early reading and writing lessons. Reading and writing actually reinforce and extend the habits and abilities acquired through listening and speaking. Each phase of language includes content, skills, abilities, and attitudes that strengthen learning in the other phases. Each stage of development prepares the child for the next stage. Failure to recognize the sequential nature of language development and the interrelationships of the areas of language impedes effective language teaching.

Writing, putting down in graphic symbols what one understands, is a partial representation of units of language expression. Although pictures convey meaning, they do not represent language units. Copying letters or setting a text in type for printing is not writing unless the person knows the language and its representation.

Prewriting

Prewriting, knowing the symbols that represent utterances and knowing how to put them down is an important step, but should not be confused with writing. Beginners are usually taught manuscript prewriting because it closely resembles printing and the contrasts are fewer and more easily learned.

The problems of teaching the grapheme–phoneme correspondence will vary, because there may be more than one spelling representing a sound but only one sound for a particular spelling, and vice versa. For example, the English phoneme /f/ is represented by *gh* in enough, *ph* in photo, and *f* in food, yet the grapheme *f* represents the single phoneme /f/. In constrast, the letter *h* can represent the phoneme /h/ in house or no sound in honor, whereas the phoneme /h/ is always represented by the grapheme *h*.

Authorities agree that children need a wealth of experience before they start to write. During initial stages children should meet in print what they have experienced and talked about. Experience charts have provided meaningful beginning reading lessons, and frequently such reading is extended to a writing experience. When an experience has particular value, the young child can be allowed to copy small groups of the words he has previously dictated to the teacher for his own book. A five-sentence story can be used by the child to make a five-page book. Each day he copies one sentence in his best handwriting, practicing prewriting skills previously taught, and illustrates it. At the end of the week his papers are stapled together, including a simple, colored construction cover or a more elaborate cover that has resulted from an art experience such as fingerpainting, to complete the child's own book.

After children are able to copy with some accuracy, they will be ready to vary the material being written. Some individuals will combine new vocabulary with former structures to introduce novelty into the early writing exercises. Because training in listening, speaking, reading, and writing is a continuing process, some children will begin to use in their writing words which they have met in reading. Others will use words which they have heard and stored in their minds. Children will have to be taught to verify words in the context of reading, reference work, or through the use of dictionaries.

Writing should be a matter of clarifying, organizing, and expressing ideas that have already become a part of the child's own thinking. Observation, experimentation, discussion, and viewing pictures, films and realia all help to prepare a child to understand and express ideas clearly. Plagiarism frequently results when the child is asked to write about something he has experienced only in reading. As previously stated, prewriting begins with manuscript for most children. The primary goal of teaching the skill of handwriting is legibility. There is now much less insistence upon uniformity of style than formerly.

Manuscript Writing

Manuscript is a kind of printing that is made up of circle and line strokes. It is relatively simple for children to learn and children make rapid progress in learning to write. Manuscript letters resemble print, so that reading and writing can be very closely related for beginning learners. Many books for young children are now published in manuscript instead of traditional print. There are few differences between manuscript and print, perhaps the most obvious one is the letter *g*. The simplicity of the manuscript as compared to the printed *g* is at once apparent. Another reason for teaching manuscript at the primary level is related to the first; manuscript writing is better suited to the motor development of young children, because it requires fewer fine coordinations.

We write this way,
straight up and down.

Much controversy over when the child should change from manuscript to cursive writing permeates educational circles. Many schools make the transition at the beginning of the third grade, giving as their reasons the following:

1. The maturity of children.
2. The need for children to write more and with increasing speed.
3. Motivation—children are asking when they are going to learn to write like older members of the family and friends.
4. The need for children to develop individuality in writing.

Actually, children in grade three have just learned to use manuscript with ease and beauty of form; at the time that writing has truly become a tool instead of a set of strokes to master, it is taken away and a new set of strokes substituted. One might question the results of such a procedure on the child's desire and ability to write creatively, on his own, without specific direction.

Concerning the need to write with increasing speed (truly an ever-increasing need of the space age), technical assistance in the form of typewriters, dictaphones, and even shorthand meet the need much more realistically than cursive writing.

In some schools children continue to use manuscript writing throughout their school years. Examples of students' writing in grades 11 and 12 demonstrate much individuality, as well as legibility and beauty of form, so that signatures in manuscript are as individual as signatures in cursive.

Of course, young children want to do what older people do. However, this is hardly a reason for changing from manuscript to cursive writing. If manuscript is more legible and beautiful, as some people claim, then older students, continuing to use it, will eventually become the models that young children wish to emulate.

Two questions need further investigation before the controversy concerning manuscript and cursive writing can be settled:

1. Why should children change from manuscript to cursive?
2. When should the change occur?

Children need regularly scheduled handwriting practice while they are learning the basic letter forms. Practice should include the use of the forms in words, phrases, and sentences as early as possible. Although instruction in handwriting proceeds continuously through the elementary grades in all written material, special periods for handwriting beyond grade three are probably a waste of time, because practice is needed only for remedial work and should be handled individually or in small groups as necessary.

Punctuation and Capitalization

From the beginning of their school life, children can be taught how correct punctuation and capitalization directly aid the process of communication. In the instances where this is not the case, the teacher should simply explain to the child that these are writing conventions of the language, making no attempt to justify them. For example, a capital letter is supposed to begin a proper noun. "Proper noun" has typically been defined as the name of a particular person, place, or thing. Yet "sun" has generally not been capitalized. Should it be? The earth has only one, and it certainly is vastly important to the well-being of human life. Tuesday, conversely, is capitalized although it rolls around every week, and there is nothing particularly significant about it. Capitalization in this sense is simply an example of a writing convention of English, and no made-up rationale will change this fact.

Punctuation and capitalization are taught early and informally. In the first grade the teacher, acting as a scribe, introduces marks for punctuation and explains their use during the writing exercise. For example, as the teacher writes the material being dictated by the children, such comments as, "I'll start this word with a capital letter to show that it is the first word in the sentence," and "I'll put a period here to show that the sentence is finished" will draw attention to the use of writing conventions that children will meet later in books and finally write themselves.

The content of writing exercises strengthens the concept of sentence structure and paragraph unity and must, therefore, be carefully planned. The content can be organized from different points of view and different levels of understanding for the various grade levels. When writing exercises are organized on familiar content, previous writing skills can be reinforced and extended, and progress in contextual analysis and understanding can also be achieved.

Although writing stages are clearly distinguishable, their sequence cannot be allocated to age or grade level. Some children come to school with few ideas to express. Others have many ideas but no notion of how to record them on paper. Still others are able to write with help in spelling, capitalization, and punctuation from the teacher, and a few children are able to write with a fair degree of ease. As children progress in the grades, the variance in writing ability increases, and for this reason individual and small group instruction is most effective.

Copying

The first writing exercises for children are usually copying exercises. The content of the copying exercise involves sentences which the children have used and read many times. As the children form letters for words and sentences that are familiar, they become aware of the general appearance of the words and finally of correct spelling. Eyes and mind work together to recall and fix the structures previously learned. The muscular activity involved in writing serves to coordinate and integrate aural and visual stimuli for the learning process.

The copying exercise should not be misconstrued as the child's beginning writing experience. The child has actually been preparing for this stage by expressing orally ideas which the teacher has then taken down and arranged into readable units. As children express their thinking in colorful and individual ways and their spontaneous expressions are recorded and used, they are developing attitudes regarding the need for writing, as well as becoming acquainted with writing conventions.

When children begin to write by copying, they should be taught to compare their finished work with the original, checking from the beginning for spelling, capitalization, punctuation, correct letter forms, and word order. Children should be encouraged to use enough space between letters, words, and lines to increase legibility and neatness. The teacher's insistence on positive habits and attitudes in early writing will be reflected in later papers only if the child understands the need for the various writing conventions.

Early writing lessons should involve very short sentences, as the purpose of copying is to produce written work with an absolute minimum of errors. Pupils may first copy only words that serve as identification markers for their papers such as their names, grade, name of school, or the titles of the various subjects.

Early copying from printed or skillfully duplicated materials at the child's desk ensures a greater degree of accuracy than copying from the chalkboard. As children's eyes move from the papers on which they are writing to the chalkboard and back again, the children frequently copy the wrong letter or word, and they become quickly discouraged. While the children copy, the teacher can move about helping individuals, calling attention to points that the children are missing.

Copying exercises can be carried on throughout the elementary grades, and absolute accuracy in copying should be required of older children. Copying focuses attention on spelling, punctuation, capitalization, and word patterns, providing excellent practice for children who have difficulty with these writing conventions.

A copying activity in the primary grades can also check comprehension. For such an exercise children are instructed orally to copy the sentence and then to draw the object or action referred to, for example:

> This is a book.
>
> This is an apple.

Such an exercise involves learning to write a pattern commonly used, using the appropriate article in front of a noun and extending the spelling vocabulary of commonly used nouns.

A later copying activity is the presenting of familiar questions and answers in random order. Children are instructed first to separate the questions from the answers, next to match the answer to its corresponding question, and finally to copy the questions with their answers.

Questions must be of a general nature for such an exercise. For example:

> What is the name of your school?
>
> My teacher is Mrs. Nelson.
>
> What is your teacher's name?
>
> My school is Kirk Elementary School.
>
> What room are you in?
>
> My principal is Mr. Towner.
>
> Who is your principal?
>
> I'm in room five.

It is important that the number of copying lessons should depend upon the individual progress of the pupil. Copying should never become busywork. Some children will be ready to move away from copying sentences very quickly, but they may need to return to copying for the introduction and practice of new forms such as paragraph writing, writing letters, and writing conversation.

When the child seems ready to write independently, he should be encouraged to do so and given all the help he needs in spelling, letter form, spacing, and other such matters. However, he should not be assigned to write on his own until he can do so with a sufficient degree of success. The child becomes discouraged when his independent writing is so poor that the corrected paper is a mass of confusion. If he utterly fails, the teacher has given him the wrong assignment. He needs to achieve accuracy in copying and studied and unstudied dictation before he is ready to move out on his own.

Dictation

Dictation is used by the teacher to check grammar points, capitalization, punctuation, and spelling as well as clarity and legibility of handwriting. Because content is given, the dictation exercise provides children an opportunity to concentrate on decisions regarding spelling, capitalization, punctuation, and even word forms, as they keep word combinations such as noun phrases and prepositional phrases in their minds while they write.

Early dictation requires selections which have been previously studied by children, but dictation in later stages of development can be unstudied, challenging the children to use previously learned rules to spell unfamiliar words and teaching them to draw meaning from context. Unstudied dictation provides children who read widely and children who enlarge both speaking and writing vocabularies through individual study an opportunity to check their progress, and it also provides the teacher an opportunity to diagnose individual writing needs.

Dictation material can be drawn from memory gems, proverbs, quotable quotes, picturesque language, or subject matter content which the children should learn and use.

Dictation exercises are brief, and each period devoted to dictation provides enough time for the children (1) to check their work against the original copy and (2) to discuss errors and reasons for making them.

When the teacher gives dictation, the selection is read first in its entirety at normal speed. Next, sentences are read in sense groups, that is, subject, predicate, prepositional phrase, etc. Each word group is read twice, and sufficient time for the children to write is given between the reading of the sense groups. After the whole selection has been dictated, it is read in its entirety again while the children check their work. A minute or two for corrections is given, then the children check their work against a written copy of the selection.

When children correct their own papers they are not distracted from the correcting task. When children exchange papers they usually pay more attention to their own paper and the child correcting it than to the paper they have been assigned to correct. Correcting their own papers has one real hazard, however, and children should be cautioned about it. They easily overlook errors. For example, the child who writes *brid* will often not notice that the word is spelled *bird* when he corrects. He does not mean to be dishonest, he simply does not notice the difference. Children will have to be taught to proofread meticulously, and teachers will always have to check papers for errors which children will miss. Added incentive can be provided through giving a special mark on each paper for proofreading, so that credit is added to the final grade of the paper for accuracy in proofreading.

After copying and dictation exercises, many children will be ready to write with increasing independence. Children during this stage learn to use self-helps, such as the dictionary or the language arts text, for writing style and form. Although a child may still get occasional help from the teacher, the independent writer usually proofreads his own material for spelling, punctuation errors, and points lacking in clarity. Eventually the writer assumes complete responsibility for his final copy.

Independent Writing

In all writing steps the emphasis is placed on purpose and content. Independent writing is best developed in an atmosphere in which children feel free to express their real thoughts and feel assured of warm acceptance and sympathetic interest.

Some children will need practice in controlled writing experiences before they are ready to write independently. Activities which allow them to construct original sentences utilizing suggested vocabulary items may help. They can be encouraged to construct new sentences on the analogy of given patterns and to construct paragraphs using a given pattern. Children can also be taught how to take notes, outline, and even how to complete a story. In all of these experiences the child writes with an increasing degree of independence. He practices correct forms, but at the same time he develops his power of self-expression through varying content, structure, and vocabulary in his own manner of thought.

As the child learns to write independently, his experiences continue to provide the content for his compositions. The need to communicate ideas is the only real motivation for clear and varied expression, correct spelling, and neatness and legibility in writing.

In early stages of independent writing, word cues such as *bad dreams, happy dreams, carols, Christmas, autumn, fear, love,* and *new shoes* can be used to motivate writing. Word cues are geared to the age and interests of children and are most effective when the writing experience is preceded by reading prose and poetry, viewing films, filmstrips, and pictures, and discussing the ideas inherent in the cues to bring them to the surface.

Paragraph writing is difficult for most children. It follows sentence writing naturally, but actual instruction in paragraphing is frequently limited to incomplete definitions presented by the teacher, plus assignments to write paragraphs. Instead the children might be given examples of well-written paragraphs and be encouraged to discover the various elements that make up a paragraph. For example, they will discover, after examining a great many paragraphs, that some are clear and easily read because they express the central thought in a topic sentence followed by sentences that develop this thought. Frequently the concluding sentence of a paragraph summarizes the points made in the paragraph, or leads into the next paragraph, or both. The patterns used in the example are found more frequently in expository writing than in narrative-descriptive writing. Whatever writing is used, children should be encouraged to discover the patterns of the paragraphs and explore possible reasons for the use of such form.

The element of continuity is extremely difficult for many young writers. They should be taught to notice how each sentence leads smoothly and logically to the next, as they listen to and read good literature. Such observation will be helpful when they are ready to write independently.

One good exercise for children beginning to write paragraphs involves the teacher's selecting a good paragraph, scrambling the sequence of the ideas, and then having the children reorder them. As they reorder, they should discuss the reasons for the choices of their particular sequence. Older children will benefit from a paragraph that can be arranged in more than one way.

After children have experienced the preceding exercise with a variety of paragraphs the teacher might list sentences from a paragraph at random, have the children order them sequentially, and then write them in paragraph form. An example from *The Adventures of Huckleberry Finn* follows: [1]

1. But she wouldn't.
2. Pretty soon I wanted to smoke, and asked the widow to let me.
3. That is just the way with some people.
4. She said it was a mean practice and wasn't clean, and I must try not to do it any more.
5. They get on a thing when they don't nothing about it.

(Key: 2, 1, 4, 3, 5)

To give practice in paragraph division, list many sentences in order. Ask the children to decide where they might make paragraph divisions and why. Are there any sentences that do not help to develop the topic sentence? Should they be omitted? Have the children rewrite the paragraphs after they have been established.

To encourage young writers to expand sentences into paragraphs give children paragraph openers that suggest development.

Examples: 1. When I grow up, I would like to be a _____ .
2. I stayed too long at my friend's house.
3. My mother was too strict.

Another exercise involves building previous events from a story ending in order (1) to develop a sense of cause and effect relationships and (2) to try to imagine what took place before.

Examples: 1. How could I have known there was a bear in the box?
2. He got the reward, but at what great cost!
3. There was never a person like him.
4. I'll never try that again!

---

[1] Mark Twain, *The Adventures of Huckleberry Finn*, eds., Kenneth S. Lynn and Arno Jewett, The Riverside Literature Series (Boston: Houghton Mifflin Co., 1962).

Notetaking

Schoolchildren need to take notes frequently throughout their school life. Notes are taken from reference materials like newspapers, journals, books, and encyclopedias. Children sometimes need to record what they have seen in films, filmstrips, selections read in class, reports of other students and lectures. The following exercises provide practice in notetaking:

1. Give a specific assignment for taking notes from reference material. Ask students to compare two articles and to record specific data such as emphasis, requirements, facilities, innovation, and objectives. From a list of the data recorded, the student can write a paragraph or several paragraphs presenting the information in his own words.

2. To provide practice in taking notes from a film, filmstrip, report, lecture, or broadcast, remind the students that all information will be presented only once and at normal speaking speed. After the presentation the student will be unable to recall all the facts given, so he needs to record in some fashion the facts which are important to him. Stress the fact that the purpose of notetaking is to help recall pertinent data, not to communicate with someone else. Hence any symbol, spelling, or fragment which clues the fact is satisfactory; no form is essential. Because the student may abbreviate or symbolize in any fashion, it is important for him to organize and rewrite the notes for permanent use as soon as possible.

To help children acquire skill in notetaking, provide fill-in outlines in early stages. As the report, film, or lecture progresses the child fills in necessary words to complete the outline. Transcribing minimal notes into complete sentences has values as a writing exercise. Sentences can be developed from notes by explaining, organizing the data chronologically, using analogies, or discussing the logic of the points involved.

When many notes have been taken, it will be necessary to organize the ideas so that each paragraph can be developed adequately and the several paragraphs developed into clear articles.

Paraphrasing

Exercises that will help children learn to transcribe written ideas into their own words can be very useful. Paraphrasing, restating the thought of the author, involves the skills of recognizing key words, discerning the author's point of view, and examining details. As the student attempts to reword statements while retaining the meaning and emphasis of the author, he will find it necessary to develop the ideas. Therefore, paraphrases are often longer than the original. Rarely can a synonym be found that is as explicit as the word the author has chosen.

Poems, proverbs, myths, and short bits of prose can be paraphrased. The child should always be encouraged to use worthy content for such an exercise.

Example: A penny saved is a penny earned.

Key words:	*penny*	*saved*	*is*	*earned*
Explanation:	*penny*	coin (may symbolize money or any substance)		
	saved	protected, preserved, redeemed, rescued, used, kept from loss		
	is	is equal to, the same as, means		
	earned	gained, merit received as compensation for labor, recompense, reward		
Paraphrase:	Anything which is protected, preserved, and available for later use can be taken advantage of when the need arises, having equal value to the rewards of labor.			

Paraphrasing provides practice in the use of the dictionary, vocabulary development, and organization of ideas.

Purpose of Writing Exercises

The ultimate goal of writing lessons is to prepare the child to write independently and fluently. Good writing requires that explanations be clear, adequate, and well-organized, that reasons and conclusions be logical and include a clear definition of terms and sufficient evidence to avoid unsupported assumptions, and that sentences and paragraphs be well developed and to the point, utilizing words and phrases that are precise in meaning and expressive when feeling is to be portrayed. Independent writing provides the child an opportunity to express his own ideas. Controlled writing equips the student to express his own thoughts freely in the most logical and effective manner possible by teaching particular use of structures and their modifications, specific vocabulary and word forms, and reducing and expanding sentence elements.

All students certainly do not have to go through all of the kinds of writing experiences previously suggested before they write on their own. Free composition or creative utilitarian writing provides excellent language practice and can be encouraged for some children as early as the first grade in school. To prepare young children for such writing, the teacher can first record the child's free oral expression and later, through skillful questioning, help children to focus attention on details that enrich expression.

The following first grade story, which resulted from a trip to the farm, illustrates the great variety of structures that children can use to express their ideas.

> We went to the farm.
> The cows were munching hay in the barn.
> A turkey said, "Gobble, gobble."
> Several dogs played together.
> We liked the farm.

Pictures that children draw themselves and mounted pictures that portray previously experienced objects and actions stimulate children to recall and express ideas in their own words.

It is futile to expect a child to express ideas when he has none to express. Very few people produce really original ideas, and teachers should be encouraged when they receive well-thought-out and well-organized analyses of ideas encountered and responded to by children.

Evaluating Writing

It is very difficult to evaluate children's writing; and, because of this, suggested practice runs the gamut from a hands-off, no-evaluation attitude to a correct-every-error attitude.

If every word, or even more than half, of a child's original writing is incorrect, that child needs a scribe to whom he can tell his original ideas, and he needs to continue with copying, dictation, and other writing exercises until he has sufficient skill to write with some degree of success.

Children should evaluate their own papers by proofreading to eliminate careless errors before papers come to the teachers. The teacher then evaluates the child's paper, not to correct and grade errors, but to "find weaknesses that need to be strengthened and strengths that need to be expanded, refined, and deepened."[2] A composition that is free from error, well organized, and worthy in content is the student's goal and responsibility, not the teacher's.

Writing Demands of Today

Written language has been affected by the space age in a variety of ways. First, and most obvious, a number of new words found in the varied technological vocabularies have come into general use. Man has completed his first landings on the moon, and new words and phrases such as *countdown, blastoff, lunar orbit, astronaut, space walk,* and *manned spacecraft center* are now common to the vocabulary of Americans.

The demands of modern culture accentuate the need for the specialized language of trades, professions, and governmental agencies. Although a great deal of levity, and often derision, is leveled against the "pedagese" of various occupational groups, the specific language helps to meet the increased need of accuracy and precision in the choice of words and phrases for clear communication.

At the same time that accuracy and precision of language are being demanded, the increased need for simplicity and directness in communication is being required because of the pressures of time. Written language of today must be quickly and accurately understood. This kind of accuracy demands a study of language structure.

Stageberg[3] provides some examples of common semantic ambiguity in writing. A noun phrase such as "a dull boy's knife," where the adjective may modify either the noun + possessive or the noun, causes confusion, and "modern language teaching," in which case the adjective may modify either noun, is not clear. In a sentence like "The hostess greeted the girl with a smile," the movable adverbial modifiers create ambiguity. Is the smile on the hostess or the girl?

Although the relationships between being able to talk about one's language and the ability to write effectively are not clear, many

[2] Ruth G. Strickland, "Evaluating Children's Composition," *Elementary English,* vol. 37, no. 5 (May, 1960), p. 330.
[3] Norman C. Stageberg, "Some Structural Ambiguities," *A Linguistic Reader,* ed., Graham Wilson (New York: Harper & Row, Publishers, 1967).

people are convinced that poor writing is directly related to grammatical incompetence. Bertrand Evans [4] makes stinging accusations against educationists for their part in the downfall of grammar instruction. He believes that educationists of the 1920s and 1930s challenged basic assumptions connected with the study of grammar on the bases that (1) grammatical knowledge had no appreciable value, and (2) the kind of study associated with learning grammar did not fit the pattern of the activity-conscious, child-centered, progressive school.

Evans continues his attack on what he calls "linguisticists" and points out that this group, too, battles against the old-fashioned study of old-fashioned grammar. Evans believes that grammar has not always been well taught, but that writing could be improved if teachers would either start from a list of the parts of speech and the several forms and functions of sentence elements, attempting to state the precise applicabilities of each to problems of writing, or start with the major problems of writing as they show on the surface in the written work of the inept, working back from these points to the particular grammatical knowledge needed to solve them. Actually Evans recommends the use of both procedures in teaching grammar.

Such a recommendation does not account for the deep structure problems that linguists are emphasizing in language study. For example, structures such as

> He is eager to please.

and

> He is easy to please.

pointed out by Noam Chomsky, seem exactly alike on the surface, but relationships within the structures are entirely different. In the first one "he" is anxious to do something that pleases, while in the second one something pleases "him."

Another example shows the same word classes in both sentences, but in the first sentence the noun phrase in the predicate is a complement, whereas in the second sentence the noun phrase in the

[4] Bertrand Evans, "Grammar and Writing," A Linguistic Reader, ed., Graham Wilson (New York: Harper & Row, Publishers, 1967).

same position is a direct object, so two different patterns are involved although both sentences look alike on the surface:

> We found him *a nuisance.*
> We found him *a job.*

Linguists have made it clear that traditional definitions do not define. For example, sentences have been defined as groups of words that express complete thoughts. How does one judge a thought as complete or incomplete? Does this definition also refer to paragraphs, or even chapters, or books?

Educationists, though under sharp attack presently, have provided valuable knowledge and obvious contributions to learning. Perhaps the most helpful and constructive direction for language development at this point is for educators, teachers, and linguists to combine their efforts to produce textbooks and programs that are linguistically respectable and pedagogically sound.

It is encouraging to note how the vernacular has taken on new respectability in recent years. Evidence of this is found in the several new translations of the Bible, such as *The New Testament in the Language of the People,*[5] and the third revision of *Webster's Third New International Dictionary of the English Language Unabridged,* which has created so much controvesy.

Functional writing of today occurs in a great variety of guises essential to fulfill the world's work. There is an increasing need for public relations people in industry, government, and educational institutions to prepare pamphlets and brochures that explain technological processes and equipment. The writing of manuals and handbooks for technical use and programs to be transmitted into cards and fed into computers is essential to life today. Writing of reports which interpret and apply computer results is in demand. Data must be translated into knowledge that can result in behavioral and attitudinal changes and this requires a new kind of writing skill. New occupations such as publications engineers demand people who can prepare handbooks, proposals for grants, written reports of completed research, and the results of projects. Copywriters for advertising continue to be increasingly in demand. The schools need to be preparing children for the writing requirements of the space age.

[5] Charles B. Williams, *The New Testament in the Language of the People* (Chicago: Moody Press, 1949).

Increased leisure, created by technological advances, provides time that can now be used to develop creative talents. Creative writing can provide man an opportunity to discover himself and his relationship to his rapidly changing environment as he gives form and meaning to his experience and ideas.

Technological Aids

To prepare children for the new writing demands of their technological society, in both work and leisure, the schools have been provided new technological aids for helping children learn about their language and extend their language use. Educational television and regularly programmed telecasts are used in schools with increasing frequency. Devices and techniques used in TV productions make possible the presentation of concepts by a master teacher to great numbers of children, while classroom teachers follow up the broadcast with learning experiences which provide children the opportunity to extend and clarify concepts and use the newly acquired information. The opaque projector has proven to be an invaluable tool for displaying various kinds of information to elicit class discussion and evaluation. Talking typewriters connected to computers, that request information and react to the typed responses of children, are being used in many schools. Programmed instruction in the form of textbooks and other written programs, as well as teaching machines, present the simple language skills of sentence structure, use of words, and many of the morphological, phonological, and syntactical aspects of grammar.

Much of the "new" English presented in simple formulae and symbols to help pupils understand English syntax can be effectively organized for programmed instruction. However, the "new" English in today's schools has a variety of approaches to the teaching of English. Sometimes the term is applied to any unified approach that treats English as a content subject, including language usage, dialects, semantics, and the history of language and lexicography.

In summary, today's teacher of English acts as a catalyst for creative thinking and expression, while providing the child with knowledge about his language, skills for effective use, and experiences for practice and language development. Such a task requires the use of the best programmed materials and technological aids now available, and if the teacher is to meet the increasing demands of society, new materials, aids, and programs must continue to be made available for use in the schools. The industrial and professional areas of society will need to cooperate with the schools more than ever before if adequate learning for the demands of life in the space age is to be achieved by today's children.

QUESTIONS FOR STUDY

1. What are some basic principles which guide writing instruction?
2. What are the developmental stages in writing?
3. What is a training lesson? How and when are training lessons used at your grade level?
4. Suggest some activities to encourage creative expression through language.

SUGGESTIONS FOR FURTHER READING

Applegate, Mauree, *Easy in English* (New York: Harper & Row, Publishers, 1960).

Burrows, Alvina, "Children's Writing: A Heritage in Education," *Elementary English,* vol. 32, no. 6 (October, 1955), pp. 385–388.

Burrows, Alvina, et al., *They All Want to Write* (Englewood Cliffs, N.J.: Prentice-Hall, Inc., 1952).

Christensen, Francis, *Notes Toward a New Rhetoric* (New York: Harper & Row, Publishers, 1967).

Friend, Mimi, "Developing A Unit in Writing Poetry," *Elementary English,* vol. 36, no. 2 (February, 1960), pp. 102–104.

Hathaway, Baxter, *A Transformational Syntax—The Grammar of Modern American English* (New York: The Ronald Press Co., 1967).

Mearns, Hughes, *Creative Power: The Education of Youth in the Creative Arts* (New York: Dover Publications, Inc., 1958).

TEACHER'S AID

Note to the Teacher:

Before this lesson can be used, the students will need a level of sophistication provided by a study of language such as that presented in the Roberts English Series, Grades 3–8. Words in the questions, such as *specific, transformation, phrases,* and *clauses,* will need discussion to assure understanding, and even words like *specific, elegant, rich, graceful, unusual,* or *flowery* must be carefully defined by the teacher and students. The grammatical structures listed in the definition of terms at the end of the lesson plan will have been previously mastered by the children, or this plan, although thorough, cannot possibly succeed.

Lesson Plan

What: To teach eighth graders to write descriptive narrative sentences.

Why: To help students discover how to generate a good, rhetorically sound sentence.

How:

1. Introduce problem

Today's problem, how to generate a good, rhetorically sound sentence, requires a definition of words. First, does anyone know exactly what rhetoric is? [Response]

Although many definitions of rhetoric can be found, the art of writing well in prose will suffice as a definition for the purposes of working toward generating a rhetorically sound sentence.

How does one write well in prose? This question takes us back to the other words of the problem which need to be defined—*good, sound,* and *generate. Good* and *sound* are adjectives of such general meaning that they tell us nothing. How can we find out what a good, rhetorically sound sentence is? How do we locate the characteristics of a good sentence?

There are books written that prescribe certain practices, telling students what to avoid in writing, how to punctuate, and how and when to incorporate mechanical rules to achieve acceptable form. There is also a vast corpus [define] of material, the writing of professionals, which we might analyze to decide what makes writing effective.

2. Analyze data

To begin, look at the sentence which you have been given from Mark Twain's *Steamboat Town.* [This sentence could be reproduced or placed on a transparency for overhead projection. If the projector is used, leave enough space to write during the discussion.]

STEAMBOAT TOWN

After all these years I can picture that old time to myself now, just as it was then: the white town drowsing in the sunshine of a summer's morning; the streets empty, or pretty nearly so; one or two clerks sitting in front of the Water Street stores, with their splint-bottomed chairs tilted back against the walls, chins on breast, hats slouched over their faces, asleep—with shingle-shavings enough around to show what broke them down; a sow and a litter of pigs loafing along the sidewalk, doing a good business in watermelon rinds and seeds; two or three lonely little freight piles scattered about the levee; a pile of skids on the slope of the stone-paved wharf, and the fragrant town drunk asleep in the shadow of them; two or three wood flats at the head of the wharf, but nobody to listen to the peaceful lapping of the wavelets against them; the great Mississippi, the majestic, the magnificent Mississippi, rolling its mile-wide tide along, shining in the sun; the dense forest away on the other side; the "point" above the town, and the "point" below, bounding the river-glimpse and turning it into a sort of sea, and withal a very still and brilliant and lonely one.

Follow along while I read the sentence. [Read] This is a very long sentence. Which words could have been omitted? How would this change the description? How has the author managed to describe a town, many of its people, some animals, the wharf, and the river in one sentence?

What is the name of the construction "the white town drowsing in the sunshine of a summer's morning"? Can you find other absolutes in the sentence?

Why is it important to say as much as possible in the fewest possible words? Look at the structure "The white town drowsing in the sun-shine." What does *drowsing* tell you? What does *white* imply? Reading on, how are the streets described? Which words are specific? Are there any unusual words? How have common words been combined to create clear pictures? From this description, do you think that elegance, richness, or grace in writing have something to do with the use of un-usual or flowery language?

What has the author done to the adjective *drowsy* to make a descriptive verb? The noun *boundary* has been transformed to a verb in "bounding the river." What phrase might the author have used in place of the verb *bounding*? [e.g., forming a boundary around the river-glimpse] How did the transformation save words and portray the same meaning? In this sentence what transformations substitute words for phrases and clauses? What phrases and clauses are added to words with general or abstract meaning?

In English, adjectives frequently precede nouns. In how many places can you find the adjective following the noun in this sentence? What is the reason for this shift? Do the added structures illustrate, amplify, or emphasize the adjective? [e.g., streets empty]

Does anyone know what we mean by *generate*? The word *generate* means to bring into being, to produce, to originate or cause to be. What is the main clause of the sentence from *Steamboat Town*? In what direc-tion does the main clause take the reader?

What is the movement of the following phrases:

with their splint-bottomed chairs tilted back against the walls

chins on breast

hats slouched over their faces

asleep—with shingle-shavings enough around to show what broke them down?

What does the author accomplish by moving the reader ahead in the first clause? How does the author help the reader to "picture that old time"? Does the picture appear in the main clause? Why is *great* in "the great Mississippi" a general term? Do the words *majestic* and *magnificent* help you to see the Mississippi? What kind of constructions are "rolling its mile-wide tide along, shining in the sun?" [verb clusters] How do these clusters add detail so that you can picture the Mississippi? What is a river-glimpse? How many noun clusters, verb clusters, prepositional phrases, and absolutes are found in this sentence? In what way does the variety of structures keep the reader involved as he completes the picture?

Is there action in this sentence? Where is the action found? Which absolutes and verb clusters provide action?

What do the noun clusters contribute to the sentence? [e.g., chins on breast, a pile of "skids" on the slope of the stone-paved wharf]

How does the absolute, "the streets empty," compare with these?

After looking at this one sentence, can we begin to establish some characteristics of a good, rhetorically sound sentence? These, of course, will have to be tested against many samples of writing before we can assume that they are valid. Think about statements we might make about writing, and we will list them on the board and in our writing notebooks for further evaluation. [List as students dictate. See the following examples.]

1. A sentence states an idea in the fewest possible words.
2. Additions follow abstract words to repeat, illustrate, amplify, or emphasize.
3. Sentence elements are shifted about, and parts of speech are changed when such changes contribute to elimination of unnecessary words or further illustration of concepts.
4. Variation in movement of the sentence modifiers takes the reader forward to advance ideas and backward to further develop the ideas.
5. The texture of a sentence is determined by the amount and quality of detail, comparison, repetition for purposes of identification, and style of writing.

Tomorrow we will begin to examine the various kinds of sentence modifiers and what they are able to contribute as a tool for the writer. But before we close the lesson for today, are all good sentences long sentences? How long should a sentence be?

Follow-up Exercise

Write one sentence to describe as accurately as possible the action taking place in this translucent corn popper while the corn is popping.

Definition of Terms

Sentence Modifier:

A free or nonrestrictive modifier which modifies the sentence itself. (It is always set off with commas.)

> *Before leaving the office,* he made several calls.
> He glanced up, *sheepishly.*

Noun Cluster (NC):

A noun, with or without other words clustering around it and modifying it in various ways.

> She saw him later, *the same wizened man.*
> He petted the deer, *a tawny doe.*

Verb Cluster (VC):

A verb, with or without words clustering around it to modify it in various ways.

> The wind blew, *bending the trees over.*
> The man left, *angered by the conversation.*
> He had been given his instructions, *to eat everything on the plate.*

Absolute (Abs):

A structure that includes a noun phrase plus a verb phrase, the verb form a participle (present or past) without the auxiliary that usually accompanies it. (If a form of *be* is used, it may be omitted from the absolute. The absolute always functions as a sentence modifier.)

> He came into the room, *sweater slung carelessly over his shoulder.*
> He looked down from the ladder, *his feet on the top rung.*

Prepositional Phrase:

A preposition followed by a noun phrase. It provides sensory images in the use of simile and metaphor for comparison and also adds exposition.

> The book was *beyond his reach.*
> He looked *with a puzzled frown.*

12

The Use of Literature in Language Study

Perhaps the two most outstanding goals of education for today's children are (1) an understanding of self and (2) a development of the self-concept in relation to others. Good literature for children will certainly help the child to find himself as a unique personality. It will also help him to lose himself as it extends his interest in other peoples, places, and times. The preceding generalizations are usually agreed on by most educators, and yet certain specific questions need to be answered if the role of literature in the elementary school language program is to become explicit.

Meeting the Needs of Individual Pupils

Because literature is so widely diversified, a wealth of good reading can be found for almost every area of interest, every stage of maturity, and every level of ability. Children who are particularly able may have their imagination and resourcefulness challenged and developed through the use of good literature. Sir Isaac Newton once said that he could see further than others because he stood on the shoulders of giants. Today's children who excel in verbal comprehension can certainly stand on the shoulders of intellectual giants of both past and present as the experiences, goals, and dreams of these men are presented in books. Fascinating stories of history, geography, science, mathematics, music, and art have the power of awakening and challenging children to pursue knowledge in these areas. Stories that describe conflict, reflect sensitivity to the needs of the physically or mentally handicapped, and tell of people who experience indignities of prejudice because of race or social class can alert future leaders and help them to identify virtues such as ambition, ability, loyalty, and valor in all peoples.

✓ Children should be encouraged to read poetry because it provides both pleasure and genuine intellectual stimulation. Poetry is par-✓ ticularly useful as a vehicle of learning for gifted children. A great deal of literature is now being written for exceptional children who enter school handicapped by the disadvantages of the environment from which they come. For these children, most of the experiences listed in typical children's books are nonexistent. These children must have experiences such as instructional walks about the neighborhood, trips to the zoo, park, and supermarket, contacts with many children and adults, and experiences in music, art, and dramatic play to accompany stories as they are presented.

Fairy tales, Mother Goose rhymes, and beautifully illustrated children's books are especially appropriate for these children. Such children may be extremely intelligent, talented in various fields, and very responsive to good teaching. Well-selected literature geared to individual needs can play a dynamic role in developing the potential of individual children.

Teachers can locate the needed materials by using the valuable book selection aids prepared by librarians and specialists in children's literature. The H. W. Wilson Company [1] publishes a *Children's Catalog* every five years which includes a brief annotated bibliography of children's books according to grade level. These are indexed by author, title, illustrator, and subject. A supplement to the catalogue is published every two years. It is estimated that there are approximately 2000 new books published every year for children. The American Library Association [2] suggests books on various subjects in its *Basic Book Collection for Elementary Grades.* This too, is an excellent source for teachers. Other sources are listed in the References at the end of this chapter.

---

[1] *Children's Catalog*, 11th ed. (New York: H. W. Wilson Co., 1966. Supplement 1968).

[2] Miriam Mathes, *A Basic Book Collection for Elementary Grades*, 7th ed. (Chicago: American Library Association, 1960).

Providing Socially Satisfying Experiences

Stories and poems are read to young children by their teachers. Following the reading, children are encouraged to talk together about the characters, events, places, and times represented in the story. As children review the sequence of events, the qualities of the characters, and the concepts which they envision regarding the times and places mentioned in the story, they have an opportunity to explore and extend social understanding. When children dramatize choice episodes of the story, they are given a chance to further explore the feelings of the characters, their own reactions to the behavior of the characters, and the events leading to the behavior.

As children get older they can share favorite books with classmates in a variety of ways such as the following:

1. Make posters to advertise their favorite books, using paint, crayons, chalk, paper sculpture, stencil, cut-out pictures, and a variety of real materials. The posters may be flat or dimensional. Printing can be taught and practiced in poster making.

2. Make dioramas to provide the setting for an exciting part of the story. Discarded materials and odds and ends can be used for props to be placed in a box or on a table. Small dolls, wire or pipe cleaner forms, papier-mâché figures, and clay may become characters. Toys can be used when they contribute to the setting.

3. Make and decorate a book jacket to attract attention as well as to protect the book.

4. Take color photographs or collect color pictures to illustrate a travel book.

5. Illustrate the high points of a story by making a "roller movie." Events are drawn on a long roll of paper or prepared individually and taped together in ordered sequences.

6. Write book reviews for the school newspapers. Write a play based on a good action story. Illustrate books with pictures they have drawn or painted.

7. Present orally, or write, a description of one character in a book.

8. Prepare a special part of the story for reading to an audience. This can be the most exciting event, the most frightening experience, the funniest incident, or the most astonishing incident, and it should titillate the listeners, making them want to read the entire book.

9. List beautifully descriptive passages or new, unusual, and interesting words during the reading of a story. These can be used later by the class in word games for vocabulary extension and by the child in his own creative writing.

10. Make pantomimes of specific events when most of the children in the class have read a book. The children can review the incident orally after guessing what has been seen.

11. Give a synopsis of a book orally to a friend or write one in a letter. This provides experience in arranging events in sequence and learning how a story progresses to a climax.

12. Give a puppet show, reviewing a book, with wooden or papier-mâché puppets, paper bag puppets, hand or finger puppets, cardboard shadow puppets, or stick puppets, depending upon the age and ability of the children.

13. Children who have read the same book can check each other's comprehension by writing questions that they think readers should be able to answer after reading the book.

14. Dress dolls authentically like the characters in the story. This will appeal only to certain children.

15. Research a favorite author, presenting a brief biography of him with sketches of his books.

16. Make an attractive display with a cord with book jackets hanging from it across a corner or an end of the classroom.

17. Prepare a chalk talk to develop the story. This is an excellent technique for the teacher also.

18. Depict the important scenes of a favorite book with large pictures or a mural.

19. Record excerpts of stories on tapes, either from notes or from prepared writing. Show illustrations to the class while they listen to the playback of the excerpt.

20. Use the excellent records, filmstrips, and films that are available. Have children read the story, compare it with the dramatization, and discuss possible reasons for the changes.

Children may also share particularly valuable and apt bits of prose and poetry by participating as group members in choral reading or verse speaking choirs.

Giving the Child Self-Insight

The child gains understanding about himself and his environment by comparing and contrasting his actions and reactions with those around him. When a child meets and identifies with someone like himself in a book, he may be helped to a more realistic appraisal of his own personality and to new aspirations for himself, whether he be lonely, timid, resentful, selfish, handicapped, deprived, or gifted. All children possess qualities such as these to some degree as they grow up, and the kind of self-evaluation that takes place as children identify with worthy characters who have obstacles to overcome and difficult goals to achieve will probably help them to establish their own personal values.

Contributing to the School Curriculum

Social studies, in addition to teaching about peoples and places, aims to teach children to appreciate and respect other persons, their cultural similarities and differences, and their contributions to human life and thought. As children identify with worthy people in fiction, they can begin to realize that human dignity and personality are of first importance in human relationships. Many books for children present worthy characters from all nationalities and walks of life. The strengths and weaknesses of these characters are honestly portrayed so that the children can identify with them. As the child becomes responsive to the needs and problems of others, he will begin to search courageously to bring about changes which are consistent with democratic ideals and processes. Anecdotes, legends, historical novels, and biography are particularly helpful in this area.

A great many informational books are being written today for children in the area of science. Such books are being read by children in great numbers, although most of them do not represent the kind of writing that is usually found in books classed as literature. Accuracy and authenticity are the prime concerns of these books, and they are geared to clarifying and extending concepts.

Many books are written that can deepen learning and create lasting interest in the work of artists, musicians, poets, and authors. Biographical sketches, picture books, song books, books of poetry, and carefully illustrated books such as the Caldecott Award books enrich the arts.

A wide variety of English language can be found in literature, from the Scottish of Burns to the picturesque talk of nineteenth century American railroaders. This great corpus of English helps children to understand the sweep and power of their language. As children meet different ways of expressing ideas, they will learn that there are many grammars within the English language, and that grammaticality is not to be equated with good and ungrammaticality with bad. The writing system of English is best presented through the use of literature. As children learn to notice how language is used by respected authors, they become aware of the need to use their own language precisely, whether in written or oral communication.

Self-expression and the misunderstood term *freedom* have for some time been the major goals in teaching children to write. Teachers' directions for writing have frequently consisted of "Write a story about _____." or "Write how you feel about the music." Such directions seem to assume that, having heard and read stories, the child can now write them. He is never taught to construct a simple plot, create a character, or write dialogue; he is rather left to write whatever comes into his head, and if nothing, then he is urged to write his "nothing!" To add insult to injury the child is frequently requested to read his nothing to the class after he has written it. The child should be taught devices for writing, how to write objective description, comparison, contrast, definition, explanation, and dialogue, and how to structure, choose, order, and evaluate his work.

Specific questions regarding literature selections which require the child to work through passages and answer from the words, rather than from pictures or flights of fancy, will help the child to become more precise in his thinking. Freedom comes only after one has mastered a discipline. Before freedom can be achieved, self must be submitted to the exacting disciplines of whatever craft one pursues. The term *self-expression*, as it is usually used by elementary educators, knows no limitations and rejects any thought of criticism of expressions as if it were a criticism of the pupil's self and hence damaging. Surely we really want the elementary pupil's self to expand. When he has achieved his mature self, through relentless and unsentimental self-examination in experience broad and deep, then and only then will he be truly able to express himself, and *he* will be something worthy of expression. Until then, his efforts at self-expression are indeed events of self-discovery, important but difficult; and he must have a great deal of instruction, as well as some opportunity for self-expression, if he is to mature and develop all his potential.

Creative Writing

This author clearly recognizes the value of creative writing in the early grades. Frequent undirected writing, however, cannot be expected to lead the pupil to an honest understanding of what writing is and how it should be done. To teach children to write with coherence and grace, teachers should induce children to write precise observations. As the student attempts to turn his observation into words, and then sharpen and organize his attempts, he is encouraged to improve both the quality of his observation and his ability to express it. Errors in observation should be noted by the teacher and the student made to look again. As the pupil labors to revise his paper, he will come to realize the relationship that language bears to the world around him. Such a view of language begins as the child is exposed to good literature, and respect for language results as the child endeavors to report faithfully what he sees.

A paper which is an observation can be dealt with rigorously because the pupil's private feelings are not involved. Observation is an objective phenomenon, and the vocabulary needed can be discussed and evaluated far more realistically than subjective papers that use words like *sad, wistful, pensive, morose, contented* or *happy*. Writing that encourages self-discovery should not be subjected to rigorous criticism. Such writing is personal, and children should be provided time to write and invited to do so, but personal writing should not be an assignment. This concept of personal writing will be discussed further in the next chapter.

Papers dealing with processes provide opportunity for combining careful observation with sequential presentations and clarity of statement. Papers that tell how to play a game, train a pet, or solve a problem in long division force the writer to select precise vocabulary and order his thinking rigorously. Such writing should be challenged until no possible misinterpretation can result, and when this occurs criticism and revision proceed simultaneously. A child who has learned to write in this fashion will have learned how to write a sentence that says exactly what he wants it to say. Objective papers, requiring the child to speak truthfully about what he sees, help the child to grow, whereas constant emphasis on self-expression forces the child back into himself instead of letting him grow into what he may become. For too long the elementary school child has been deprived of the chance to get down to the business of learning how to use his language in a serious and controlled manner. This learning can best be brought about through a careful examination of how fine writers use vocabulary and syntax to write with integrity in clean, eloquently simple lines. The accurate use of writing conventions such as spelling, capitalization, and punctuation can be developed by copying appropriate passages of literature directly from the book. Absolute accuracy is emphasized during such an exercise. New English programs are emphasizing a serious approach to writing for elementary pupils.

Reading with Accuracy and Understanding

Literature can also be used to teach the child to read more accurately and more sensitively. It is possible to get the gist of an argument by reacting to key words here and there, while missing the precise meaning in literature of any difficulty. Because it is difficult to learn to read accurately, much time must be devoted to it. Vocabulary can be taught through the use of familiar contexts, pictures, analogies, and the use of the dictionary. Literature presents a variety of content and subject matter and should be presented on a level that the child can understand with effort and aid. The literature selections presented to teach the child to read accurately should have value in themselves as well as provide the source from which new knowledge or skills will be drawn. Because they will be read carefully and many times, selections presented to teach the child to read accurately should have value in themselves as well as provide the source from which new knowledge or skills will be drawn. Because they will be read carefully and many times, they should be selections worthy of the time and effort spent on them. Literature selections also provide topics for work in composition, reports, and discussions, and illustrate the use of language in a variety of ways.

Accuracy is stressed in reading to develop an awareness of grammar and sentence structure. Complete understanding of the new words presented in each selection of literature should be stressed. Studying the etymology of words provides essential background for developing vocabulary, and a structural or syntactical analysis of the words can add to their meaning.

Literature that includes rhyme and rhythm frequently connects sound and spelling. Emphasis is placed on sound when this is appropriate. After sound and letter relationships have been introduced, opportunity should be provided for spelling practice in writing.

Each selection of literature to be studied by children should be read to them before they read it so that they can hear it first as spoken English. From listening to the language, they can move to answering questions about what they have heard. Questions should be designed to force them to read the selection themselves in order to answer the questions. At first, the entire class reads the selection together, then some of the class members can read one part and some another. Eventually it is time for individual reading. Questions must be answered by reading the exact response, rather than guessing, reading the pictures, or providing an answer from the child's own experience. As the children move into studying the specific aspects of the story or poem, they begin to apply grammar to the literature and are helped to discover new structures of increasing complexity. Structural meaning is important to reading. As the child is able to discern the verb, discuss its function, and explain how the noun phrase is functioning in relationship to it, he is beginning to read with much accuracy. Certain passages in literature, most often poetry, display a deliberate departure from normal forms, and children should become acquainted with special uses of language as they learn to read.

Selecting and Using Literature

As previously stated, the selections of literature will become the corpus from which new knowledge and skills are drawn; they must therefore contain examples of what needs to be taught. They must also be at a reading level that pupils can handle with effort and help. Experts in the field insist that language development is sequential, and that concepts need to be developed sequentially so that they move from basic principles and simple analyses into increasingly complex combinations. Linguistics has provided data which make programming language learning possible, and the new texts and materials are demonstrating the use of such knowledge.

The other criterion of great importance for the selection of literature involves the value of the selection. Because the selection will be used in depth, and often memorized by the pupil, it must be a selection worthy of the time and effort spent on it.

Criteria for Evaluating Children's Stories

1. The plot should possess an orderly sequence of events with few and clearly marked transitions in time and place. Children's stories—

    (a) grow out of a strong theme.

    (b) support vigorous action.

    (c) offer heroes who have obstacles to overcome, conflicts to settle, and difficult goals to win.

    (d) provide suspense which keeps children reading to find out how the hero achieves his ends.

    (e) present a clear-cut conclusion to help children build both the courage to try difficult tasks and the faith to believe that high endeavor succeeds when reinforced with industry and persistence.

2. The content and theme of children's stories should—

    (a) be appropriate to the background and age of the children for whom the stories are written.

    (b) set in action truths worthy of inspiring and being remembered.

    (c) possess integrity and morality but not be overburdened by moralistic and didactic emphasis.

3. Characterization should be well-drawn and convincing:

    (a) Strengths and weaknesses should be portrayed so that children can identify with the characters.

    (b) Character development takes place within the story.

    (c) Characters offer children insight into their own personal problems and their relationships with other people.

4. Style:

    (a) Meaningful words fall into patterns that are comfortable and pleasant to read aloud.

    (b) Children want lots of action, little description. They enjoy conversation.

    (c) The author must not talk down to children.

5. Format:

    (a) The pictures should convey the message of the story.

    (b) The title page, the spacing of the print, the kind of print used, and the illustrations should be in harmony with the desired effect of the story.

Poetry

Poetry is one form of literature that is rich linguistically, and can afford the child an understanding of language possibilities, as he becomes acquainted with the great variety of ways in which language can be used. Poetry requires the child to read accurately and sensitively, as it enriches his sensory experience and builds vocabulary. When children become aware of how form, imagery, and sound combine to make meaning, their appreciation of poetry as an art form begins to develop. Through questioning, they can recognize the skill with which the poet expresses depth of meaning in his reaction to the world around him.

Children need to have poetry read to them. Rhythm and rhyme are conveyed most easily through the ear, and children are delighted by the sounds of alliteration, assonance, consonance, and onomatopoeia. They also respond to the repetition of words. In reading poetry to children, it is important to speak all of the words clearly and in a natural voice. If the teacher gets the feeling of the poem and follows the rhythm, the meter will take care of itself.

Choral speaking provides an effective opportunity for group interpretations and presentation of poetry. Choral speaking allows every child to participate. The timid child and the over-aggressive child become as one, developing empathy with all others as they participate in choral speaking. Voices blend, articulation and enunciation become vital, and pitch, stress, and juncture are emphasized. Children memorize poetry easily because of the repetition necessary for effective presentation. The meaning of poetry is analyzed for dramatic interpretation, and as children help in planning and arranging poetry for choral speaking, the understanding which they gain leads to a sincere and deep appreciation of the poetry.

Choral speaking can begin for children when they speak the refrain of a poem with the teacher. During refrain speaking, if the selection is long, the children usually begin to repeat the refrain with the teacher about the third time it is spoken. They continue this chanting of the refrain until the end of the poem. If the teacher wishes to structure refrain speaking, the following steps can be used:

1. The teacher motivates the poem by relating a recent experience, a picture, or some realia to the main idea of the selection.
2. The teacher reads the poem and asks the children to listen for their part of the poem, paying special attention to words, intonation, and

timing. This is done through specific questions geared to bring out these three elements:

(a) What word in the line was emphasized?

(b) Which words went together in a phrase?

(c) Which words or sounds received the least amount of emphasis?

3. The teacher may need to reread parts of the poem to help the children answer the questions.

4. The teacher reads the poem again and the class joins in on the refrain. Eventually the teacher or one class member reads the poems while the class does the refrain without the teacher.

Beginners in choral speaking should speak couplets rather than single lines to avoid loss of rhythm and meaning. In some poems certain children may be responsible for one line, if this does not hamper the meaning. Movement from one section to another, or one voice to another, is effective, but again, such movement must not hamper the rhythm or meaning of the entire selection.

Antiphonal choral speaking is the most intricate and effective way of blending voices into a verse choir. High, low, medium, light, and heavy voices will be used to form groupings for special blends and effects. Poems featuring contrasts can be spoken by these groups. The more vigorous sections of the poetry will be spoken by the heavier voices. In question-answer poetry the heavier voices will take parts that have predominately long vowels. The teacher trying antiphonal speaking for the first time might use only two groups, boys and girls or high and low, and the poetry should be presented to the class in much the same way as it was for the refrain.

Children should be encouraged to interpret the selections and make suggestions for the intonation of the poetry, for the organization and use of the voices, and for gestures or movements to accompany the poetry. It is imperative that discussion provides each child with the meaning of all the words, and that all of the children learn the entire selection. It is helpful to spend ten to twenty minutes daily on choral reading rather than a longer period of time less frequently. Children should be encouraged to bring in favorite poems for learning. A list of material suggested for the teacher follows at the end of this chapter.

Writing poetry should be encouraged in the primary and intermediate grades. As children begin to express ideas in poetic form, the teacher can act as a scribe and record these for class poetry books. As children increase in their ability to use repetition and rhyme effectively, they can begin to copy their own poems and become aware of form. Children should be invited to write poetry, never assigned to do it. As their interest and ability grows, they may read and copy poems from the literature. After they have become acquainted with many forms of poetry such as couplets, triplets, quatrains, limericks and Haiku, they can begin to make choices regarding how they will write. Poetry is personal. It can discuss any subject, and it contains many forms. Poetry evokes pictures and mental images that attract attention and demand response. Poetry is related to music, and it is the relationship of sound and meter that delights young children as they listen to rhymes and jingles during their first exposure to poetic forms.

As children express themselves in poetic form, their own books of poetry can be made for class use. These are either handwritten and illustrated for the class or duplicated so that each child can have his own copy. Encouragement should be the key word, and the extension of skills and knowledge about form, content, and style should be handled through related lessons rather than in an analysis of the child's own poem.

Criteria for Evaluating Poetry

Poetry which appeals to children has these elements:

1. Rhythm. The rhythm is suited to the subject matter and the mood of the poem, and these receive the emphasis rather than the rhythmic pattern. Children prefer emphatic, regular rhythm, but they should become familiar with the cadenced and unrhymed rhythm as well as with the metrical and rhymed. The best poetry for children sings with rhythm, true unforced rhymes, and a happy compatibility of sound and subject.

2. Word and Sound Patterns. Children enjoy alliteration, rhyming words, and repetition of words and phrases. Good poetry for children uses strong, vigorous words, warm, rich words, or delicate, precise words that may be exact and descriptive or sensory and connotative in their meanings.

3. Imagery. Children enjoy imagery and metaphors that are within the realm of their background and within the limits of their imagination. Only under these circumstances can imagery excite sensory scenes and sensations and evoke emotional response to the attitudes and moods of the poem. Sense appeal and imaginative

comparisons resulting in fresh, unexpected resemblances make poetry come alive for children.

4. Content. Although poetry is largely emotional in its appeal, it includes subjects or ideas that appeal to the intellect as well as the emotions. Poetry has varied subject matter, but it invests the content with arresting significance. Poetry takes the strange or everyday facts of life and gives them fresh meaning, and the content of the poem elicits from the child a feeling of personal kinship with the poet, a share in an emotional experience, or an urge for self-expression. Poetry has the power to capture and extend experience, thought, and emotion. Children enjoy hearing about their world in a simple vivid manner that is to the point.

5. Story Elements. Children enjoy story poems. Narrative poems for children use comparisons, figurative language, analogies, and various types of sensory appeals.

6. Humor. Nonsense rhyme and humorous poetry that evoke an emotional response, a certain gaiety of heart, and a beginning appreciation for serious poetry have long been popular with children.

Myths and Fables

Myths and fables also contribute to the reading and writing experiences of children. From the fifth century B.C. the Greeks took myth to mean everything which was legendary and miraculous and which could not be proven as fact or demonstrated through reason. The word retained this meaning, equating mythical with unreal. For this reason the poetry, gods, and heroes of the ancients were tolerated in the Christian faith. It had aesthetic significance but was acknowledged not to be true.

Fables are short, to the point, and highly moral. Aesop is so much a part of our culture that our language includes foxes and sour grapes, dogs in the manger, and boys who cry "wolf" without our consciously relating these forms to the ancient writer. Fables are strong. They have weathered many powerful voices raised against them and are ideally suited to inculcate concepts of morals, ethics, and social behavior. They should be used sparingly, for they can lose their significance if too many are read at one time.

In summary, a thorough study of the corpus of language found in good literature will teach children to read accurately and write effectively and perceptively. Such a study must include a careful analysis of vocabulary, and the phonological and syntactical components of form and content.

QUESTIONS FOR STUDY

1. How are literature selections used to demonstrate the spellings, punctuation, and capitalization conventions of English in the language arts textbooks of your elementary schools?
2. How are literature selections used by teachers to teach vocabulary, etymology, and syntax?

SUGGESTIONS FOR FURTHER READING

Arbuthnot, May Hill, *Children and Books*, 3d ed. (Chicago: Scott, Foresman and Co., 1964).

Arnstein, Flora J., *Poetry in the Elementary Classroom* (New York: Appleton-Century-Crofts, 1962).

Barrows, Herbert, et al., *How Does a Poem Mean?* (Boston: Houghton Mifflin Co., 1959).

The Children's Book Council, *The Calendar*, vol. 25, no. 2 (May–August, 1968).

Cianciolo, P. J., and Reid, V. M., "Poetry for Today's Children," *Elementary English*, vol. 41, no. 5 (May, 1964), pp. 484–502.

Eaton, Annie T., *Treasure for the Taking* (New York: The Viking Press, Inc., 1946).

Fenwick, Sara I., ed., *Bulletin of the Center for Children's Books*, vol. 21, no. 7 (Chicago: The University of Chicago Press, March, 1968).

Frank, Josette, *Your Child's Reading Today* (Garden City, N.Y.: Doubleday & Co., Inc., 1960).

Galisdorfer, Lorraine, *Educational Reading Guide for the Partially Seeing* (Buffalo, N.Y.: Foster and Stewart, 1951).

Guilfoile, Elizabeth, *Books for Beginning Readers* (Champaign, Ill.: National Council of Teachers of English, 1962).

Hallowell, Lillian, *A Book of Children's Literature*, 3d ed. (New York: Holt, Rinehart & Winston, Inc., 1966).

Harrington, Mildred P., *The Southwest in Children's Books* (Baton Rouge: Louisiana State University Press, 1952).

Heaton, Margaret M., *Reading Ladders for Human Relations* (Washington, D.C.: American Council on Education, 1955).

Johnson, E., et al., *Anthology of Children's Literature* (Boston: Houghton Mifflin Co., 1959).

Logasa, Hannah, *Historical Fiction* (Brooklawn, N.J.: McKinley Publishing Co., 1964).

Logasa, Hannah, *Historical Non-Fiction* (Brooklawn, N.J.: McKinley Publishing Co., 1964).

Long, Harriet G., *Rich the Treasure: Public Library Service to Children* (Chicago: American Library Association, 1953).

Mathes, Miriam, *A Basic Book Collection for Elementary Grades*, 7th ed. (Chicago: American Library Association, 1960).

Smith, Dora Valentine, *50 Years of Children's Books*, 1910–1960 (Champaign, Ill.: National Council of Teachers of English, 1963).

Spache, George D., *Good Reading for Poor Readers* (Champaign, Ill.: Garrad Publishing Co., 1964).

Turner, Mary C., *Best Books for Children* (New York: R. R. Bowker Co., 1966).

The reader will find current and past issues of the following magazines helpful: *Library Journal, The Hornbook Magazine*, and *Publisher's Weekly*.

GENERAL REFERENCES:

Bibliography of Books for Children (Washington, D.C.: Association of Childhood Education, 1965).

The Booklist and Subscription Books Bulletin (Chicago: American Library Association). A bimonthly publication.

Books on Exhibit (Mt. Kisco, N.Y.: 1968).

Children's Catalog (New York: H. W. Wilson Co., 1969).

Fuller, Muriel, *More Junior Authors* (New York: H. W. Wilson Co., 1963).

Kingman, Lee, et al., *Illustrators of Children's Books, 1957–1966* (Boston: The Horn Book, Inc., 1968).

Kunitz, S. J., and Haycroft, *The Junior Book of Authors* (New York: H. W. Wilson Co., 1951).

Paperbound Book Guide for High School (New York: R. R. Bowker Co). An annual publication.

TEACHER'S AID

A. Jingles and Poems for Choral Reading in the Primary Grades

TWOS

Why are lots of things in twos?
Hands on clocks, gloves and shoes
Scissors blades and water taps,
Collar studs and luggage straps,
Walnut shells, and pigeon's eggs,
Arms and eyes and ears and legs—
Will you kindly tell me who's
So fond of making things in twos?

—John Drinkwater

THE ELEPHANT'S SKIN

I think they had no pattern
When they cut out the elephant's skin
Some places it needs letting out
And others taking in!

—Edna Baecker

THE BEAR

"I think," said the bear,
With a mighty yawn,
"That it's time for my winter's sleep."
So he set his alarm clock
for half past spring
And curled himself up in a heap.

—Cushman Mitchell

THE SEASONS

Spring is showery, flowery, bowery;
Summer: hoppy, croppy, poppy;
Autumn: wheezy, sneezy, freezy;
Winter: slippy, drippy, nippy.

MY SHADOW

My shadow is a funny fellow
He never wears bright green or
    yellow,
He dresses all in black you see
And never wanders far from me.

—Cox

SNOW

The snow fell softly all the night
It made a blanket soft and white
It covered houses, flowers, and
    ground,
But did not make a single sound.

—Alice Wilkins

DAWN

Night folded up the stars
And put them all away
A rooster woke the sun up.
And then—it was day!

—Alfred Tooke

CONSCIENCE

The jar on the shelf
Was full of jam;
It isn't now—
But I am.

The jar looked happy,
I never knew
That it felt queer—
But I do.

THIS OLD MAN

This old man,
He played one.
He played nicknack on my thumb.
Nicknack, paddy whack
Give a dog a bone.
This old man came rolling home.

This old man
He played two
He played nicknack on my shoe
Nicknack, paddy whack
Give a dog a bone.
This old man came rolling home.

This old man,
He played three
He played nicknack on my knee,
Nicknack, paddy whack,
Give a dog a bone.
This old man came rolling home.

This old man,
He played four,
He played nicknack on the floor
Nicknack, paddy whack
Give a dog a bone,
This old man came rolling home.

THE REASON

Rabbits and squirrels
Are furry and fat
And all of the chickens
Have feathers, and that
Is why when it's raining
They need not stay in
The way children do
Who have only their skin.

—Aldis

LAWN MOWER

I'm the gardener today
I push the lawn mower across the grass
Zuzz, wish, zuzz, wish.
I'm the lawn's barber.
I'm cutting its green hair short.
I push the lawn mower across the grass
Zuzz, wissh, zuzz, wissh.

—Baruch

MERRY-GO-ROUND

I climbed up on the merry-go-round
And it went round and round
I climbed up on a big brown horse
And it went up and down
Around and around
And up and down
Around and around
And up and down
I sat up high on a big brown horse
And rode around on the merry-go-round
and rode around
And round
And round.

RIDING

I ride on the trolley,
   I ride on the train,
I ride in the sunshine,
   I ride in the rain.

I ride in the auto,
   I ride on my bike,
I ride in my wagon
   With Bobbie and Mike.

I ride on my kiddy-car
   Morning and noon;
If I had an airship
   I'd ride to the moon.

I'd better go walking
   To see how it feels;
Or my poor lazy feet
   May turn into wheels.

           —Mabel Walton

FLOWERS

A little yellow cup
   A little yellow frill
A little yellow star
   And that's a daffodil.

The golden crocus reaches up
To catch a sunbeam
In her cup.

Tulips,
orange,
red,
and pink,
Hold honey and dew
For fairies to drink.

A KITE

I often sit and wish that I
Could be a kite up in the sky
And ride upon the breeze and go
Whichever way I chanced to blow.

B. Poetry Selections

1. Poetry to Read Aloud (selected for rhythm, humor, narrative):

Aldis, Dorothy	*The Clown*
Anonymous	*Whisky Frisky*
Frost, Robert	*The Road Not Taken*
Fyleman, Rose	*I Think Mice Are Nice*
Herford, Oliver	*The Elf and the Dormouse*
Jacques, Florence P.	*There Once Was a Puffin*
Masefield, John	*Sea Fever*
Milne, A. A.	*Aneezles*
Richards, Laura E.	*Antonio*
	Eletelephony
Roberts, Elizabeth M.	*The Woodpecker*
Rossetti, Christina	*Who Has Seen the Wind*
Stevenson, Robert Louis	*My Shadow*
Tippett, James S.	*Trains*
Wordsworth, William	*Daffodils*

2. Poems Suited to Dramatization:

Browning, Robert	*The Pied Piper of Hamelin*
Emerson, Ralph Waldo	*Concord Hymn*
Taylor, Ernest Laurence	*Casey at the Bat*
Von Chamisso, Albert	*A Tragic Story*

3. Poems Which Lend Themselves to Pantomime:

Hunt, Leigh	*Abou Ben Adhem*
Longfellow, Henry Wadsworth	*The Village Blacksmith*
Saxe, John Godfrey	*The Blind Men and the Elephant*
Trowbridge, John Townsend	*Evening at the Fair*
Whittier, John Greenleaf	*In School Days*

4. Poems Suited to Puppet Shows:

Ballad	*Robin Hood and Little John*
Browning, Robert	*The Pied Piper of Hamelin*
Cary, Phoebe	*The Leak in the Dike*
Field, Eugene	*The Duel*

5. Poems Suited for Shadow Plays:

Herford, Oliver	*The Elf and the Dormouse*
Lear, Edward	*The Owl and the Pussycat*
Longfellow, Henry Wadsworth	*The Courtship of Miles Standish*
Moore, Clement Clarke	*The Night Before Christmas*

6. Holiday Poems:

Child, Lydia Maria	*Thanksgiving Day*
Chute, Marchette	*Birthdays*
Longfellow, Henry Wadsworth	*Christmas Bells*
Stevenson, Robert Lewis	*At the Seaside*

7. Fun Poems:

Burgess, Gelett	*The Purple Cow*
Carryl, Charles Edward	*The Plaint of the Camel*
Lear, Edward	*The Owl and the Pussycat*
Richards, Laura E.	*Eletelephony*
Stevenson, Robert Louis	*Mr. Nobody*

C. Books on Poetry and Verse (for Primary and Intermediate Grades)

Aldis, Dorothy	*All Together*
Behn, Harry	*The Little Hill*
	The Windy Morning
Belloc, Hilaire	*Cautionary Verses*
Benet, Rosemary and Stephen	*A Book of Americans*
Blake, William	*Songs of Innocence*
Eliot, T. S.	*Old Possum's Book of Practical Cats*
Farjeon, Eleanor	*Sing for Your Supper*
Field, Eugene	*Poems of Childhood*
Field, Rachel	*Taxis and Toadstools*
Frasconi	*The Snow and the Sun*
Gilbert, W. S.	*The Bab Ballads*
Lear, Edward	*The Complete Nonsense Book*
Manning, Saunders	*A Bundle of Ballads*
Masefield, John	*Salt-Water Poems and Ballads*
Milne, A. A.	*When We Were Very Young*
	Now We Are Six
	The World of Christopher Robin
Nash, Ogden	*The New Nutcracker Suite*
Reeves, James	*The Wandering Moon*
Rossetti, Christina	*Sing-Song*
Stevenson, Robert Louis	*A Child's Garden of Verses*

D. Anthologies

Adshead, Gladys & A. Duff	*An Inheritance of Poetry*
Auslander, Joseph & F. Hill	*The Winged Horse Anthology*
Brewton, John	*Under the Tent of the Sky*
	Gaily the Parade
Day-Lewis, Cecil	*The Echoing Green*

Ferris, Helen	*Favorite Poems, Old and New*
Garnett, Eve	*A Book of the Seasons*
Graham, Eleanor	*A Puffin Book of Verse*
	A Puffin Quartet of Poets
Nash, Ogden	*The Moon Is Shining Bright as Day*
Opie, Iona and Peter	*The Oxford Dictionary of Nursery Rhymes*
Thompson, Blanche	*Silver Pennies*

E. Books Containing Nonsense Verse:

Carroll, Lewis	*Alice's Adventures in Wonderland*
	Through the Looking Glass
Charles, Robert Henry	*Roundabout Turn*
Lear, Edward	*The Jumblies and Other Nonsense Verses*
Rhys, Ernest	*Book of Nonsense Verses, Prose and Pictures*
Richards, Laura E.	*Tirra Lirra*

An excellent book for suggestions in specific lesson planning in poetry for the primary grades is Rosalind Hughes' book *Let's Enjoy Poetry* (Boston: Houghton Mifflin Co., 1966).

F. Selections for Choral Speaking:

1. Refrain:

Anonymous	*Gallop Away*
	Grasshopper Green
	Poor Old Woman
de la Mare, Walter	*The Cupboard*
Lear, Edward	*The Owl and the Pussycat*
Milne, A. A.	*Shoes and Stockings*
Stevenson, Robert Louis	*The Wind*
Tennyson, Alfred Lord	*Bugle Song*

2. Line-a-child:

Anonymous	*Monday's Child*
	The Squirrel
Burnham, Maude	*Farmer's Day*
Chute, Marchette	*Undersea*
Farjeon, Eleanor	*Boys' Names*
	Girls' Names
Greenaway, Kate	*School Is Over*
Hopper, Queenie	*Amy Elizabeth Armuntrude Annie*
Kilmer, Joyce	*Trees*

Mathias, Eileen	*Zoo Manners*
Mother Goose	*Solomon Grundy*
Rands, William B.	*Godfrey Gordon Gustavus Gore*
Tippet, James	*Trains*

3. Antiphonal:

Bennett, Henry H.	*The Flag Goes By*
Bennett, Rowena	*Conversation Between Mr. and Mrs. Santa Claus*
Coatsworth, Elizabeth	*"Who Are You?" Asked the Cat of the Bear*
Cole, Charlotte D.	*The Spider's Web*
Fyleman, Rose	*Momotara*
Lawson, Marie	*Halloween*
Milne, A. A.	*Puppy and I*
Mother Goose	*Baa, Baa, Black Sheep*
Richards, Laura E.	*The Monkeys and the Crocodile* *"Talents Differ"*
Rossetti, Christina	*What Does the Bee Do?*

4. Unison:

Austin, Mary	*Grizzly Bear*
Burgess, Gelett	*The Purple Cow*
Coatsworth, Elizabeth	*He Who Has Never Known Hunger*
Conklin, Hilda	*Weather*
de la Mare, Walter	*Poor Tired Tim*
Mother Goose	*Daffadowndilly*
Nash, Ogden	*Nonsense Verses*
Rossetti, Christina	*Who Has Seen the Wind?*
Stevenson, Robert Louis	*The Swing* *Windy Nights*
Teasdale, Sara	*The Coin*

G. Selections for Choral Speaking of Prose
  1. Children's stories such as Wanda Gage *Millions of Cats* to be used as refrain speaking.
  2. The Bible:
     (a) Psalms
     (b) Beatitudes
  3. Gettysburg Address
  4. Desiderata

Consider the following statements. Do you agree or disagree with them? What other reasons can you give for encouraging children to read mythology?

Greek mythology should be included in children's literature because

(1) The music and rhythm of its poetry express the nature of a people gifted with a fine and artistic soul;

(2) Our own thought and art are in great part a heritage from the civilization of Greece;

(3) The stories provide entertainment and act as a stimulus to the child's imagination.

In light of the statements regarding the fable in this chapter, how would you evaluate the inclusion of myths and fables in your language texts?

13

Creativity in
Language Teaching

A Story

This chapter begins with a story. The story began when, as a supervisor of student teachers, I walked into a classroom to watch a student teacher present a lessson. The student teacher was extremely enthusiastic about her school, class, and resident teacher, so I had been anticipating the visit with great expectancy. I arrived at the school a few minutes before class was to begin and went directly to the classroom.

The classroom was unlocked, so I walked in to find some inconspicuous place to sit. No one was in the room, and as I took in the details of the physical environment, I began to wonder if the student teacher had been hearing any of the points I had been so deftly pursuing in my lectures! The bulletin boards were not skillfully captioned, nor were they carefully arranged in terms of color scheme, design, or even the information being presented. The desks were in five long rows of eight as though the teacher had never discovered that modern desks are movable and that a great variety of desk arrangements are possible and necessary to facilitate classroom discussion, small group discussion, group activities, and a number of individual activities that require specific arrangements.

Near the seat which I had taken in the back part of the room, a table was piled high with papers of a variety of shapes and sizes. I remembered my lecture on the necessity of good housekeeping in the classroom and wondered how such an able student could have missed my clearly articulated principles!

"How could a good student teacher be enthusiastic about *this* classroom? Well, of course, it must be the teacher—she must be so charming that the student has been completely blinded to the appearance of the classroom!" So ran my thoughts as the class of sixth graders began to fill the room.

They came in as sixth graders would be expected to enter a classroom—breathless, full of vitality, a happy confusion of excited voices and noisy shoes. One boy, in particular, caught my attention immediately. In shoes chosen unquestionably for their ear shattering effect, he clumped past me and fell into a desk in the corner opposite my seat.

Now the door opened and the student teacher and resident teacher entered. The resident teacher was a very plain woman, nothing noteworthy about her appearance, who moved quite unobstrusively to her desk—squarely in front of the class.

"Good morning, John." she called out, and the returning "Good morning, Mrs. _____," left me reeling with "Good morning, Miss Dove," ringing in my mind as I watched her take roll call and thought, "Oh no! A teacher can take roll with a sweep of her eyes. Why should this kind of time be wasted when there are so many important things that children could be doing in these first precious five or ten minutes of the school day?"

After roll call the teacher stood and introduced the student teacher, preparing the class for the special lesson in which they were about to participate. She did this with great skill and quiet dignity, and for the first time since I had entered the classroom door, I felt a ray of hope.

After the introduction, the resident teacher came back to sit beside me and began to talk to me, which of course is something just not done during a student teacher's lesson. I tried to be pleasant, at least civil, as I gave her a frozen smile before turning to look straight ahead toward the student teacher, in a studied pose of utter concentration.

It was no use. She began to thumb noisily through a stack of papers on the table. The student teacher, meanwhile, was moving along with great confidence and with the attention of every child in the classroom. Suddenly, the rattling of paper subsided, and a sheet was placed in front of me. With feigned total absorption in the student teacher, I ignored the paper. I felt the eyes of the resident teacher on me, and I also felt her resignation combined with patient assurance that I would read when the opportunity provided itself—and so she sat and waited. Finally, in an attitude of combined desperation and exasperation at the insensitivity and lack of awareness of this "clod" who dared to call herself a teacher, I looked down, and this is what I read:

LONELINESS

Loneliness is a haunted passage straight
Through a deep black forest
Where nobody has ever ventured except me.
And as I walk down this passage
Strange ghosts haunt my thoughts.
Hurt from sorrow and pain that
Wander endlessly in my mind,
I feel as though I have no destiny
Or love to accompany me.
I walk in endless pain.

I was impressed, and the teacher had watched every movement as my immobile glare had changed to startled incredulity. I looked at her. She was waiting, eyes shining, for my response, and she pointed to the "hulk" who was sitting across from me in the corner. My eyes registered further surprise, and thus reassured that the "old girl" wasn't quite dead yet, she began to rummage quickly through a second stack. This time when she handed me a paper I glanced down at once, and here is the second poem I read:

WINGED DEVILS

The deep of night faded into
A pale grey as the dawn unfolded
And the trees seemed to draw apart.
Towards the west black wings pressed
Against the sky.
All Germany seemed to awake in a hollow cry.
Huge winged devils focused in the twilight
Heaving capsules of terror into
The ransacked streets
In which not one voice lingered.
Minutes later the vibrations faded
And ended at the horizon.
Not a creature murmured.
Darkness fell, hiding the vengeance
That threatens all mankind.

In triumph she nodded again toward the "hulk" and began to pull out artwork that portrayed an unbelievable talent in this area as well. Then she began to put the poetry of other children in my range of vision. The entire class was writing, and writing well. I was amazed at the quality of the poetry written by the boys. Of course, I was hooked. I had taught sixth grade for years and nothing like this had ever come from any of my children, much less from such an obvious problem as the boy in the corner. Oh yes, my bulletin boards were noteworthy, my classroom was neat, and I used all the latest techniques and materials with great skill and pride. My principal pointed to me as a "shining light," and many teachers visited my classroom, but I had never had a child write poetry like this!

At recess time I told the student that her lesson had been fine and that we would discuss it at the college in the afternoon. I don't like to do this—the student teacher is anxious about the supervisor's reactions and deserves to know them at once, if possible, rather than wait and wonder. But I *had* to talk to that resident! I had to know how she got this kind of writing from her students.

"Well," she began, "I really don't know anything about teaching. I'm an English major from Cal (Berkeley), and I'm sure that I do lots of things wrong."

My mind was racing furiously. "This teacher knows nothing about teaching? Just how to teach—that's all! Oh, I do hope that she'll share with me a few of these things she does 'wrong,' so that I can try them and share them with other teachers!"

She continued, "In September I discovered that sixth graders are interested in lots of things that aren't in the curriculum guides. They want to know about death, and war, and loneliness, and their emotions. So, when someone brought up one of these topics I asked if the other members of the class were interested. If the class showed interest, I asked if anyone had any ideas on the topic. I gave the children about five minutes to react; then I told them that I'd see what I could find to extend their ideas. For about a week I brought poetry that dealt with the topic into the classroom and read it to the children for five to ten minutes a day. This poetry was always the poetry of men such as Frost, Keats, Shelley, E. E. Cummings, and Ciardi, so that boys would never think of poetry as sissy or silly. Sometimes a paragraph or brief excerpt of prose from men such as Lincoln, T. S. Eliot, and Churchill helped us to extend our horizons. After each brief reading, the selection was discussed to ensure understanding of what the poet was saying. After a number of short discussion periods, I gave the children a chance to write and tell me what they now thought about the topic. No child had to write. Each child was invited to. If a child did not want to write, he could read or occupy himself in any way he chose. The only stipulation was that he was not to disturb anyone who was writing."

The teacher explained that it was during one of these writing sessions in mid-November that "the hulk" responded to an assignment for the first time since school had opened in September. After the children were involved in writing, he opened his desk, took out a crumpled piece of paper, and went to work with his thoroughly chewed and nearly pointless pencil. It was so very quiet during these periods that the teacher was sure that everyone in the room would hear the pounding of her heart. She tried not to look in his direction, giving only an occasional swift glance as her eyes swept the room, but as she caught him completely absorbed in his labor, she had to hold her breath to calm the rapid rhythm of her excited breathing. Suddenly he was through! He looked the paper over carefully, crumpled it disdainfully, and got up to clump to the wastebasket and throw it in.

After the recess bell rang and the students were dismissed, the teacher dashed to the wastebasket to retrieve the crumpled mess. As she told the story, I thought of my "high standards" for papers which were to be turned in. I insisted on careful handwriting and spelling, and a sincere attempt (whatever that is) at proofreading, correcting errors of capitalization, punctuation, and sentence fragments. Now, here was a teacher groveling in the wastebasket for a chance to communicate with a child.

When she had retrieved and opened the paper, she couldn't read it! Not one thing the boy had written resembled traditional orthography. The next period was an eternity for the teacher, but as the recess bell rang she bent over to ask the boy to remain for just a minute after the others had been dismissed. When they were alone, she showed him the crumpled paper.

"Please, I know that you have written something. I've tried to read it and I can't. Won't you tell me what it says?"

As he told her, she wrote, acting as a scribe in the same way a primary teacher would record a child's story, and she wrote the poem *Loneliness*. She was so moved, astonished, and excited that she literally used the poem as a club, telling the boy that anyone with such great talent was no longer going to sit passively in the classroom. She insisted that he come before school and stay after school, and she worked furiously with him to help him develop the learning tools and skills that he was without. He was, of course, willing to try now—his teacher thought he had merit!

As she worked with him she learned a great deal about him. He had spent all of his school life in the same school. He lived in an attractive house in a fairly middle class neighborhood. His mother had been placed in a mental institution when he was in third grade. His father was a truck driver, and he was left in the care of an older brother when the father was away, or so his father thought. In reality when the father left the brother did too, and the eight-year-old boy wandered from door to door ringing doorbells. Mothers opened doors and upon seeing who was there closed them quickly. In addition to the magnificent vocabulary which is evident in the poetry, this child had another vocabulary, acquired from his truck driver father and older brother, and mothers did not want the language of their children thus contaminated. Teachers had for years commiserated with each other over this child and the mere mention of his name in the faculty room brought forth spontaneous combustion! Had this child experienced loneliness by the time he was twelve years old? In a most complete and remarkable way.

I wish there were a happy ending to this story. Unfortunately one year's patient pedagogy could not make up for five wasted years, and when the year-end tests were given the boy placed below average. He was placed in a class with children who had made similar scores on the tests, and he immediately became disheartened. When he moved from the classroom to one of California's penal institutions, society suffered a tragic loss of talent.

There is no desire to place blame in the telling of this incident. My only reason for telling this tale is to help beginning teachers to understand the preciousness of human beings and the real nature of teaching. Methods and techniques do indeed make life run smoothly for the teacher, but getting children to respond to their experiences is the heart of teaching. This great teacher was not defeated by what happened to the boy outside the classroom or in other years, and she made every effort to relate as completely as possible to each child she taught. How proud I was of the student teacher who had recognized the qualities of a great teacher in spite of the narrow picture which I had been painting. This resident teacher saw teaching as discerning rather than dismissing, as sharing rather than demanding, and as instructing rather than telling. She recognized teaching as taking the responsibility of organizing and presenting materials in such fashion that children could discover information and develop skills rather than assigning and placing the burden of learning on the children.

Children and Poetry

Let me share with you another delightful poem, this one dictated by a six-year-old kindergarten child:

TWO TEA-PARTIES

Molly and I made cookies yesterday
(Molly's Mandy's daughter, and Mandy washes for us)
We rolled out the dough,
And rolled it,
And rolled it,
And then made little cookie stars from it,
And pushed them in the oven.
When they came out all nice and brown,
Molly put some on a yellow plate
And put some milk in a blue pitcher,
And Teddy and I had a party
Under the cottonwoods along the canal.

Last night, when I was in bed,
The fairies were having a tea-party.
But they were awfully messy.
They spilt the milk from the blue pitcher
All across the sky,
And dropped cookie stars from the yellow moon-plate.
And then someone—
Someone much bigger than Molly—
Took a big dark cloud and washed the sky.
I heard the water dripping all night,
And when I awoke this morning,
Wasn't the sky clean?

> (Oral story told by a kindergarten girl,
> submitted by Hetti Lou Downing)

Remarkable, you say? Yes, indeed! But even more remarkable is the fact that this child had a teacher who was "tuned in" to listen to such stories. How many busy teachers would have interrupted after the second "and rolled it," with "That's very nice dear, but you run on outside now while I get the activity centers ready for the children. Perhaps you can tell your story to the class later!"

Two Tea-Parties was recorded by a teacher, Mrs. Hetti Lou Downing, who was herself a writer of poetry. Here is just one of her poems:

FAMILIAR PATHS

How many times I've walked the way
Along this road which leads me down
The mountainside and past the creek,
Across the bridge, and into town.
I know the names upon each gate,
Each little garden that I pass,
Each friendly path, each stately tree,
Each fragrant rose upon the grass.
And yet I know that I could walk
This way a thousand times or more
And never really know my town
Until I've looked beyond each door
And found each heart that dwells within,
And lingered long enough to share
His overflowing bowl of joy,
Or bitter cup of black despair.
    And so
    I seek to know
    my neighbor's heart.

(First verse of a poem
by Hetti Lou Downing)

Obviously a creative, sensitive teacher is going to be aware of creative possibilities in others, and I have discovered in working with teachers that they are, for the most part, an extremely sensitive and creative group. This is doubtless the reason that most teachers have chosen their profession. Teaching provides an opportunity for creativity that is unequaled. Creative approaches to working with individuals, with materials, with content, and with organizing and presenting information are not only desirable but absolutely essential to good teaching. No two children respond to an experience in exactly the same way, and the teacher is constantly changing and enhancing learning experiences.

Here is a seasonal poem written by a teacher in a night class in creative writing.

AUTUMN'S CHILD

Last week the Autumn sent to me
A flask of blood-red burgundy.
And penned in russet words was this:
"Remember our October's tryst."

And I sent back a sun-drenched jot
To let Fall know I'd not forgot.
"Could I forget my month of birth!"
October-forget, I'm part of earth.
My birthstone flashing opal fire
Vies Autumn's opulent attire.

The quiet haze, the flaming tree,
The fragrant mists are part of me.
And more things, too, myself define
And drown my soul in Autumn's wine.

The grapes brought low, emitting musk
In day's last warmth that parts at dusk,
The soaring golden aspen leaf
Lifts domed skies—blue beyond belief.

I've harvested the summer sun
And stored the songs the grass has sung.
And all earth's fragrant nourishment
Has filled my drab husk past content.
Till, bursting with this wealth—sky piled!
I thrust out new—an Autumn Child.

—Anonymous

True, this is perhaps the most exquisitely written poem that I have received from a teacher, but had I the time and space, I could share many delightful bits of writing from teachers.

The Creative Act

David Holbrook [1] states that whole powers of intuition are developed by creative work and in response to creative work. He believes that children working in clay or with music, watching the creative work of others, or listening to others making music, are intuitively learning about the inward life. For this reason the activity of creating, from the first expressions of children to creative-writing courses in the universities, is essential. Writing creatively is a way of understanding experience. Experience and expression are the same thing, in the way that clay and form become the final product. Experience is therefore not complete until one has given form to it through words and invested it with something of oneself.

One teacher tells of a third grade child who was a nonentity in a class of thirty-six. The child was quiet, unobtrusive, obedient, an average student with nothing to make her noticeable. She became interested and responded with enthusiasm when the teacher read poetry to the class. The teacher's first invitation to the children to write brought this response from her!

> When Ann and I go out to walk
> We hold each other's hand and talk
> Of all the things we mean to do
> When Ann and I are forty-two.

Even though this poem was not original with the child (an A. A. Milne poem), it was satisfying to her to have been able to share something she knew and loved with the class, and her second contribution, her own, displayed great sensitivity.

> If you were a bird and lived on high,
> You'd lean on the wind when the wind came by.
> You'd say to the wind when it took you away,
> That's where I wanted to go today. [2]

Christians can read into this poem the same spiritual significance that many haiku contain for the Buddhist religion. Probably the child did not intend all of this deep meaning—but it is there, none the less.

[1] David Holbrook, *The Exploring Word* (London: Cambridge University Press, 1967).

[2] Laura Walker, pupil of Janice Siegel (Grade 3, Serra School, Cupertino School District, San Jose, Calif.).

Poetry, says Cecil Day-Lewis, poet laureate of England, makes it possible for people to explore their inner life, and self-discovery is the most important of all human discoveries.[3]

Poetry can be instrumental in illuminating and giving quality to life. Reading poetry to children about their own experiences helps them to satisfy their curiosity about the world in which they live, provides variety that encourages growth in different abilities and capacities, and also encourages them to continue to reach out for knowledge and understanding.

If children are to express themselves poetically, they will need to become genuinely aware of themselves and their environments. Reading poetry to them will help them accomplish this awareness by awakening dormant senses and helping them to discover new sense experiences. Teachers can also snatch ideas that are expressed creatively by the children and challenge them to further develop these ideas.

Writing poetry comes last and requires a careful sifting of words, because poetry distills the essence of an impression to its clearest, purest form.

Teachers can develop sensitivity to the truly creative expressions of children by building their own background of knowledge and appreciation of the wide variety of creative expressions available in various media. The teacher who is familiar with the paintings of Lautrec as well as Reubens, with the poetry of Dylan Thomas as well as that of Longfellow, and with the music of Benjamin Britten as well as Bach will be more likely to appreciate the unusual when it is found in children.

Developing Creativity

Developing creativity has long been considered one of the important tasks of an elementary school. Teachers, however, have sometimes thought of creativity as a trait to be developed only in connection with stories which children write and pictures they paint, rather than a quality which can infuse all aspects of life.

Richard DeMille [4] advocates a dimensional approach to the understanding of creativity. He states that aptitude traits are found

---

[3] Cecil Day-Lewis, "The Poem and the Lesson," *Elementary English*, vol. 45, no. 4 (April, 1968).

[4] Richard DeMille, "Creativity Is Illusive," *News Briefs*, California Teachers Association, vol. 5, no. 4 (October, 1964).

in varying degrees throughout the population, and that everyone has some degree—small, moderate, or great—of each trait. DeMille points out that creative thinking characteristically involves the ability to change one's approach to a problem, to express ideas that are both relevant and unusual, to go beyond the immediate situation, and to define and redefine the problem or any part of it. Such abilities are not limited to art or science but are found in every kind of human activity.

Celia Stendler isolates some factors which contribute to creativity.[5] Using Terman's famous study of gifted children and his earlier study of Sir Francis Galton as her evidence, Stendler lists *intelligence* as perhaps the most important genetic factor contributing to creativity. She points out that the estimated intelligence of the creative people of history has been high. Her example follows:

> Terman's study estimated that the intelligence quotient of Sir Francis Galton, the English scientist, between the ages of 3 and 8 years was "not far from double his actual age." Galton, taught by his sister Adele, herself a mere child, knew his capital letters by 12 months; could read a little book at 2½ years, and was able to read any English book, say all the Latin substantives, adjectives and active verbs, read French a little, and multiply by any number from 2 through 11 before he was five.

Stendler cautions that not all people thought to be highly intelligent on the basis of intelligence test scores are creative. In Terman's study of gifted children, which included over 1500 boys and girls with I.Q.s of 135 or over, as measured by the Stanford-Binet Intelligence Test, not one person made a highly creative contribution to society, although many became superior adults, educationally, vocationally, and socially.

Torrance and Getzels report that abilities related to creativity tend to be unrelated to or to have only a low relationship with the types of items included in our current intelligence tests.[6] They estimate that if talent is to be located on the basis of I.Q. score, only thirty percent of those with high creative ability will be found.

A second factor contributing to creativity is *energy*. Highly cre-

---

[5] Celia B. Stendler, *Teaching in the Elementary School* (New York: Harcourt, Brace & World, Inc., 1958), pp. 343–348.

[6] E. Paul Torrance, "Explanations in Creative Thinking in the Early School Years: A Progressive Report," and J. W. Getzels and P. W. Jackson, "The Highly Intelligent and the Highly Creative Adolescent: A Summary of Research Findings," *The Third University of Utah Research Conference on the Identification of Creative Scientific Talent*, ed., Calvin W. Taylor (Salt Lake City: University of Utah Press, 1959).

ative people are capable of producing many ideas in a single unit of time. They have a high energy level.

Another factor found in creative people is *special ability and aptitude*. Patterns of high-order ability frequently appear in students at the secondary school level. A child who is gifted in the language field, for example, may read widely, learn foreign languages easily, show an aptitude for history and related subjects, and write well.

Brandwein [7] studied gifted students in science and listed some personality characteristics he found prevalent in the students. He described the more creative students as quiet, reflective, and inward-looking. They showed a greater tendency toward introversion than the norm and were persistent and questing. Their outside hobbies consisted of science projects, chess, music, and serious reading, and they preferred self-initiated projects to social activities.

Foshay [8] describes an important characteristic of the creative process as *openness* and defines it as deliberately opening the self to new experiences. Openness involves suspension of judgment, since to judge is to structure. The creative person apparently accepts situations in which he does not understand everything; he tolerates gaps and lack of closure and uses these to formulate hypotheses.

The last personality characteristic associated with creativity to be discussed in this chapter is *lack of conformity*. Of necessity, the creative individual must depart from the conventional. If to be creative means to make form out of what is formless, then the creative individual has to discover new solutions, forms, and processes. When one is too concerned about what others will think of him, he will be unwilling to depart from the safe, accepted patterns of behavior. There is an important difference between the individual who departs from the conventional because he has an original idea which must be tested and the professional nonconformist. The professional nonconformist ignores the conventional simply because he wants to be different. He is really a conformist who likes the art, literature, music, and hair styles admired by other professional nonconformists with whom he identifies.

To be creative in a society which stresses conformity requires a

[7] Paul F. Brandwein, *The Gifted Student As Future Scientist* (New York: Harcourt, Brace & World, Inc., 1955).

[8] Arthur W. Foshay, "The Creative Process Described," *Creativity in Teaching*, ed., Alice Miel (Belmont, Calif.: Wadsworth Publishing Co., Inc., 1961), pp. 22–32.

great amount of self-discipline. Discipline includes inhibition, limitation, rigor, ordering, codifying, following the rules, and being accountable and responsible. Creative people work hard and unremittingly, and although the work may be unpleasant, the drive to accomplish the goal reaches beyond all distracting or discomforting influences.

In summary, although, according to recent research,[9] there is no valid way to spot highly creative children, the following characteristics reflect the kind of behavior teachers might look for in children who are considered to be highly creative:

1. Awareness of the existence of problems and desire to solve them
2. Ability to produce many novel ideas in a given period of time
3. Persistence in the face of frustration or distraction
4. Ability to use initial failure as a step toward success
5. Preference for individual rather than group activities

Most of these behavior characteristics can be taught. The highly creative child is frequently not near the top in school achievement. Teachers can examine their programs to determine whether or not the learning experiences being provided offer opportunity for the development of positive attitudes toward life and learning for each child. Helping each child to develop fully his potential for creative living is a tremendous responsibility and there are no clever gimmicks or unusual activities that can remove the responsibility from the teacher. The learning environment will nourish or stifle individual growth for each child.

QUESTIONS FOR STUDY

1. How can unusual contributions of children be rewarded in the classroom setting?
2. What kinds of activities can be provided for both boys and girls to encourage them to enjoy art, music, poetry, and the various areas of the sciences?
3. How can creative children be helped to adjust to group situations?
4. What methods and materials can be used to stimulate a classroom atmosphere which is conducive to creative living?

[9] Jacob W. Getzels and Philip W. Jackson, *Creativity and Intelligence* (New York: John Wiley & Sons, Inc., 1962), pp. 13–132.

SUGGESTIONS FOR FURTHER READING

Heinrich, June S., *Creativity in the Classroom*, Unit Two: SRA Teacher Extension Service (Chicago: Science Research Associates, 1964). A unit of study for use in in-service programs.

Kneller, George F., *The Art and Science of Creativity* (New York: Holt, Rinehart & Winston, Inc., 1965).

Mearns, Hughes, *Creative Power: The Education of Youth in the Creative Arts*, 2d ed. (New York: Dover Publications, Inc., 1958).

Taylor, Calvin W., ed., *Creativity: Progress and Potential* (New York: McGraw-Hill Book Co., 1964).

Torrance, E. Paul, *Guiding Creative Talent* (Englewood Cliffs, N.J.: Prentice-Hall, Inc., 1962).

TEACHER'S AID

Encourage originality on the part of children in *all* classroom experiences. Although children often enjoy writing in privacy, stories are invented to share with others. Because of previous experiences with dictating and telling ideas, stories, and poems, children often bring writing to the teacher. If the writing is accepted with warmth and appreciation, children will continue to write. Such writing is not "assigned" or "collected," just encouraged. When the teacher receives a story, he does not talk of periods, paragraphs, spelling, or neat writing. He accepts the contribution eagerly, reads it, and expresses appreciation.

If the child wishes the teacher to read the story to the class, he should do so. The teacher might then encourage the child to read future stories to the class, if the stories seem to contain something that the class will appreciate.

A class book that holds the original writing of the children provides some children an added incentive for writing. If the teacher wants to type a child's story for the class book, permission should be asked of the child, and spelling and form should be corrected, so that it will be accurate for the sake of those who read it. The child who is able to rewrite his own story in his own best handwriting, after the teacher has discussed with him necessary writing conventions including punctuation and spelling, should be encouraged to do so.

For suggestions for creative activities to use with children see:

Applegate, Mauree, *Easy in English* (New York: Harper & Row, Publishers, 1960). See the Cupboard of Ideas at the end of each chapter.

Myers, R. E., and Torrance, E. Paul, *Just Imagine* (Boston: Ginn and Co., 1961). This is one of a series of workbooks designed to stimulate creativity.

Tiedt, Sidney W., and Tiedt, Iris M., *Creative Writing Ideas* (San Jose, Calif.: Contemporary Press, 1964).

14

Teaching English
as a Second Language

Teaching English as a Second Language, also known as TESL, is the procedure employed in countries where English is used for all the formal schooling of children except native language classes in the upper elementary and high school grades, and where English is the language of government and trade. In such countries, non-native speakers of English use this language as their linguistic bridge to the outside world in the areas of science, technology, research, philosophy, art, and culture. The national language of such countries is considered to be very important also, and the two languages complement each other. Often they perform different functions, and sometimes their functions overlap. Both languages are important.

TESL techniques can make a significant contribution in helping elementary schoolteachers meet the language needs of bilingual children in their classrooms. Knowing something of the history, principles, and goals of second language teaching will help teachers use the techniques with skill and purpose. Many TESL techniques can also be applied to the child who needs to learn the English used in the classroom as a second dialect.

Approaches to Language Teaching in American Schools

The traditional approach to teaching a foreign language is called the grammar-translation method. In this approach, students define parts of speech, memorize conjugations, declensions, and grammar rules, and translate selections, using a bilingual dictionary or glossary. Although translation is a valuable skill in itself, it cannot be equated with any of the skills of understanding, speaking, reading, and writing a language. Students who have devoted years to this kind of study of a foreign language are rarely able to use the language with any facility.

As a reaction against the grammar-translation approach, a reform was instigated in Europe called the direct method. This method attempts to use the language in meaningful situations. It substitutes language contact for grammar recitation and language use for translation. The direct method, also called the natural or oral method, attempts to associate words and sentences with their meaning through demonstration, dramatization, and pointing.

The direct method is based on the assumption that learning a foreign language is like learning the native language, and so it exposes the student directly to the language for imitation and practice. This procedure has not proven to be very effective because the student already has recourse to his own language and therefore does not need the new language to express his desires. In addition to having no real motivation for learning the language, the student is further hampered by having to perceive the new language through previously ingrained habit patterns of his native tongue. Therefore, he has not learned the language with the facility and ease hoped for. Nevertheless, the method is still being used as a means of teaching a reading knowledge of foreign languages.

After the Second World War the importance of teaching a foreign language for full communication was recognized. This recognition gave rise to the linguistic approach of foreign language teaching. The linguistic approach emphasizes the imitation and memorization of basic conversational sentences used by native speakers. It also describes the distinctive elements of the structure of the language: intonation, morphology, and syntax. Pattern practice, practice of specific grammar points, has been developed to establish and build patterns. Teaching materials include:

1. Basic conversation for memorization.

2. Structural notes to help the student perceive and produce the speech and sentence patterns of the foreign language.

3. Pattern practice exercises to establish the patterns as habits.

4. Language laboratory materials for oral–aural practice so that the student can listen to and repeat the language.

5. An opportunity to use the language in communication rather than translation.[1]

Accepted Principles of Second Language Teaching

Because of the increased interest in language and language learning and the continued improvement of electronic devices, the changes in language teaching already in motion will undoubtedly continue. A scientific view of language and learning recognizes the complexity of language, ranging from the acquisition of simple automatic skills to an understanding of abstract conceptual and esthetic meaning. All of this learning, occurring in the same utterances, involves hundreds of articulatory changes and grammatical and lexical selections per minute. Therefore, any single development could not be expected to solve all the problems of language learning. Scientific investigation and training must continue to apply the best that is known to language teaching and language learning.

The following points of view are presently accepted and recommended as guides for second language teaching:

1. A study of the language should begin with oral activity. Reading and writing should be deferred until reasonable mastery has been achieved orally.

2. Dialogue, taken from forms naturally used by native speakers, provides an excellent vehicle for presenting conversational speed, intonation patterns and stress, terms, and structures. Dialogue presented in textbooks in phonetically based transcription may be accompanied by idiomatic translation into the student's mother tongue.

3. Audio-visual aids are used extensively in second language teaching.

4. The teacher should set the quality of speech by being a good model. If the teacher is not a native speaker of English, he should provide the student with tapes or records of native speakers or if possible bring native speakers into the classroom.

5. Learners may begin early to read previously memorized materials, but reasonable control of phonological and grammatical patterns should precede reading new material.

[1] Robert Lado, *Language Teaching: A Scientific Approach* (New York: McGraw-Hill Book Co., 1964).

6. The framework of teaching English as a second language involves a sequence of structural pattern logically arranged and selected on the basis of a contrastive analysis of the mother tongue and English, with emphasis on the patterns known to be most difficult.

7. Drill should be related to the method and content used in the presentation. For example, the structural point to be studied may be introduced and studied in a dialogue and then related to the grammatical drills that follow.

8. A great amount of drill material is essential. Pattern practice includes substitution, minimal pair, transformation, response, and translation drills. Practice should include only a few drills with which students can become quickly familiar.

9. Presentation of new material and drills should be based on real classroom situations whenever possible. Relating language instruction to experience helps bridge the gap between the manipulative use of language to communicating ideas.

10. Teaching pronunciation is an integral part of teaching grammar. Students learn to pronounce by imitating a good model. Although great emphasis is given to pronouncing patterns, separate drills such as minimal pair sound contrasts are used for specific pronunciation problems.

11. The content of the lesson should be the language itself. Statements about the language are given only when needed by the student to help him imitate and practice the new forms correctly. The teacher's role is to guide the student's practice in the language, not to expound in the language or on the language. Cultural values and patterns of native speakers form a significant part of the content from the beginning in second language study.

12. Vocabulary is always presented in cultural and linguistic context. A minimum number of words are introduced in the earlier stages because frequent reintroduction of known items is preferred to the acquisition of a large number of words. Vocabulary selection is based on usefulness and frequency.

13. Writing of orally mastered materials occurs only in the early stages. Later, at more advanced levels, extensive preparation is given for writing exercises.

The preceding points of view regarding the teaching of a second language are based on the nature of language and language learning analyzed by linguists and summarized by Fe R. Dacanay as follows: [2]

(1) Language is speech, not writing.
(2) A language is a set of habits.
(3) The language itself should be taught, not information about it.
(4) The language is what the native speakers say, not what someone thinks they should say.
(5) Languages are different. Each language should be analyzed in terms of its own structure.

Although transformational grammarians are still busy investigating the nature of man that makes it possible for him to learn language and the nature of language that man can learn it, there are some guidelines from the discipline of psychology that provide direction for second language teaching.

First, Gestalt psychology, which affirms that the response of an organism to a situation is a complete whole rather than a sum of the responses to specific elements in the situation, provides the rationale for suggesting that sounds are learned in words which are in turn learned in sentences or situations.

Second, it seems to be more important to link the foreign words with objects, pictures, demonstrations, and actual experiences than with corresponding words in the mother tongue.

Third, learning must be specific. Generalizations about how language behaves are nearly meaningless unless the learner has experienced the phenomenon before he generalizes. The best way to learn a skill is to perform the skill, and it is certainly easier to learn something correctly in the first place than to unlearn and relearn it. This means that free conversation and writing should not be encouraged until the child is ready.

Fourth, people learn through various senses, but sight and hearing seem to be the most efficient for learning. For this reason the use of visual aids is extremely important in teaching a second language.

Last, practice is mandatory, as it provides the opportunity for language performance. Although the types of pattern practice need to vary frequently (thirty minutes should be a maximum for prac-

[2] Fe R. Dacanay and J. Donald Bowen, *Techniques and Procedures in Second Language Teaching* (Quezon City, Philippines: Phoenix Publishing House, 1963).

ticing a single drill), practice seems most effective if spread over longer periods of time. As the learner tires and his native habit patterns begin to break down, the new patterns seem to take on more force and to be substituted at a less conscious level.

The correlation between knowledge about a language and skills in reading and writing is currently under study. Denby[3] reports a recent study which indicated that fifth grade students understood the concepts of structural and generative grammar and that such knowledge enabled them to produce longer syntactic structures of greater complexity and to use a wider variety of transformational operations than students taught traditional grammar. The study concluded that a carefully planned and efficiently taught linguistically oriented language arts program for the upper elementary grades might accelerate the rather unimpressive progress that has been made by traditionally oriented grammatical approaches toward improving children's control of syntax. The emphasis on learning to use the language rather than learning about the language indicates that most authorities agree that effective language learning is concerned with habit formation and performance rather than with knowledge or problem solving, so facility in the use of language must precede learning about it.

Although most children come to school today with greater language facility than ever, the children who come from non-English-speaking homes or bilingual backgrounds find learning English increasingly difficult because of the accelerated language ability of their peers. As nonnative speakers begin to learn English, they are both hearers and speakers. Recognition and discrimination are for them followed by imitation, repetition, and memorization. Many classrooms include children who are nonnative speakers of English, and their language needs require a careful analysis of the native language and English to provide ammunition for a direct attack on the problem areas.

Needs of Spanish-Speaking Pupils Learning English

Learning the sound of a second language is a difficult problem. Habits of pronunciation require an extended program of presentation and practice, because the learner will transfer the sound system

[3] Robert V. Denby, "Linguistics Instruction in Elementary School Classrooms, An NCTE/ERIC Report," *Elementary English*, vol. 46, no. 1 (January, 1969).

of his first language (Spanish) to the second system (English). Some elements and patterns will be similar and need not be taught. However, even when both languages contain the same phonemes there are often phonetic differences within. For example, /d/ in Spanish has two variants. In the first, which occurs initially in a word or after *l* or *n*, as in *doctor* or *ando*, the /d/ is like the English /d/ except farther forward, with the tongue touching the back of the upper teeth instead of the alveolar ridge. The other variant of /d/, occurring in all other positions (*lado, medico*), is formed like the English voiced /th/, as in *the*.

Table 5 shows the contrasts between English and Spanish phonology. The symbol − means that the sound does not exist. The glottal /x/ in Spanish is a kind of guttural /kh/ sound, whereas the /h/ in English is considered to be a voiceless glottal fricative sound by many linguists, although it is shown with the resonants on the chart of English consonant phonemes. This group of resonants contain the sounds which are described by different linguists in a variety of ways.

The elements and patterns that differ structurally from the first language represent the real problems. Spanish speakers learning English have great difficulty with English /ē/ and /i/. Hearing English for years and receiving detailed phonetic explanation with examples do not eliminate the problem. Strategy requires that such problems be brought to consciousness, understood, practiced consciously, and then practiced extensively with attention on communication. Minimal pairs are very helpful for this purpose.

The features that constitute the problems should be emphasized and practiced. Spanish speakers have trouble pronouncing the English beginnings /sp/, /sk/, and /st/, as in *speak, school,* and *study*. They introduce an initial /e/ and produce *espeak, eschool,* and *estudy*. It would be confusing to teach this problem by describing /s/, /p/, /k/, /t/ and the clusters /sp/, /sk/, /st/. The students already know these phonemes and sequences from Spanish, as in *español, escuela, estudiar*. The problem is their occurrence initially without a preceding vowel. This is what the students cannot pronounce and probably do not hear.

By contrasting a description of the sound system of the target language with that of the first language, the problems that need to be taught and the particular features that are difficult are anticipated. Increasing numbers of such comparisons are becoming avail-

TABLE 5

Comparison of English and Spanish Phonemes

ENGLISH CONSONANTS

	Labials		Dentals		Palatals	Velars	
Stops	P			t	ch	k	Vl
(Affricates)	b			d	j	g	Vd
Fricatives		f	th	s	sh	—	Vl
		v	~~th~~	z	zh	—	Vd
Nasals	m			n	—	ng	
Resonants	w		(r)	l	y	h	

Bilabials · Labiodentals · Interdentals · Alveolars

SPANISH CONSONANTS

	Labials		Dentals		Palatals	Velars	
Stops	p		t		ch	k	Vl
(Affricates)	b		d		—	g	Vd
Fricatives		f	—	s	—	x(kh)	Vl
		—	—	—	—	—	Vd
Nasals	m			n	ñ	—	
Resonants	—		r rr l		y	—	

Bilabials · Labiodentals · Interdentals · Alveolars

ENGLISH VOWELS

Simple Nuclei

	Front	Center	Back
High	i	(ɨ)	oo
Mid	e	u	(o)
Low	a	o	au

Complex Nuclei

ē
ā
ī
ō (Mid back)
ū
oy
ou (Low center)

SPANISH VOWELS

/ē/ Front   Back /ū/
/ā/   i   u
       e   o   /ō/
/ā/   a
/o/
Mid

(The symbols are those used in the Roberts English Series.)

able in print and should be studied by teachers. The teacher must also have a thorough understanding of contrastive problems, because dialect and individual differences among students will produce differences in learning.

Sound systems cannot be taught all at once; therefore, the teacher must decide in what order to teach not just the consonant and vowel phonemes, but also intonation, stress, rhythm, tone, juncture, and sequence. These need not be specifically taught to children in kindergarten through third grade.

Since intonation, stress, rhythm, and juncture affect consonants and vowels, they should be taught with consonants and vowels from the beginning where they constitute learning problems. The correlations between pitch, stress, and terminal juncture and vowels and consonants are different in English and Spanish, and, as a result, produce different rhythmic effects. Syllable length and stress do not have the same relationship in Spanish and English. Spanish rhythm tends to give each syllable approximately the same duration of time, whereas English gives the syllable receiving the heaviest stress a greater amount of time. The intonation pattern of a common Spanish statement is low-mid-low in contrast to the English mid-high-low pattern.[4] The following examples of the mid-high-low patterns in English show the relationship between intonation and stress:

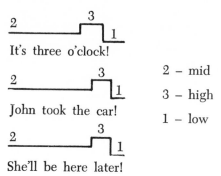

It's three o'clock!

John took the car!

She'll be here later!

2 – mid

3 – high

1 – low

Notice in each case that the high intonation pattern is on the vowel sound carrying primary stress, and the low intonation pattern correlates with the drop in voice or weak stress.

The entire intonation system does not need to be taught. Problems should be selected and taught one at a time, while other in-

[4] Donald L. Fabian, *Essentials of Spanish* (Boston: Houghton Mifflin Co., 1957).

tonations that are not problems may simply be used. The system should not be distorted in an attempt to simplify it. A common intonation pattern represented by 2 3′ 1, as in

$$\overline{2} \quad \overline{\underset{\underline{1}}{\overset{3}{\rceil}}}$$

I need a car

where 2 = mid, 3 = high, 1 = low, or fade-out juncture, and the stress mark on 3 represents the center of prominence or stress, needs to be taught specifically to Spanish speakers learning English.

Intonation, stress, and rhythm in English are complex and constitute major problems for many language backgrounds. With intonation and rhythm, the vowels need to be taught gradually because of their difficulty and frequency. Semivowels such as /r/, /y/, and /w/ should come at the stage when vowels are being taught. A special problem for Spanish speakers is /y/ vs. /j/. Systematic drill on consonants and consonant clusters should be withheld long enough to permit basic work on intonation, rhythm, and the vowels.

One problem should be taught at a time. Progress should be cumulative, using, insofar as possible, what has been previously taught.

Vocabulary problems should be withheld when pupils are concentrating on a pronunciation problem. When an unusual word is needed to illustrate a minimal contrast between phonemes, the word can be taught as form only, not necessarily meaning, although with young children this device must be used sparingly.

When a grammatical problem that needs to be taught involves a pronunciation problem as well, the pronunciation problem should be taught even if it does not fit the order of presentation of the sound system. For example, the automatic alternation of the plural /s/, /z/, / z/ in English, as in *books*, eggs, and boxes, should be taught early enough to facilitate the grammar problem, even if it does not fit neatly into the order of presentation of the consonants and vowels.

When a vocabulary item is necessary to operate a grammatical pattern, and the vocabulary also contains a pronunciation problem, the pronunciation problem should be taught for that word. Only when the speaker is thoroughly familiar with sounds, arrangements, and forms is he ready to center his attention on enlarging his vocabulary. As the learner acquires control of structure he will make conscious choices which will eventually be used habitually and un-consciously. Throughout the study of English the learner will con-centrate on gaining accuracy before striving for fluency.

The personal pronouns in English have to be taught early. This involves pronunciation problems such as /sh/ as in *she* or /z/ as in *his*. The verb *be* also introduces the problem of /z/, as in *is* and *was*.

Although a high degree of audio-comprehension can be obtained with tapes and records, fluency in speaking is another matter. With-out guided imitation, the student who is left to his own devices in a laboratory or simply listening to tapes tends to superimpose the speech habits of his native language on utterances of the target language.

As previously stated, the ability to understand and use a language is the possession of the habits that make up the language. The learner's Spanish habits have been deeply embedded by long prac-tice, correction, and renewed practice under correction. English, to be usable, must also consist of a set of habits which are as deep as the opportunities for practice and correction allow. Modern lin-guists have shown the extent to which language behavior is uncon-scious, not merely the movement of physical organs to produce sounds and sound sequences, but also the manner of signaling grammatical meanings by words, endings, sequence features, certain melodies, timing factors, or stresses. The user of language is usually unaware of any of these at an intellectual level while he is speaking.

The Teacher's Roles

Because the formation of language habits involves practice, cor-rection, and more practice, the teacher needs to understand the stages of recognition, imitation, repetition, variation, and selection in language use. To build language habits, the teacher must guide the pupils to a thorough control of a very limited part of the new language being taught. This will provide a firm, secure foundation for later rapid progress.

In the development of the pupils' first new language habits, the teacher has three indispensable roles. First, he serves as a model for his pupils' imitation. For this role he needs an accurate control of the pronunciation and the sentence structures of the material his pupils are to learn. He need not and should not use any more English in his pupils' hearing than they are to imitate. He may use his tapes as aids, but his own voice supplies freedom from mechanical defects, flexibility, and important facial postures and gestures. Second, the teacher must judge the pupils' accuracy in imitation. As he listens for departures from the correct desired response, he must draw upon theoretical knowledge of the nature of both Spanish and English as well as his control of the desired responses in both languages. His knowledge of the points of conflict between the pupils' native language habits and the structure of the new language will enable him to foresee and understand the pupils' difficulties as well as to determine the appropriate kind and intensity of practice to overcome them.

Spanish speakers learning English will be faced with certain grammatical problems because of structural differences in English and Spanish. First, questions that are signaled in Spanish by intonation contrast are signaled in English by means of word order. Because the Spanish speaker has learned to react to intonation signals and to ignore word order, which in his language is not structurally relevant, he will have to learn different reactions and new responses, and this will be difficult.

Second, the Spanish speaker will frequently omit the pronoun subject in both statements and questions as its inclusion is not necessary in Spanish. When learning to include the pronoun in English, the Spanish speaker will sometimes overcompensate and use two subjects such as, "Mary she called my mother."

Third, the article will often be placed erroneously in front of proper nouns, because Spanish speakers use articles with titles, e.g., *el señor, el professor, el doctor,* and *el presidente,* as well as with many proper nouns.

The teacher's third role is to decide how much teaching and practice is essential for each individual in the class. The length of time during which pupils will hear English incorrectly and imitate inaccurately depends on the amount and kind of difference between the sound systems of English and Spanish and on teaching techniques. It will also vary from pupil to pupil. Throughout the initial stages of practice in discriminating and producing unfamiliar sounds and patterns of rhythm and melody, the pupil is dependent on a teacher who is monitoring to detect errors at the predictable points of difficulty and to direct the needed corrective practice. Certainly contrastive phonology and morphology are important for this. To supplement the text of a beginning class, for example, English word classes that function like Spanish adverbs, prepositions, and conjunctions should be presented and the likenesses pointed out. This kind of presentation can be followed by a comparison drill, which allows the students to match the points of similarity in both languages. Next, the principal differences in word order should be taught, for example, Spanish pronouns usually precede the verb, and adjectives usually follow the verb. In addition, the differences in grammatical structure shown on page 246 should be taught.

Techniques for Teaching a Second Language

There are many techniques for presenting the language to children in situations that approximate normal life experiences so that the structures have meaning to the learners.

Dialogue. First, new terms and new structures can be presented by means of dialogue. The situation around which the dialogue is built can be explained with the use of pictures, puppets, or realia. After the introduction, the dialogue is presented by the teacher or by a few students who have memorized it and are able to do it without error.

Following the presentation, questions are asked to ascertain the degree to which the students understand the dialogue. Next, memorization of the dialogue takes place, and this can be accomplished by:

1. Having the class repeat the lines after each line modeled by the teacher.
2. Having the teacher take one part while the class takes the other.
3. Exchanging roles.
4. Having the class act out the various roles in groups, in rows, and individually.

Repetition is essential to language learning and can be cued by the teacher through questions, directions, or presenting the immediately preceding line of the dialogue and asking the child to repeat the line that follows. If the child is able to learn the dialogue without all of the steps, some of them may be omitted. As children learn more vocabulary and structures, memorization of dialogue will take less time.

English	*Spanish*

NOUNS

Four forms:

	Subject	Possessive
Singular	cat	cat's
Plural	cats	cats'

Two forms, two genders:

	Masculine	Feminine
Singular	niño	niña
Plural	niños	niñas

ADJECTIVES

Three forms:

slow	(positive)
slower	(comparative)
slowest	(superlative)

Two forms, two numbers, two genders:

lento	lenta
más	más
el más lentisimo	or lentisima

PRONOUNS

1 subject form, 1 object form, 2 possessives:

I	me	my	mine
he	him	his	his
you	you	your	yours

1 subject form, ½ prepositional form, ½ verb-object forms, 1 possessive plus status and intimacy:

(I)	(give me)	(with me)	(he loves me)	(my, mine)
yo	dame	conmigo	me quiere	(el) mio
(he)	(him)	(him)	(his)	
el	le	lo	(el) suyo	(de él)
(you-Obj)	(NV + Obj form)	(Ind 3rd Obj)		
tu-ti-te,	vosotres—as, os	se		

usted (es), lo (s), la (s), le (s)

VERBS

1 person, number marked form, 1 mood, 2 simple tenses:

| V | Vs | Ved | Ven | Ving |
| speak | speaks | spoke | spoken | speaking |

3 persons, 2 numbers, 2 moods, 5 simple tenses:

hablo-as-a, -amos-áis-an,
hablaba, hablé, hablaré, .hablaría

It is also important to break sentences up into small sense groups of not more than six syllables for beginning students, since they have difficulty imitating more than six syllables of a new utterance.

The Direct Method. Vocabulary and structure can also be presented by the direct method. This method involves teaching by association an object, an action, or an idea with the word or expression that names, describes, or explains it. This method is the one most often used, because it requires the least amount of preparation on the part of the teachers. The prepositions *in* and *on* can be presented by locating objects in or on desks, tables, or bookshelves in the classroom. There are some aspects of the direct method that deserve consideration. First, there is often no clear-cut division between the presentation and the drill that follows. This creates problems when the drill is not geared to the kind of communication that elicits meaning and approximates realism in language, or when there is no real motivation for repetition. Frequently, the method is combined with other methods to ensure good communication and motivation. An example of the direct method is given at the end of this chapter.

The Picture Story. The picture story provides an effective vehicle for presenting new vocabulary and structures. Pictures can be displayed on the bulletin board before the presentation to arouse interest, or held up at the time of presentation. The pictures must be large enough to be easily seen and should show the action without clutter so that children can interpret the pictures without confusion. The teacher presents the new structures in an identification exercise, moving children from known concepts to the new structure. The story is then presented and followed by specific comprehension questions. Cooperative storytelling follows as the children (1) show the appropriate pictures or point to the appropriate parts of a picture as the story is being retold and (2) take turns telling parts of the story as the pictures are shown.

Poetry and Verse. Poems, rhymes, and light verse can also be used to teach new structures and vocabulary. In using poetry the teacher reads a poem and asks specific check-up questions to test the children's understanding of it. The questions can be followed by a rereading of the poem or sections of the poem until the children can answer the questions accurately. The poem can then be read by the entire class, by groups, and finally by individuals. Memorization will usually automatically follow such procedures because of the number of repetitions. If not, special memorization drills may be used when memorization of the structures has value.

Advertisements. Children learn the jingles and songs used in advertisements almost unconsciously. Because advertisements are so much a part of the lives of pupils, they can be used in a limited manner as a means of presenting new vocabulary and structure. Usually the advertisement text expresses an idea forcefully and in the fewest words possible. Although the artistic layout in newspaper and magazine advertisements can be evaluated to help pupils judge critically the claims of the advertiser in relation to the qualities of the product, the emphasis of the lesson must be placed on the structure and vocabulary being presented.

After the new vocabulary and structure have been introduced, the teacher presents the advertisement by pointing out the forceful caption and the layout and by reading the content which includes the structures to be studied. Check-up questions follow which test the child's understanding of the advertisement and force him to use the new structures (e.g., comparative and superlative forms of adjectives) as he compares the claims of the product with the product itself.

The next step requires the child to interpret other advertisements and make comparisons. Finally, generalizations and original statements can be made about the advertisement. Children can be encouraged to evaluate radio and TV commercials as well as newspaper and magazine advertisements. The study of the advertisement can be entirely oral or oral with the introduction of some reading.

Several recommended methods which present new structures in experiences involving reading include the use of short stories, news stories, comic strips, and diaries.

Reading Stories. The story reading presentation begins with the introduction of new vocabulary and structures. A short story that illustrates the structure to be presented may be read to the class or presented on tape. This is followed by comprehension questions that test understanding and elicit the structures being presented. Although the story might have literary, cultural, or personal goal value for a reading lesson, the language lesson is designed to concentrate on introducing, reviewing, or extending some grammatical concepts or structures.

After the questioning, the story is read by the pupils. The story can be divided into parts with each part given to a group for preparation for presentation to the rest of the class, or one representative from each group might be chosen to present a part to the class, in correct story sequence. As a follow-up, the structure should be used in other situations.

News Items. A news story is presented in much the same manner as the story. Several short news items are presented during a news presentation. The pupil might be reminded that the word *news* consists of the initial letters of the four main directions, north, east, west, and south. Also, to make news articles brief, accurate, truthful and clear, the *wh* questions—who, what, where, when, and why—frequently the how question, are answered.

The news items can be presented one at a time, with comprehension questions, oral reading, and interpretation following the reading of each item. Structures should be used in other situations as a follow-up.

Comic Strips. The presentation of new vocabulary and structures in comic strips requires an explanation of the situation around which the conversation is built. If possible, the children should read the strip silently, after the teacher introduces the new vocabulary and structures. Check-up questions to test comprehension follow, and then the child is ready for repetition of the conversation. The conversation might be repeated first by the entire class, then by groups, then rows, and finally by individuals. Dramatic readings by groups or individuals can provide a vehicle for repeating the conversation. Parts may be memorized for a dramatization of the situation.

Finally, the conversation can be varied by the pupils through the use of substitutions in the dialogue created by new situations presented by the teacher or suggested by the class. The dialogue of the comic strip should be a faithful reproduction of informal conversational language.

Keeping a Diary. Some older children are interested in recording experiences which they want to remember, and the presentation of new structures by means of a diary provides them a recommended activity for future writing.

After the teacher has introduced the new vocabulary and structures, the situation in which the diary incident occurs should be explained. The diary is then read to the class, and the reading is followed by questions to check comprehension. As the diary incident is read a second time, the pupils are asked to listen for the particular structure to be studied. Then the diary is read by the children. Next, questions that elicit the structure encourage the child to analyze the meaning of each structure in its context. After children have discovered the use of the new structures, they can be encouraged to generalize rules concerning them. For follow-up activities, children can make a cooperative diary about a long-range science project or experiment, such as planting a lima bean on cotton. They write daily the changes that take place. The writing for the diary may be dictated to the teacher and then copied by the pupils, or if the children have sufficient skill they keep individual logs on the process.

Letter Writing. Letter writing provides a useful and realistic way to present certain structures and new vocabulary. In using a letter to present new vocabulary and structure, copies of a letter are given to the class. The children are told about the situation in which the letter was written before the teacher reads the letter to them. Questions which check comprehension follow, and the class then reads sections of the letter by groups or individually. Letter variations are presented, and finally the children are encouraged to write their own letters. Obviously, this method of presentation will not be used before children can read and write with some degree of skill. This exercise has great composition value because it puts grammar structure in a realistic learning situation that requires clarity and naturalness of expression.

The previously suggested techniques for presenting new vocabulary and structure are designed to teach the pupils the meaning of the new vocabulary, structure, and pronunciation and the appropriate occasions for their use. After vocabulary and structure have been analyzed and understood, drill provides the pupils an opportunity to internalize the new structures and to integrate them with previously learned material. A number of vocabulary items and two or three new grammatical structures may occur in one presentation, depending on the normal speech situation in which they are presented, but these items are drilled one at a time. Wherever possible, the drills should include previously learned vocabulary and structure to help pupils relate old and new material.

Drills

Drill provides practice and repetition by applying the same structure in a variety of situations. Drill should be simple and easy, and it should give the pupils an opportunity to use the language successfully.

Pattern drills focus on stress and intonations. They include substitution drills, transformation drills (T-drills), response drills, and translation drills. In substitution drills the pupil is given a cue which requires a change in the sentence. For example, if one is drilling adverbial expressions the cues would be presented as follows:

> Teacher: I'm going home.
> Response: I'm going home.
> Teacher: _____ away.
> Response: I'm going away.
> Teacher: back
> Response: I'm going back.
> Teacher: there
> Response: I'm going there.
> Teacher: somewhere.
> Response: I'm going somewhere.

Transformation drills (T-drills) change word order, expand the elements in the original sentence, reduce the original sentence elements, or integrate two sentences into one. Statements can be changed to questions, the position of sentence modifiers can be changed, and a variety of structures can be used in different ways. An example of a transformation drill using possessives follows:

> Teacher: The boy has a bat.
> The bat is broken.
> Response: The boy's bat is broken.
> Teacher: John had a book.
> The book was lost.
> Response: John's book was lost.

These are advanced T-drills of the double base variety. Simple T-drills include the positive–negative drill:

> Teacher: The boy has a bat.
> Response: The boy hasn't a bat.

the statement–question drill:

> Teacher: The boy has a bat.
> Response: Has the boy a bat?

and the tag question response drill:

> Teacher: The boy has a bat.
> Response: The boy has a bat, hasn't he?

Response drills are designed to test comprehension and provide pattern practice. For this type of drill, the teacher, one pupil, or a group of pupils provide the stimulus while the rest of the class responds. A number of short answer patterns such as the following need drill:

Yes, I do.	No, I don't.
Yes, he would.	No, he wouldn't.
Yes, we have.	No, we haven't.
Yes, they are.	No, they aren't.

Questions or statements eliciting either the positive or negative response for these and other English response patterns are presented as stimuli for response drills.

Translation drills give a model in the pupil's native language and the pupil repeats the statement in the target language. The use of such drills has been questioned, but if the cue to translate is standardized, the drill can be effective. An example of this kind of drill follows. This drill[5] demonstrates the correlation between subject pronouns and possessive forms.

Teacher (Spanish)	*Response* (Target Language)
El va a traer su coche.	He's going to bring his car.
Yo voy a traer mi coche.	I'm going to bring my car.
Ella va a traer su coche.	She's going to bring her car.
Usted va a traer su coche.	You're going to bring your car.
Nosotros vamos a traer nuestro coche.	We're going to bring our car.
Ellos van a traer su coche.	They're going to bring their car.

Contrast drills are perhaps the most important drills for learning the pronunciation of the language. They consist of minimal pair

---

[5] J. Donald Bowen, "The Modern Language Association College Language Manual Project," *P.M.L.A.*, vol. 74, no. 7 (September, 1959), p. 24. Reprinted by permission of the Modern Language Association of America.

contrast in words, phrases, or sentences. In each of these cases the entire context is exactly the same except for one sound.

Some examples of minimal pair contrast drills follow:

Words: leave   live   Sentences: He's going to leave.
Phrases: if we leave   He's going to live.
         if we live

Comparison drills match similar sounds in the native language and the target language. These drills usually involve lists of words that have similar sounds. An example is the comparison between the simple vowels /i/ in Spanish and the complex vowel or diphthong /ē/ in English. In comparison drills, as in contrast drills, the pupils are urged to listen carefully, note likenesses and differences, and imitate accurately.

A detailed lesson plan, using the direct method to deal with the pronunciation problem of English /i/ and /ē/ for Spanish speakers, is included in the Teacher's Aid section at the end of this chapter.

In summary, the primary goal of second language teaching is to teach the pupil to understand what he hears and to be understood when he speaks. Literacy follows the ability to communicate orally. Young children are usually able to hear and imitate effectively if they have good models. Older children tend to have more rigid habits of pronunciation and need specific instruction in the making of sounds. They sometimes need to become consciously aware of the problems resulting from conflict in the patterns of the two languages involved. The teacher will select, devise, and plan the most efficient way to present structures and vocabulary which will help each child to a sufficient mastery of English as a second language.

QUESTIONS FOR STUDY

1. How can nonnative speakers of English make automatic the systems of the phonology, morphology, and syntax of the language? How does this apply to speakers of a second dialect?
2. What is a contrastive analysis? Why is it important for the teacher to be able to contrast the native vs. the target language? What are the implications for constructing analysis of the phonology, morphology, and syntax of the native vs. the target language?
3. Why are audio-visual aids used extensively in teaching children for whom classroom English is either a second language or a second dialect?

4. What basic principles are considered in planning and using drills in language teaching?

SUGGESTIONS FOR FURTHER READING

Allen, Harold Byron, *Teaching English as a Second Language: A Book of Readings* (New York: McGraw-Hill Book Co., 1965).

Allen, Harold Byron, *A Survey of the Teaching of English to Non-English Speakers in the United States* (Champaign, Ill.: National Council of Teachers of English, 1966).

Bloomfield, Leonard, *Language* (New York: Henry Holt and Co., 1933).

Bowen, J. Donald, "Characteristics of an Effective Program of Teaching English as a Second Language," *California Education,* vol. 12, no. 6 (February, 1966).

Bowen, J. D., "TESOL: The Groundwork," *Audio-Visual Instruction,* vol. 2, no. 8 (October, 1966), 618–620.

Brooks, Nelson, *Language and Language Learning: Theory and Practice,* 2d ed. (New York: Harcourt, Brace & World, Inc., 1964).

Dacanay, Fe R., and Bowen, J. Donald, eds., *Techniques and Procedures in Second Language Teaching* (Quezon City, Philippines: Phoenix Publishing House, 1963).

Finocchiaro, Mary B., *English as a Second Language: From Theory to Practice* (New York: Regents Publishing Co., Inc., 1964).

Lado, Robert, *Language Teaching: A Scientific Approach* (New York: McGraw-Hill Book Co., 1964).

Strain, Jeris E., "Teaching a Pronunciation Problem," *Language Learning,* vol. 12, no. 3 (1962), pp. 231–240.

TEACHER'S AID

Lesson Plan

WHAT: A pronunciation problem: to teach English vowel contrasts of /i/ and /ē/ to Spanish speakers.

WHY:

1. The elements /i/ and /ē/ function significantly as carriers of meaning in English.

2. The elements of sound are not the same in English and Spanish. The Spanish /i/ is a high front vowel sound which resembles /ē/ except that there is no off glide or diphthongizing. English /i/ is a slightly lower front vowel sound, and English /ē/ is a high front vowel sound plus a glide. Therefore, Spanish speakers will have to learn a new sound /i/, and the /ē/ will be phonetically different from the sound which resembles it most clearly in their language.

3. Skill in pronunciation consists of automatic hearing and speaking responses which include the ability to recognize significant sounds and to react to them in an appropriate manner.

4. Oral language habits, hearing and speaking, can be best developed through drill. The classroom procedure will therefore include maximum practice and very little explanation.

5. Conscious drilling of a specific point will be followed by focusing the learner's attention on a related but irrelevant point so that the practiced response of the specific point can become automatic.

6. Learning the necessary automatic habits involved in this pronunciation problem requires a limited number of vocabulary items. Words such as *ship–sheep* and *gyp–jeep* will be avoided because the Spanish speaker does not have /sh/ and /j/ in his sound system.

PROCEDURE:

1. Motivation
   Call the students' attention to the learning point by showing a picture of *Pete* and a picture of a *pit*. With the flannel board demonstrate how *Pete* fell into the *pit*, using the words in contrast several times, as the action is pictured. "*Pete* fell into the *pit*. Lift *Pete* out of the *pit*."

2. Following the introduction show the pictures to the children and let them say *Pete* and *pit* as appropriate responses to the pictures. Be sure that the sounds are being made correctly. Walk about the room using the words and listening to the response of the children.

3. To further focus attention on the sounds, place the figures of *Pete* and a *pit* on the flannel board with the appropriate phonemic /ē/ and /i/ directly below them. To each child give a red card (3 × 5 in.) bearing /ē/, boldly written with a felt-tip pen, and a blue card with /i/. Ask the children to hold up the appropriate card for Pete (red /ē/) and the appropriate card for pit (blue /i/). Check responses for accuracy.

4. [Teacher addresses class.] "Listen to the following words. They all contain this sound." [Teacher points to /ē/ on the flannel board then shows pictures for first four while saying the word.]

bean	meat	seat	feet
green	seen	leap	beat
seek	read	heat	deep

[The initial /s/ may present an added problem.]
"Now listen for this sound." [Points to /i/. Shows pictures or action to give meaning to first four.]

bin	mitt	sit	fit
grin	sin	lip	bit
sick	rid	hit	dip

"Now listen to the sounds in contrast."

meat–mitt	meat–mitt
feet–fit	feet–fit
seat–sit	seat–sit

"Can you hear the difference?"

5. "Now identify the vowel sounds in the following words by holding up the red card /ē/ for the *ē* sound, and the blue card /i/ for the *i* sound as I read the following words." [Teacher checks responses.]

meat (/ē/)	mitt (/i/)	mitt (/i/)
heat (/ē/)	seat (/ē/)	meat (/ē/)
sit (/i/)	hit (/i/)	sit (/i/)

seek (/ē/)	bit (/i/)	leap (/ē/)	feet (/ē/)
seem (/ē/)	beat (/ē/)	fit (/i/)	rid (/i/)
sick (/i/)	lip (/i/)	read (/ē/)	seen (/ē/)

6. "Well done! Tell me, how are /ē/ and /i/ different?"

   (a) "Say *it* and *eat* to yourself. Where is your tongue for the first part of *it*? for *eat*?"
   (b) "Now say *ī* and *ē* again."
   (c) "Do you feel your tongue move?"
   (d) "Where is your tongue when you say /ē/?" [High and close to the top of the mouth.]
   (e) "Say it again. Do you feel it? Notice how the tongue glides up to the top. Where is your tongue when you say /i/?" [Seems lower and toward the middle of the mouth because it does not glide to the top as /ē/ does.]
   (f) "Pronounce /ē/ after me: /ē/" [response], "/ē/" [response],
                        "/ē/" [response], "/ē/" [response].
       [Teacher walks around and checks responses. Moves quickly.]
   (g) "Pronounce /i/ after me." [The same procedure as with /ē/ is followed.]

7. Developing facility
   "Now, let's practice. Pronounce these word pairs after me."

seek–sick	seek–sick
meat–mitt	meat–mitt
beat–bit	beat–bit
seen–sin	seen–sin
deed–did	deed–did
feet–fit	feet–fit

"Good! Pronounce each word after me."

beat	it	me	mill
bit	if	him	in
sin	tea	see	did
seen	he	fill	lit

8. Pattern practice
"Now, say these phrases after me."

[ē–ē]	[i–i]	[contrast]
he eats	it did	he did
he sleeps	Tim did	it's tea
he leaps	Lynn did	beat him

"Pronounce these sentences after me."

Potato *chips* are *cheap*. [contrast]
Did the shoes *fit* his *feet?* [contrast]
Sit in your *seat*. [contrast]
Pete fell into a *pit*. [contrast]

9. Perception check
"I am going to read some sentences in pairs. If the sentences sound the same, do not raise your hands. If they sound different, raise your hands." [Teacher carefully stresses the target words while reading the following sentences.]

He bit me. He beat me. [different]
The sandals fit her feet. The sandals fit her feet. [same]
Did you buy the meat? Did you buy the mitt? [different]
He bit his lip. He bit his lip. [same]
Fill it. Feel it. [different]
The pit is deep. The pit is deep. [same]
He was bitten on the leg. He was beaten on the leg. [different]

Notice that in sentences that are different there is only one difference and the difference pertains to the target sound. /Th/ and /z/, sounds that have been previously avoided because they are not in the student's native sound system, are used in these sentences where they need not be identified or repeated.

10. Substitution drill
Using pictures, review and develop the following vocabulary: mitt, beet, seat, bean, key, lip, chin. Hold up each picture in turn, saying, "It's a mitt," for example, and the students reply, "It's a mitt." A picture of a face can serve for both lip and chin if you point to the particular part.

During this drill have students say the following sentences using the pictures to cue the responses.

Teacher (holding up picture of key): It's a key.
Response: It's a key.
Teacher (holding up picture of a beet): It's a beet.
Response: It's a beet.
Teacher (holding up picture of a seat): It's a seat.
Response: It's a seat.
Teacher (holding up picture of bean): It's a bean.
Response: It's a bean.
Teacher (holding up large picture of face and pointing to one lip): It's a lip.
Response: It's a lip.
Teacher (holding up same picture and pointing to chin): It's a chin.
Response: It's a chin.

During this drill it is important to correct pronunciation. Meaning is essential, but items must be carefully selected to avoid pronunciation problems other than the ones being practiced, such as the /sh/ and /j/ sounds. For example, *ship, sheep* would create an /sh/ problem in addition to /i/, /ē/ problem for Spanish speakers and are thus omitted.

11. Reinforcement
    This exercise can be taped for the listening post and used by the pupils individually for practice. The pictures used for the substitution drill are bound with ring binders in the order they are mentioned on the tape. The words might be given in manuscript underneath the pictures to begin to prepare the child for future reading and writing exercises using the same material.

    Picture 1   Taped voice: It's a _____ .
                        Student: Key. It's a key.
                        Taped voice: It's a key.
                        Student: It's a key.
    Picture 2   Taped voice: It's a _____ .

Continue as above, using all of the items from the previous drill.

12. Follow-up

    (a) Copy the words from the book. Circle the letters that spell the /ē/ and /i/ sounds. (ey, ee, ea, i)
    (b) Give children worksheet with

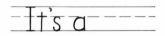

written in manuscript on first line. Have them fill in the first word in the book and then write sentences using all of the other words.

The preceding lesson on the /ē/, /i/ sounds should take from fifteen to twenty minutes to present. The reinforcement and follow-up are individual activities that can be done during the child's work periods following the oral presentation.

15

Tomorrow's Challenge
to Language Teachers

New needs in education are continually being created by the tremendous technological developments that are taking place. Education must meet these needs and keep pace with the changing demands of society. As needs in civilization change, goals and procedures in education must change. If the elementary school curriculum is to prepare children to meet new conditions and new opportunities in the space age, it must incorporate activities that teach them how to think, how to communicate, how to adapt to new situations, and how to create new solutions. To do this, new frontiers in education are currently being explored. If he is to help all children attain their potential, the language arts teacher in the elementary school has a great responsibility in this conquest. Elementary school language programs will provide wider accommodation and guidance for the gifted child, the child who is bilingual, the child who speaks nonstandard English, and the child who speaks standard English.

Torrance,[1] in writing on curriculum frontiers for the gifted pupil, discusses six areas that should be emphasized. These include self-initiated learning, learning on one's own, creating the responsive environment, revising concepts of readiness, searching for self (self-concepts), and searching for one's uniqueness. He continues this

---

[1] E. Paul Torrance, "Flying Monkeys and Silent Lions," *Exceptional Children*, vol. 28 (November, 1961), pp. 119–127.

discussion with suggestions on opening these six frontiers, and the suggestions, if acted upon, would provide valuable opportunities for language development in the elementary school.

Today's world calls for the acquisition of new subject matter almost daily and for the development of new understanding and the solving of new problems. Tomorrow will add to these needs and make new demands upon children, who must be equipped to cope with the vast technological changes that are forecast, such as exploration of the moon and planets. Teachers will become more responsible for helping each individual pupil in their classrooms to think clearly and creatively, to speak and write effectively, and to observe, listen, and read accurately. Furthermore, in this age of technological change and development, the job opportunities of tomorrow will be increasingly limited to those who have acquired the best and highest education. It is the responsibility of the elementary school so to prepare and motivate the schoolchild, particularly in the communication skills, that he will want to forge ahead and acquire the kind of education needed for tomorrow's world.

Leaders in education and classroom teachers continue to place increasing emphasis on creativity in oral and written communication in the curriculum in order to help children learn the fundamentals of better human relationships. From the heads of nations to the members of families, from the community and the school to the teacher and the child, the demand for better communication lines continues to increase. Children of today and tomorrow must understand the significance of communication in their daily experiences with language in the classroom.

Future schools will provide various opportunities and incentives for observing and listening to electronic and mechanical devices, such as television, radio, films, records, tapes, and perhaps "voice printers" that can turn pupils' dictated words into print. Teaching machines will improve and be used to greater advantage in the schools. They will not replace the teacher as some fear but will serve as a supplement to his work, giving him more time for creative work with his pupils. Better television programs will be made available to more schools so that children's listening and observing activities can be guided through planning, viewing, and follow-up experiences, including evaluation.

In the elementary schools of tomorrow, well-equipped libraries in every elementary school, which can serve as a "hub" for much of the work of classes, will provide greater incentives for reading. Children will use them for:

1. Research in solving problems and answering questions that arise in large units of experience and other activities.
2. Seeking information that satisfies their curiosity.
3. Reading well-written books of fiction, poetry, and biography for sheer enjoyment.

Beginners in reading will continue to be given delightful stories which are beautifully illustrated, but tapes, microfilm, and other media will doubtless become standard equipment in addition to books.

"Head Start" programs are becoming more widespread. These programs, designed to enrich the experiences of disadvantaged children before they reach first grade, offer a variety of activities that build concepts and help to develop oral language ability. Children who come from poverty-stricken areas seem to profit from such programs.

More attention is being given to the problem of how to teach bilingual children to speak, read, and write English. Increasing emphasis on developing a better understanding of the various cultures and problems of children should continue to precede language instruction. Today's interest in teaching a second language at the elementary school level is expected to deepen. With the close interrelationship of more and more people in other countries as technological advances bring world communities together, children in American schools will have increasing need to understand and to speak other languagues.

Language Programs of Tomorrow

English programs have previously focused on ideas being communicated rather than the way in which communication occurs. Linguists have pointed out the essential relationship between structure and meaning; that is, the manner in which the structure of the language actually defines and illuminates the message being communicated. Scholars are presently shifting attention from the relationship of meanings within the English sentence to the relationship of structures and sound. Stress on the relationship of sense and substance is being superseded by stress on form and structure.

Although linguistic scholars are still disagreeing among themselves regarding the value of each new discovery, research in language is demonstrating the importance of form in the communication of ideas. Hopefully, as pupils are taught the structural elements of the language (i.e., sounds, structural units of meaning morphemes, basic patterns, and transformational rules), they will not only be able to develop greater understanding of the English sentence but greater facility in its use as well.

Several studies have been made and some are still being carried out to determine the usefulness of linguistic analysis in the teaching of listening, speaking, reading, and writing in the elementary school. One recent study made use of linguistic data as it developed a reading curriculum for a computer-assisted instructional system. This study tested various psycholinguistic propositions about contrasting dominant subordinate patterns and phonological regularity. It also investigated a number of syntactic and semantic questions concerning general reading comprehension.[2]

Two older studies that have provided much direction for language instruction at the elementary school level are studies done by Ruth G. Strickland[3] and Walter D. Loban.[4]

Strickland's study of language development and reading achievement of children at the sixth-grade level produced a significant relationship between the use of movables and elements of subordination in oral language and oral reading interpretation. Children with high rankings on measures of comprehension in listening and silent reading made a greater use of movables and elements of subordination in their oral language than did children who ranked low on measures of these variables. This suggests a significant relationship between a child's ability to comprehend written language and his ability to utilize subordination and movables in oral expression.

Loban made a longitudinal study of children's language development and found that children who were advanced in general language ability were also advanced in reading ability. General

[2] Richard C. Atkinson, project director, *Progress Report, A Reading Curriculum for a Computer-Assisted Instructional System: The Stanford Project* (Stanford, Calif.: Stanford University Press, August, 1966).

[3] Ruth G. Strickland, "The Language of Elementary School Children: Its Relationship to the Language of Reading Textbooks and the Quality of Reading of Selected Children," Bulletin of the School of Education, no. 38 (Bloomington: Indiana University Press, July, 1962).

[4] Walter D. Loban, *The Language of Elementary School Children* (Champaign, Ill.: National Council of Teachers of English, 1963).

language ability was determined by vocabulary scores at the kindergarten level and language ratings by teachers. Language achievement differences between high and low groups were found to increase from year to year, with the low group using many more partial expressions or incomplete sentence patterns. Loban's study provided evidence that competency in spoken language appears to be significantly correlated with competency in reading.

A curriculum for grades seven through twelve has been developed by the Oregon Curriculum Study Center.[5] It was used in the classroom of 150 pilot teachers in seven cities of the Pacific Northwest. This program is a curriculum in rhetoric, one strand of a comprehensive program that includes six-year sequences in language and literature.

The rhetoric curriculum attempts to remedy the following deficiencies and errors which have made the teaching of writing so unsuccessful in American education:

1. The four forms of discourse (description, narration, exposition, and argumentation), which specified rules for writing paragraphs, including topic sentences, modes of development, and transition, have provided limited and barren instruction.

2. Textbooks have frequently been dull, repetitious, ill-informed, and not infrequently poorly written as they have presented dogmatic generalizations and assigned students to write autobiographies or tell what they did during vacation.

3. Almost no serious instruction has been offered in the use of oral language.

Through the identification and organization of principles underlying skill development, the rhetoric curriculum uses purpose, audience, substance, structure, and style to improve writing.

Linguistic Contributions to Listening Programs

Linguistics has provided the direction which results in a new emphasis on the audio-lingual approach to language teaching. Listening and speaking are being increasingly emphasized in the primary grades in addition to reading and writing. Language, most completely expressed in speech, represents intonation, rhythm,

---

[5] Albert R. Kitzhaber, "A Search for Better Ways to Teach Writing," *CTA Journal*, vol. 63, no. 2 (March, 1967), pp. 13–15.

stress, and juncture patterns that can be recorded only in part by written language. Schools no longer assume that children have learned all they need to know about listening and speaking before they come to school. The old concept that the primary language emphases of the classroom are reading and writing is still prevalent. However, there is some evidence today that any attempt to decipher written material without first knowing the language patterns as speech is not only incomplete and imperfect but inefficient as well. A recent psychological study shows greater transfer from audio to visual learning than the reverse! [6]

The listening process starts with expression as heard in context, followed by recall of content through various associations between expression, content, and the listener's background of experience. Great facility is required for listening at conversational speed, approximately 500 sounds per minute,[7] and for retaining the content of what is heard.

Memory, facility, fluency, and needs are involved simultaneously when a person is listening and speaking. The elementary school teacher needs to understand each of these areas and know how to ensure their development in children. Linguistic emphasis suggests early training in listening comprehension, because the ear dominates the learning and use of speech sounds. The tongue and other organs are used to reproduce the speech sounds that the ear has learned to recognize, and the process of listening–speaking is so closely related that often the listener grasps the content of an expression before the speaker finishes it.

To account for the process of listening, recall and memory bring patterns to attention and hold or reproduce patterns as needed. A memory store within the nervous system retains each unit and pattern of expression and content for instant use. Under normal speech conditions, the speaker manipulates expression through the use of bundles of habits without conscious effort. Attention may be focused on a particular word, sound, or other element of expression. Attention is focused partly by the need or will of the listener or speaker and partly by habits, attitudes, intensity of sound, duration, repetition, relative movement, change, and con-

[6] Paul Pimsleur and Robert J. Bonkowski, "Transfer of Verbal Material Across Sense Modalities," *Journal of Education Psychology*, vol. 52, no. 2 (1961), pp. 104–107.

[7] Robert Lado, *Language Teaching, A Scientific Approach* (New York: McGraw-Hill Book Co., 1964).

trast. Attention must be directed to as many items as possible at any given time. Facility in listening and speaking involves selection of inflections, words, phrases and sentence types, new arrangements of words and structures, and habit formation of the phonemes and variants.

The current emphasis on oral language experiences, listening and speaking, found in today's courses of study, language textbooks, and experimental programs for children in the primary grades is witness to the influence of linguistics on the language program. However, in many schools, despite this emphasis on oral language and the awareness of its importance to language development, most of the child's time is still devoted to deciphering written words and doing seat work, copying words, writing on his own, coloring, filling in blanks, drawing lines from word to word and completing sentences or paragraphs. Elementary schoolteachers have problems making time for oral expression in classroom situations with thirty to forty children. Activities must be skillfully organized so that small groups of children may work together to provide opportunity for greater participation. In a classroom of thirty-six children, six groups will permit six children to speak at one time and to be heard and receive the kind of attention and response that a speaker deserves. For certain experiences, more groups with fewer children can be utilized. New examples of written work that involve emphasis on sound relationships are appearing in textbooks. Texts which assume some reading ability emphasize oral reading and discussion as well as written work. Much of the written work concentrates on the need for being conscious of sounds. For example, the student is instructed to say a group of words to himself and underline those with the same beginning, medial, or ending sounds. He is in fact listening to himself in the exercise as he speaks the words silently.

Linguistics and Speaking

The units and patterns of speech as described by linguists are available to the teacher. Phonemes are examined in words, as parts of words, and as morphemes rather than in isolation. For example, the /p/, /i/, and /n/ phonemes are expressed automatically in a habit bundle as the word is elicited. Phonemic variants are effected by their phonetic environments. The /p/ of *pin* is exploded as an initial stop; the /i/ is rather drawn out before the /n/ nasal continuant in final position. However, if the phonemes are reversed as in the word "nip," a different phonetic environment for each phoneme results in different phonetic emphasis; /n/ as an initial nasal moves toward /i/ which is not quite so long as it rushes to /p/, now in the position of an unreleased stop. Expression is associated with content, as content is in turn associated with expression; one elicits the other. Such information helps the teacher select sounds for drill as they occur in normal patterns of discourse, and when the teacher of a second language is aware of the various patterns used by children in their native language or dialect as well as the patterns of the target language, he can isolate areas that need emphasis.

Linguistics and Reading

Because hearing and speaking are both members of the audio-lingual facet of language, it is important to separate them from reading and writing during the early stages. When the transition from the *hear–say, gesture–see* language experience is made to graphic *read–write* material, it must be made in terms familiar to the student, and the relationships must be clear. For example, as previously mentioned, /g/ is not the sound of g, as has frequently been taught, but rather g is a grapheme which represents the sound /g/ in get and /j/ in gin and ju*d*ge. As children move into graphic material they need to be taught the relationship of the receptive skills involved in speaking and writing.

Changes are taking place in reading texts as a result of linguistic investigation. For example, one of the first texts to show change was Slager's [8] series of texts, *English for Today,* in which careful attention was given to the sequential introduction of language structures and sounds in each of the first three texts. Vocabulary control was achieved primarily in terms of the cultural basis for the concepts.

Another linguistic approach to reading has been presented by Leonard Bloomfield and Clarence L. Barnhart.[9] This program,

[8] William Slager, ed., *English for Today* (New York: McGraw-Hill Book Co., 1962). Six volumes on the teaching of English as a second language.

[9] Leonard Bloomfield and Clarence L. Barnhart, *Let's Read, A Linguistic Approach* (Detroit: Wayne State University Press, 1961).

based on a careful phonological analysis of English sound structures, is very different from phonics programs which have been
developed with little regard to the nature of the English language.
In *Let's Read*, Bloomfield is concerned with transforming written
symbols into sounds. Since he stresses the substitution of emphasis
on form for preoccupation with meaning, and since the relationship
of letter(s) to sound is central, his approach is sometimes equated
with what is called a phonic approach. Phonics, however, con-
fuses writing with speech and also expects the child to produce on
cue isolated speech sounds. Children practicing the /g/ sound,
for example, attempt to make it alone or follow it by a schwa.
Bloomfield is uncompromising in rejecting the phonic method.[10]

> English speaking people . . . are not accustomed to making that kind
> of noise. Learning to pronounce such things is something in the nature
> of a stunt, and has nothing to do with learning to read. We intend to
> apply phonetics to our reading instruction; this does not mean that we
> are going to try to teach phonetics to young children. In this absurdity
> lies the greatest fault of the so-called phonic method.

Bloomfield's method presents words in which the contrasts in
sound can be easily identified with differences in the letters used to
form the contrasting sounds. Vocabulary is controlled so that each
sound is represented by only one letter and each letter represents
one sound. Irregular spellings are carefully screened out of initial
reading instruction, and the beginning reader works with minimal
pairs such as *man* and *nan, fan* and *van, pan* and *tan*. In each case
only one difference in sound occurs. This method helps children
to discover the speech sounds that serve as phonemes in the language. The correspondence of phonemes and graphemes is stressed
on the thesis that the ability to read must be built on what is basic
to the expressive structure of the language. Such a foundation is
expected to provide children the optimum opportunity to succeed
in becoming independent readers.

Bloomfield suggests that the motivating factor of content is likely
irrelevant and may even be harmful. He believes that the beginning reader is so busy changing printed symbols into sounds that
he has neither interest nor energy left for the message. According
to Bloomfield, knowing that he has responded appropriately to the
symbols is motivation enough to keep the beginning reader at work.

[10] *Ibid.*, p. 28.

Both listening and reading as intake processes of language have been organized into levels. The first level of listening is called hearing. This involves the physical process by which speech sounds in the form of sound waves are received and modified by the ear. This process is similar to that of seeing, looking at symbols, in reading. The second stage of listening, identifying and recognizing the sound sequences, compares to recognizing the symbols as different graphemes in reading. The third stage of listening is called auding and refers to the process by which the continuous flow of sounds is translated into meaning, just as reading, at its highest level, occurs when the symbols are interpreted and translated into meaning.

Although it does seem less than productive to think of "the accurate calling of words" and "getting meaning from the printed page" as mutually exclusive alternatives in reading, certainly recognizing that beginners need to progress through levels to achieve the highest degree of language development does not seem illogical or unusual. Trying to start at the top level, emphasizing meaning, before any foundation has been laid, seems much more likely to cause problems. Controlled sound introduction and extension of experience with basic sentence patterns may hold much promise for future reading programs.

Thus linguistic reading programs:

1. Teach children a systematic decoding system at the beginning of their reading experience.

2. Place a systematic control over the introduction and patterning of consonant and vowel combinations.

3. Introduce letters, letter names, and corresponding sounds.

4. Focus on decoding behaviors, leaving comprehension and story interpretation skills for later.

5. Introduce morphological rules such as the pluralization of nouns and syntactic concepts such as word order differences in declarative and interrogative sentences.

6. Consider picture clues and content clues as separate skills which are not part of the decoding system.

Linguistic programs are based on linguistic criteria involving the structural nature of the phonological, morphological, and syntactic systems of English rather than on criteria of word frequency, experiential familiarity, pictorial nature of the vocabulary, and story content.

Linguistics and Grammar

The kind of English grammar frequently taught in schools has been based largely on written usage and consequently fails to describe the sound system, the stress and intonation patterns, and the junctural features of the spoken language. Its categories have been derived from Latin grammar and are therefore not wholly appropriate to English, and its mixture of semantic and relational definitions gives an imprecise picture of how the language actually works.

In addition, school grammar often fails to recognize that there are various standards of usage which are acceptable to different people, or which are appropriate for different occasions. It tends to impose an arbitrary and often artificial concept of correctness.

Linguists have for some time been attempting to influence school grammar and to show the relevance of both their objective attitudes toward language and their findings about language, including phonology, grammatical analysis, dialect geography, and language history. Leonard Bloomfield devoted the final chapter of his book *Language* [11] to the applications of linguistics in the school curriculum. Charles Fries [12] and W. Nelson Francis [13] followed this precedent and urged a better use of linguistic knowledge by the schools. John B. Carroll [14] has a chapter on the actual and potential relationship of linguistics and education in his book *The Study of Language*. Henry Lee Smith, Jr.,[15] points out the dependency of understanding how language functions on an accurate description of the sound system of English, while Gleason [16] offers a survey of approaches to grammatical analysis, going on to relate the study of grammar to composition and literary appreciation.

[11] Leonard Bloomfield, *Language* (New York: Holt, Rinehart & Winston, Inc., 1933).

[12] Charles C. Fries, *The Structure of English* (New York: Harcourt, Brace & World, Inc., 1952).

[13] W. Nelson Francis, *The Structure of American English* (New York: The Ronald Press Co., 1958).

[14] John B. Carroll, *The Study of Language* (Cambridge, Mass.: Harvard University Press, 1956).

[15] Henry L. Smith, Jr., *Linguistic Science and the Teaching of English* (Cambridge, Mass.: Harvard University Press, 1956).

[16] H. A. Gleason, Jr., *Linguistics and English Grammar* (New York: Holt, Rinehart & Winston, Inc., 1965).

Whatever impact such books have had or will have, articles published in professional journals and papers read at meetings of professional societies probably influence the practicing teacher more directly. For example, Robert Moore uses a journal article to present an approach for introducing word classes, inflected and uninflected, to third grade children. He also introduces the basic sentence patterns and in this manner provides teachers specific data which they can use in the classroom.[17]

The National Council of Teachers of English has unquestionably been very influential in bringing about change in English teaching, where it has occurred, by publishing articles, reprints, monographs, and books to disseminate new ideas, and by sponsoring institutes, workshops, and study groups in applied linguistics. The Council may also be given credit for the fact that several state departments of education have recently revised their requirements for the certification of teachers of English as well as their English curriculums.

In California, for example, the Report of the California State Advisory Committee for an English Framework [18] recommends the teaching of the rhythmical and structural patterns in English, which include the sounds and visual forms of standard English (morphology, syntax, and intonation patterns). The report also recommends the inclusion of some analytical study of regional and social differences in American English and discrimination of standard from nonstandard usage.

The effect of all this activity on teachers in the classrooms is nevertheless questionable. Continuous and consistent use of new ideas in the classrooms requires well-planned programs which utilize such ideas. Whether these programs appear in the form of textbooks or other teaching devices, teachers who have discovered new concepts and approaches must have suitable materials for carrying out learning experiences. Such programs should include not merely a means of analyzing English but also a way of applying such analysis in developing critical listening, appreciative reading, and effective speaking and writing. Materials for teaching vocabulary, the mechanics of prepared speeches and written composition, the organization of ideas, and the appropriateness of different language forms to their intended communicative function are essential if grammar is to be related to literature and composition.

---

[17] Robert P. Moore, "A Structural Approach for the Third Grade," *Elementary English*, vol. 64, no. 2 (February, 1967), pp. 138–147.

[18] Preliminary draft (June, 1967).

Charles Kreidler [19] examined thirty English language textbooks published over a ten-year period and found that in two-thirds of them at least the term "linguistics" was used. Several of the publications had a linguistic consultant in addition to the staffs of authors. Although the effect of linguistics is generally stronger at the high school level, several texts have been prepared for elementary school use. *The Macmillan English Series,* by Thomas Clark Pollack and others (2nd edition, New York: Macmillan, 1963; grades 2–12) and *The New Building Better English* by Norma W. Biedenharn and others (4th edition, New York: Harper & Row, 1966, grades 2–12) include some emphasis in linguistics. However, in both cases grammatical analysis is limited to the high school texts. The work of *Language for Daily Use,* by Mildred A. Dawson and others (New York: Harcourt, Brace and World, 1964; grades 1–8) contains optional lessons on sentence patterns with appropriate symbols, but it is so arranged that teachers can concentrate on traditional elements.

The Roberts English Series: A Linguistics Program, Grades 3–9 (New York: Harcourt, Brace and World, 1966) applies linguistics to the relation of sound and spelling, an understanding of sentence formation, and an appreciation of what can be said in English through examining literature. The relationship of sound and spelling is developed through a presentation of the concept of phonemes and includes, over a four-year period, all the phonemes of English, correlating each with the traditional orthography (English spelling) which represents it. Sentence formation is explained by a battery of generative-transformational categories and rules, and reading selections include a variety of literary forms that display dialectic as well as stylistic differences. These literary selections are taught in order to develop the child's ability to get meaning from a written passage.

The Roberts series attempts to use the familiar terms of traditional language, using a structural linguistic approach to phonology and morphology and a transformational approach to syntax. Many of the valid assumptions of traditional grammar overlap what structural and transformational linguists have discovered about English, making possible the eclectic approach to language used in the Roberts series.

[19] Charles W. Kreidler, "The Influence of Linguistics in School Grammar," *The Linguistic Reporter,* vol. 8 (Washington, D.C.: Center for Applied Linguistics, December, 1966).

Since the major language goals of the early grades in school (approximately grades 1–3) include teaching the child to listen, express himself adequately, and read and write, basic concepts of phonology and morphology are most relevant at this level. Syntax should be built upon a sound foundation of phonology and morphology, as the child progresses through the middle grades and becomes ready for it.

Within the various grade groups there are additional groups, speakers of standard English, speakers of nonstandard English, and speakers of other languages. These children have different language needs, and varying emphases within the same body of knowledge is rarely a solution to their problems. They have the right to be taught what they need to know in order to develop essential language facility. For example, contrastive linguistics is useful for contrasting structures of Spanish and English. The Spanish child has a palatal nasal /n/ in his vocabulary but no velar /n/. Spanish nouns have two forms and two genders as contrasted to English nouns with four forms.

	Spanish		*English*	
	Masculine	Feminine	Subject	Possessive
Singular	*niño*	*niña*	*cat*	*cat's*
Plural	*niños*	*niñas*	*cats*	*cats'*

Pointing out these basic contrasting elements directs the student, at once, to reasons for problems that arise in both pronunciation and sentence structure as he attempts to learn the new language.

Perhaps one of the greatest contributions of linguistics to school language programs has been the resulting generalizations of language study that provide schools some basic principles on which to base the formulation of new instruction goals and procedures.

John Carroll suggests the following as the major perspectives that linguists have contributed to language study: [20]

1. Recognition of the primacy of speech as contrasted with written communication as a proper orientation for instruction in oral communication and in the teaching of reading.

2. Acquaintance with the phonemic structure of the language and its relation (or lack of relation) to orthography as a preparation for the teaching of reading, writing, and spelling.

[20] John B. Carroll, *The Study of Language* (Cambridge, Mass.: Harvard University Press, 1959), p. 144.

3. Awareness of the dynamic character of a language system and its changes through time and space as a background for the teaching of grammar and usage.

4. Knowledge of the nature of meaning and its genesis as a background for vocabulary development and the teaching of listening, understanding, and interpretation.

5. Concern with the role of language in mediating virtually every kind of learning as an aid to capitalizing on the advantages of verbal learning and at the same time avoiding the excesses of "mere verbalism."

6. Understanding the psychological processes involved in encoding and decoding information through a culturally determined linguistic system as a background for the teaching of all communication skills.

From such directives as the above, the following goals for elementary school language programs of the future may be suggested:

Give more emphasis to oral language as it is interrelated with other experiences through the day so that each individual pupil can learn to speak with ease, competency, and pleasure.

Teach standard usage by providing each child the opportunity to speak it daily.

Help the child become competent in listening through participation in purposeful listening situations.

Guide the child's reading activities so that he will learn to enjoy reading while mastering the skills.

Help the child find esthetic enjoyment and therapeutic value in literature.

Encourage creative writing by providing rich and broad experiences in living, and by helping the child to develop skills sufficient to enjoy creating on paper in the early years, and later, to write with correctness and power.

Give more attention to personal development of every child as an individual personality.

See that language skills are learned as needed.

Make greater use of mass media for instructional purposes.

Help children grow in an awareness of the beauty and power of words.

See and use obvious interrelationships of subject matter and relating activities throughout the day as opportunities in developing skills and power in all language areas.

Language programs of tomorrow will prepare a child to analyze his own style of speech and writing, his usage, and his appreciation of literature on the basis of systematic knowledge of the system underlying the sounds he utters and the meanings they convey. Learning how language works to provide meaning, a study of man's most characteristic activity which may one day help him to understand himself, is a fascinating and valuable study. Great programs in language can indeed result in great programs in living.

Language programs of the future will continue to ask probing questions. What are the goals of individual students? In what ways are language programs educative as well as social forces? How many programs are needed to fit large, diversified communities, and how do these programs provide for different needs and varying rates of progress? To answer such questions, parents, teachers, scholars, researchers, and administrators will decide jointly what is best for boys and girls. On this basis, judgments concerning what to accept and reject in language study will be made. Both the creative and functional aspects of language must be carefully considered as choices are made. Creativity, often instrumental in changing behavior and in illuminating and giving quality to life, will continue to be an integral part of language development. Experiences which help young persons satisfy their curiosity about the world in which they live, which provide them with enough variety to permit their growth in different abilities and capacities, and which encourage their reaching out for knowledge and understanding, result in creative-functional language growth.

> Great programs in living are made only by men who stand back and look over their universe as an artist retreats to look over his canvas. And from that point they know where the high lights are to be placed. There is nothing precious about it all; it is not the idleness of the indolent. It is a profound and rugged challenge to those who are tempted to wear out their strength in futility.[21]

[21] E. D. Hutchinson, "The Period of Frustration in Creative Endeavor," A Study of Interpersonal Relations, ed., Patrick Mullahy (New York: Hermitage Press, Inc., 1949), p. 419.

QUESTIONS FOR STUDY

1. How can the various parts of the English program (such as poetry or syntax) be coordinated and articulated through the school program from elementary school to college?
2. How can the less able students in English be taught effectively to appreciate their language and use it with facility?
3. How can research programs, institutes, and other activities help the English program at the elementary school level? (Although many such programs are designed for the secondary level, little money is being spent on English in the elementary school.)

SUGGESTIONS FOR FURTHER READING

Bloomfield, Leonard, *Language* (New York: Henry Holt and Co., 1933), pp. 3–547.

Brooks, Nelson, *Language and Language Learning*, 2d ed. (New York: Harcourt, Brace & World, Inc., 1964).

Carroll, John, *The Study of Language* (Cambridge, Mass.: Harvard University Press, 1959).

Chomsky, Noam, *Syntactic Structures* (The Hague: Mouton and Co., 1957).

Fries, Charles C., *Linguistics and Reading* (New York: Holt, Rinehart & Winston, Inc., 1963), pp. 35–112, 133–158.

Hathaway, Baxter, *A Transformational Syntax: The Grammar of Modern American English* (New York: The Ronald Press Co., 1967).

Lado, Robert, *Linguistics Across Cultures* (Ann Arbor, Mich.: University of Michigan Press, 1957), pp. 51–74.

Rycenga, John A., and Schwartz, Joseph, *Perspectives on Language—An Anthology* (New York: Ronald Press Co., 1963).

Sapir, Edward, *Language—An Introduction to the Study of Speech* (New York: Harcourt, Brace & World, Inc., 1921), pp. 1–247.

TEACHER'S AID

For a complete listing of Language Arts publications, journals, literary maps, filmstrips and recordings for the various age levels, request *Resources for the Teaching of English* (1968–1969) from the National Council of Teachers of English, Champaign, Illinois.

Index

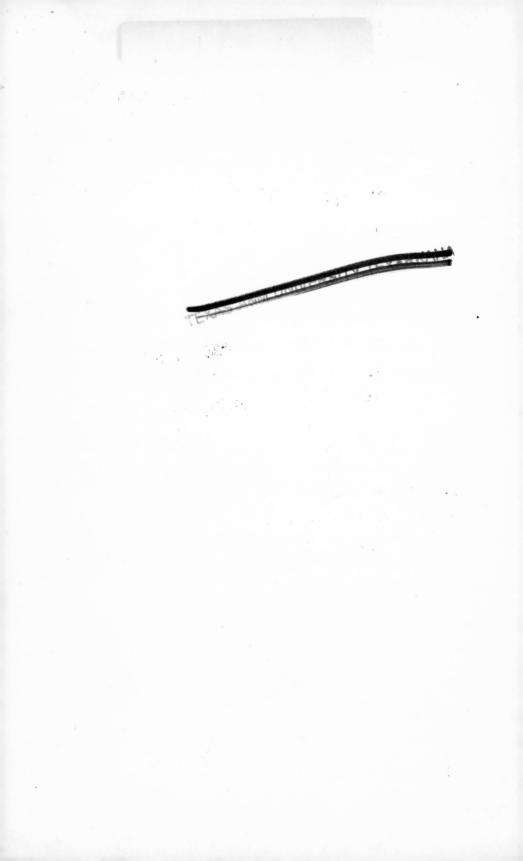